99 Crazy Mazes

Puzzle Book For Adults

Copyright 2019 Vibrant Puzzle Books

Build problem solving skills and Confidence by solving puzzle mazes!

PUT A HEX ON IT #1

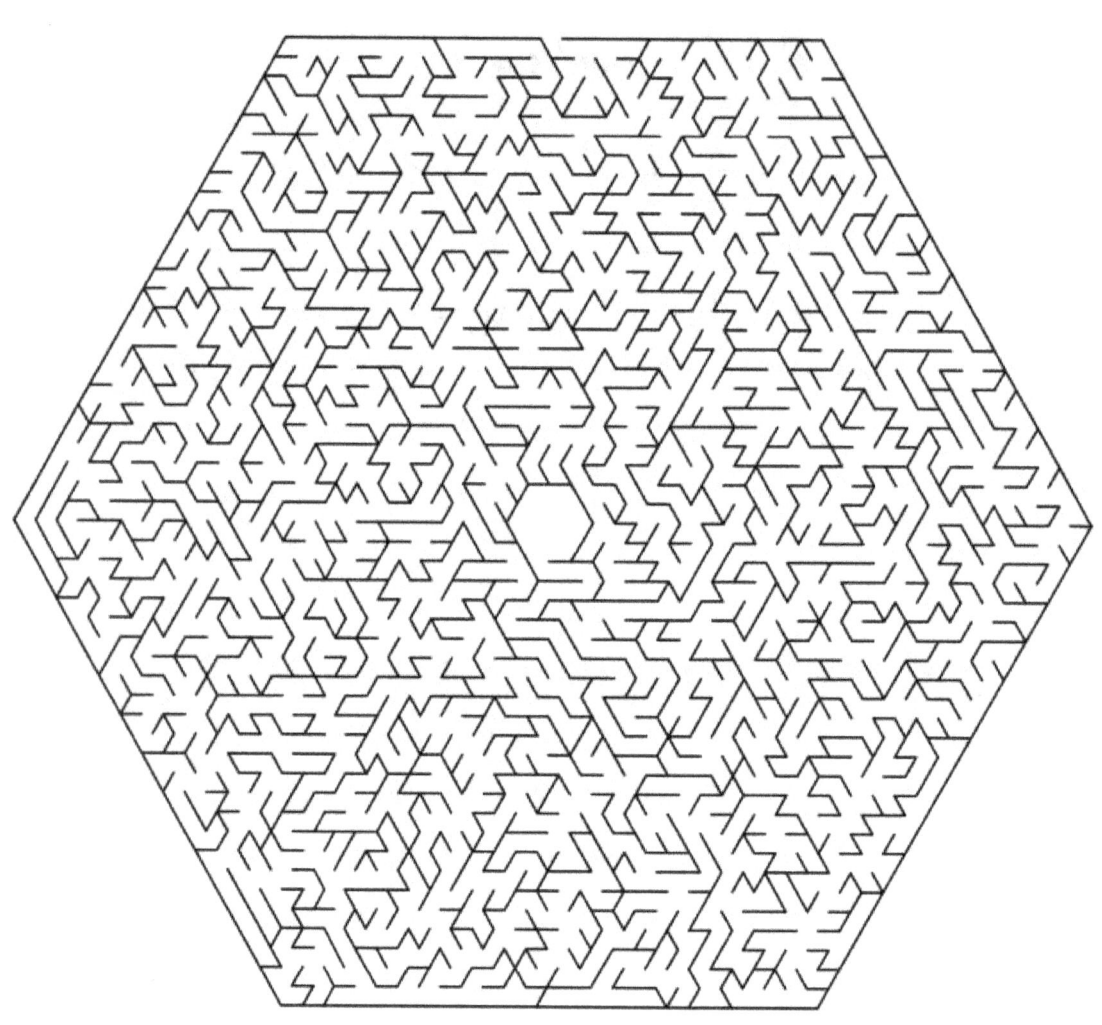

PUT A HEX ON IT #2

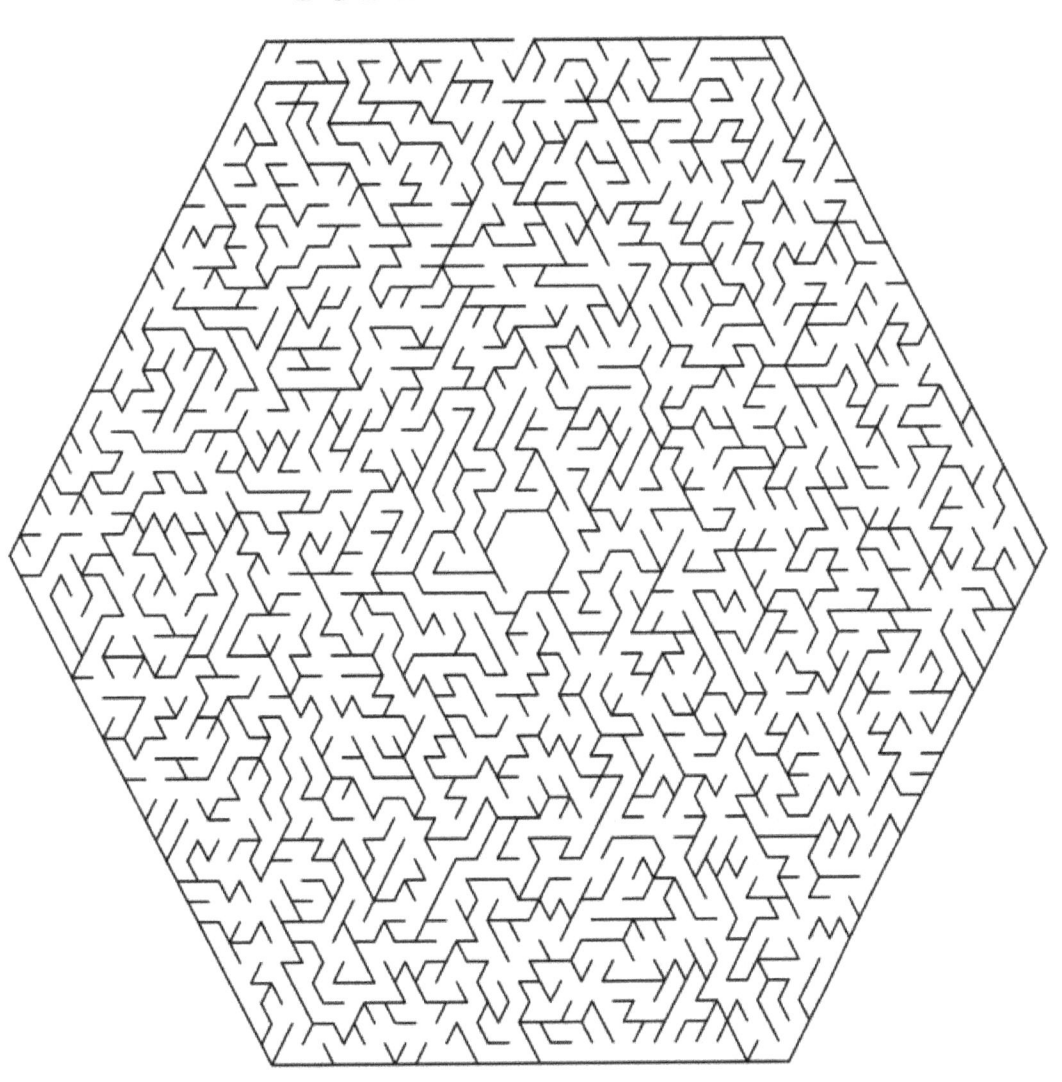

PUT A HEX ON IT #3

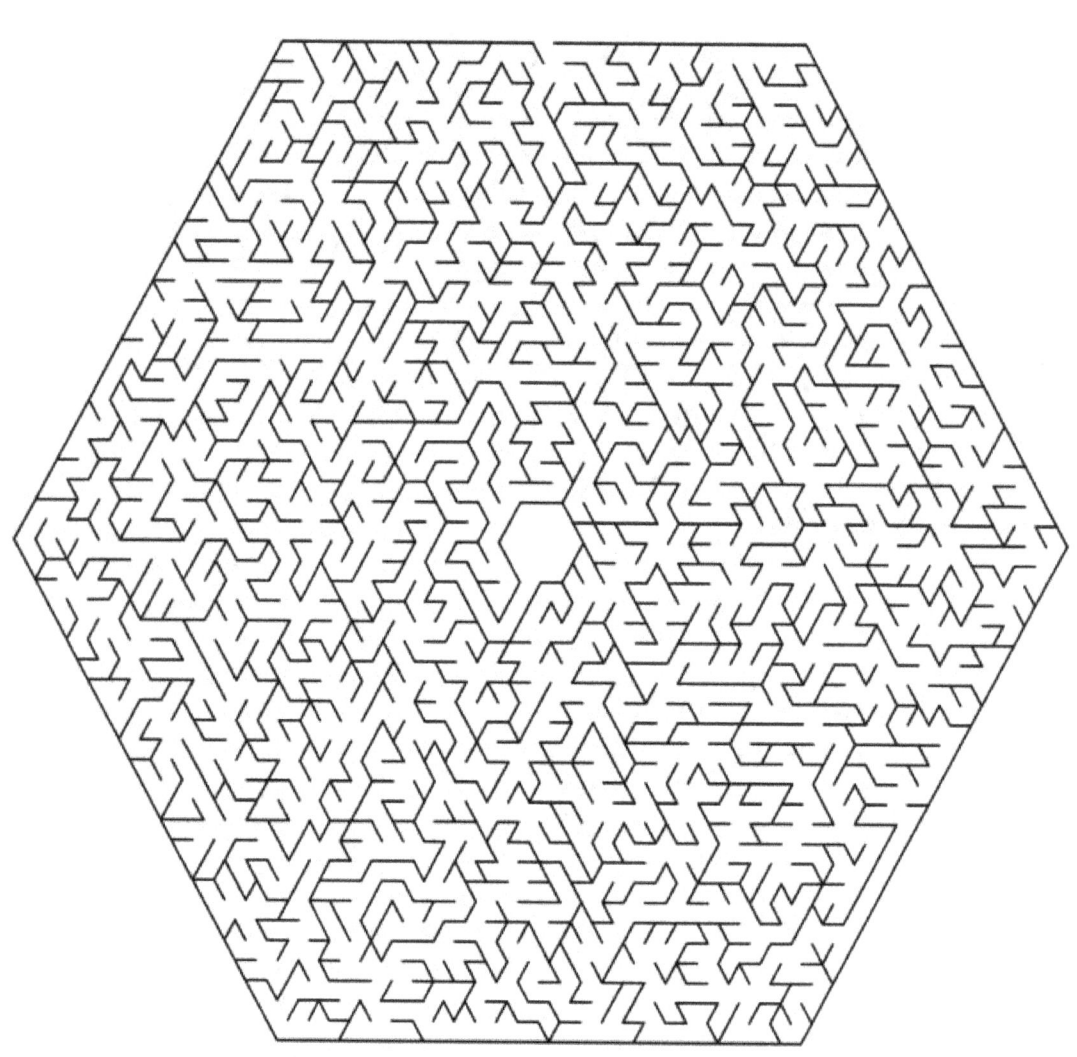

PUT A HEX ON IT #4

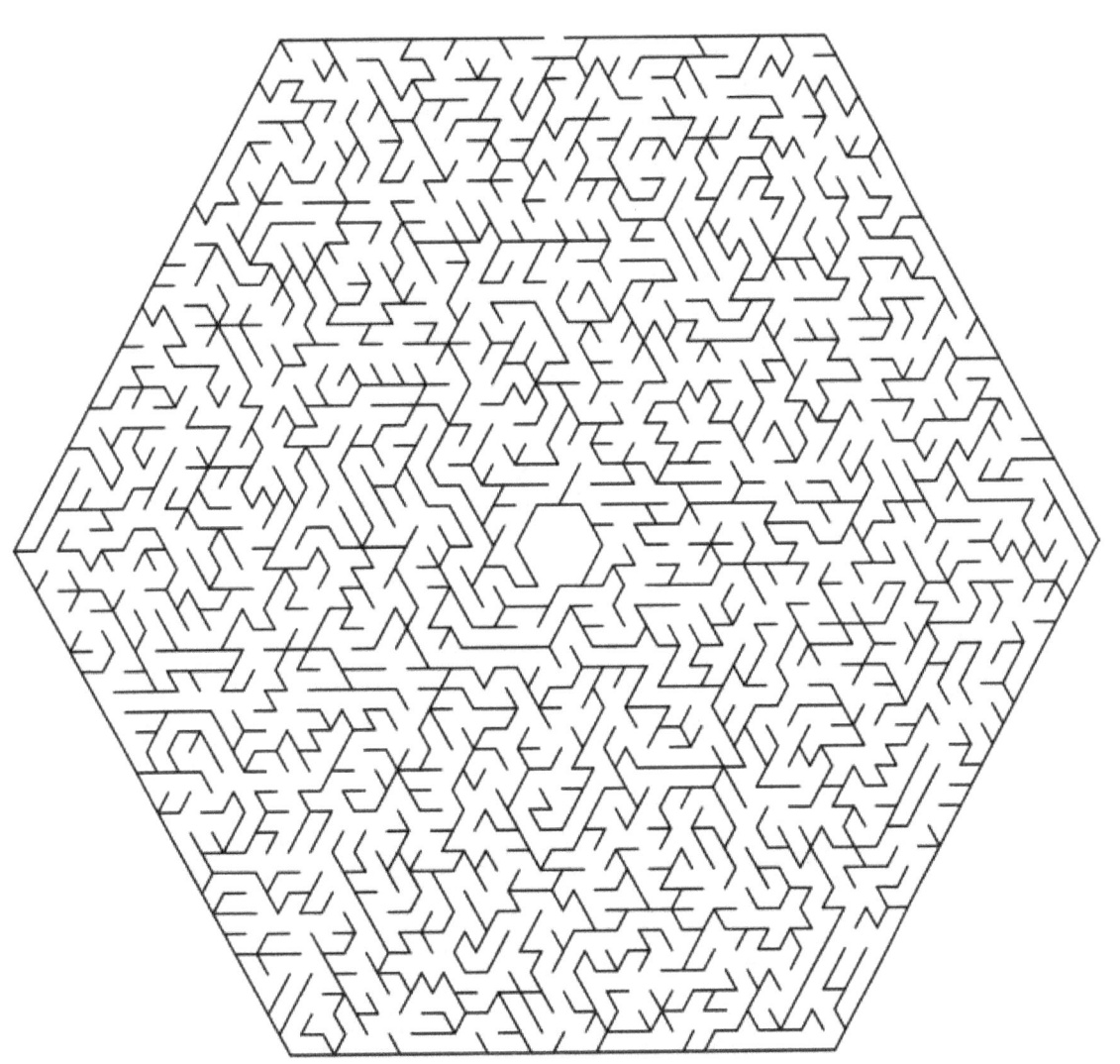

PUT A HEX ON IT #5

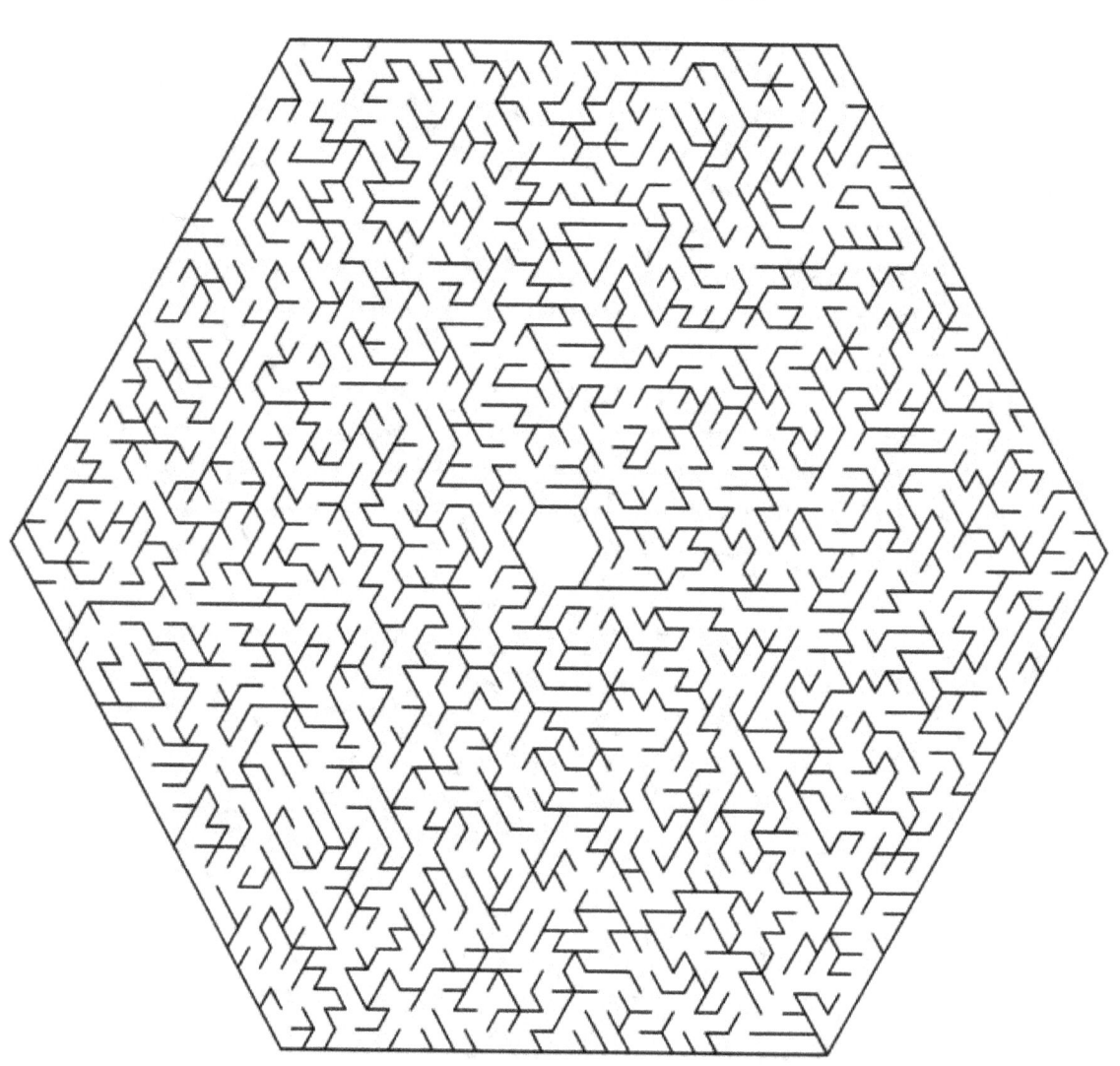

PUT A HEX ON IT #6

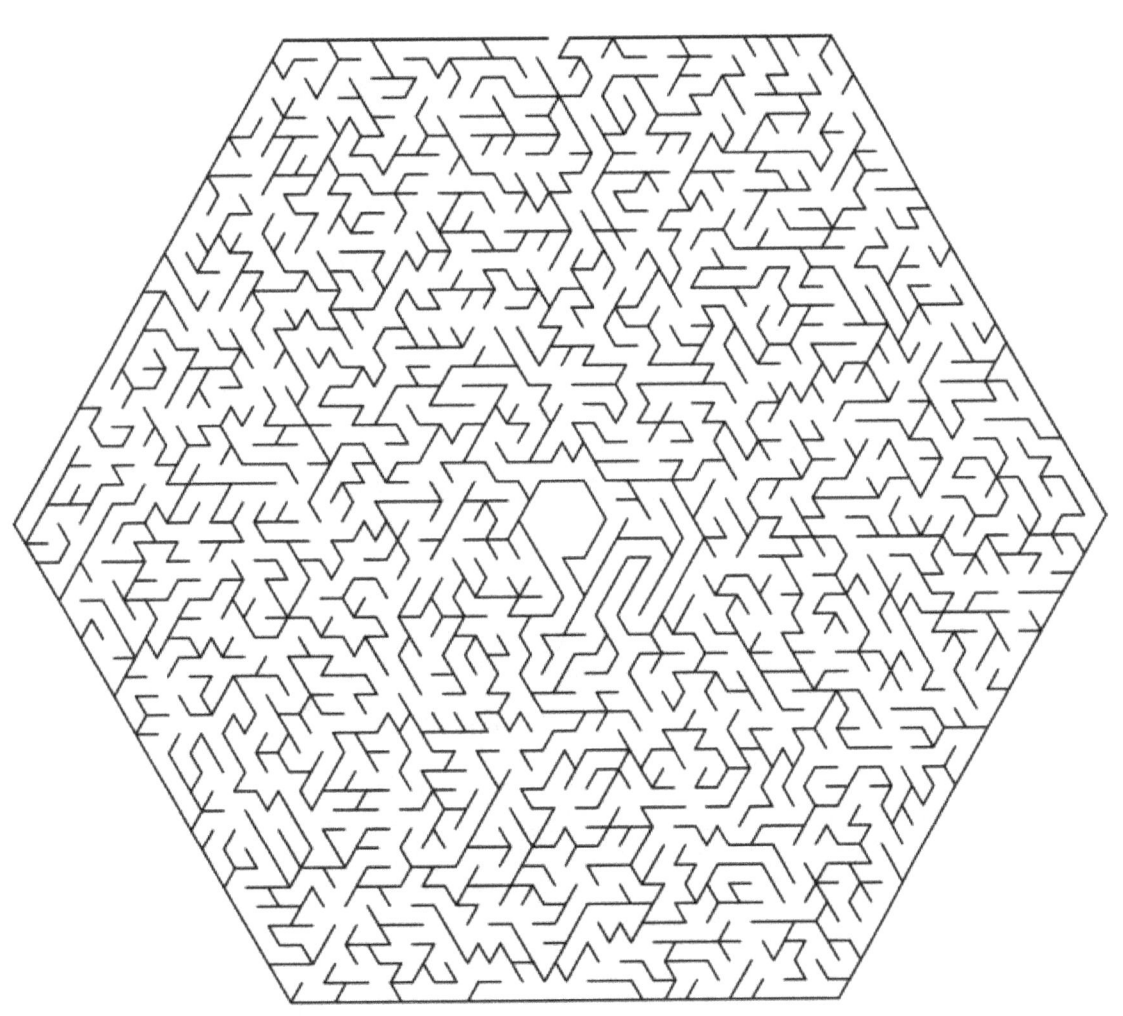

PUT A HEX ON IT #7

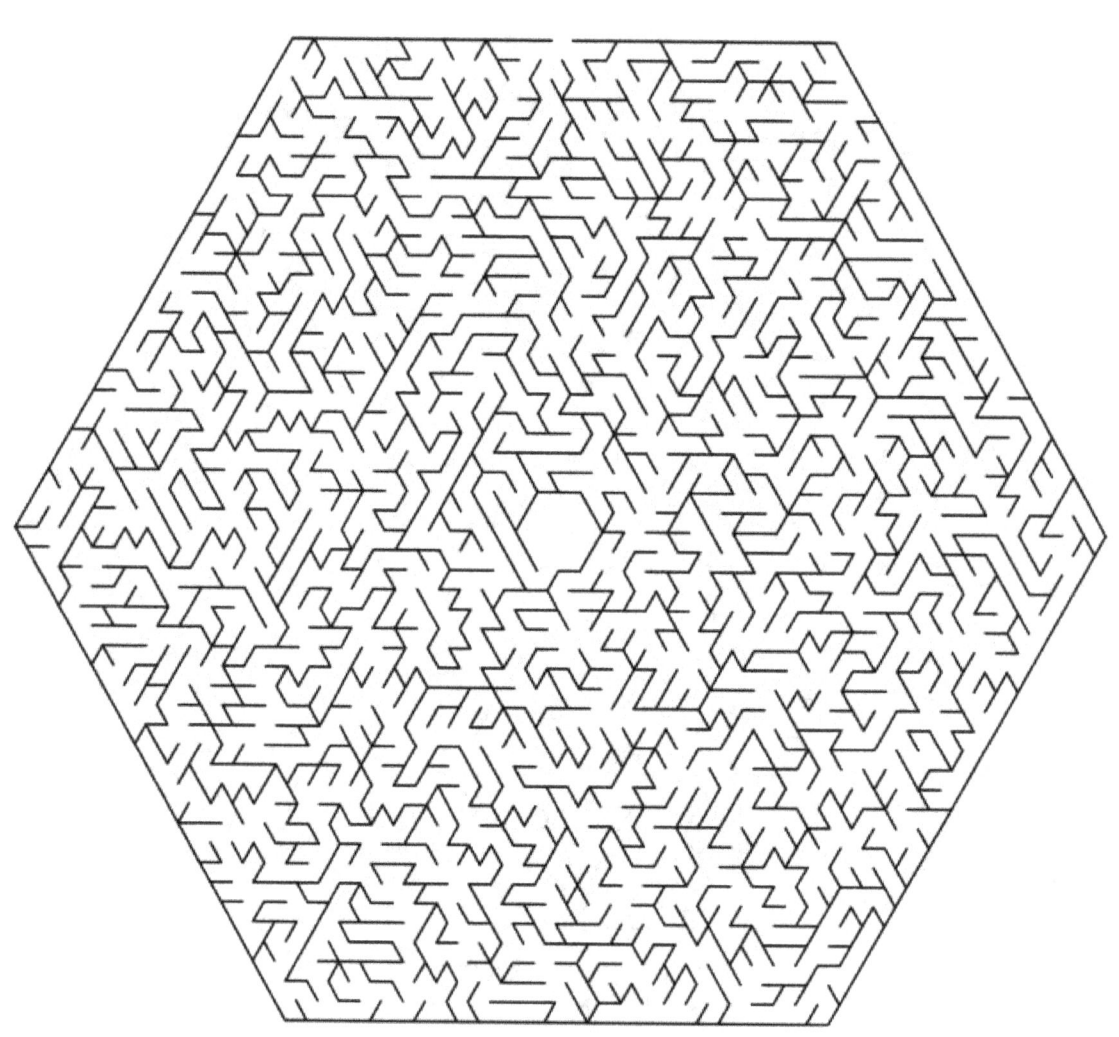

PUT A HEX ON IT #8

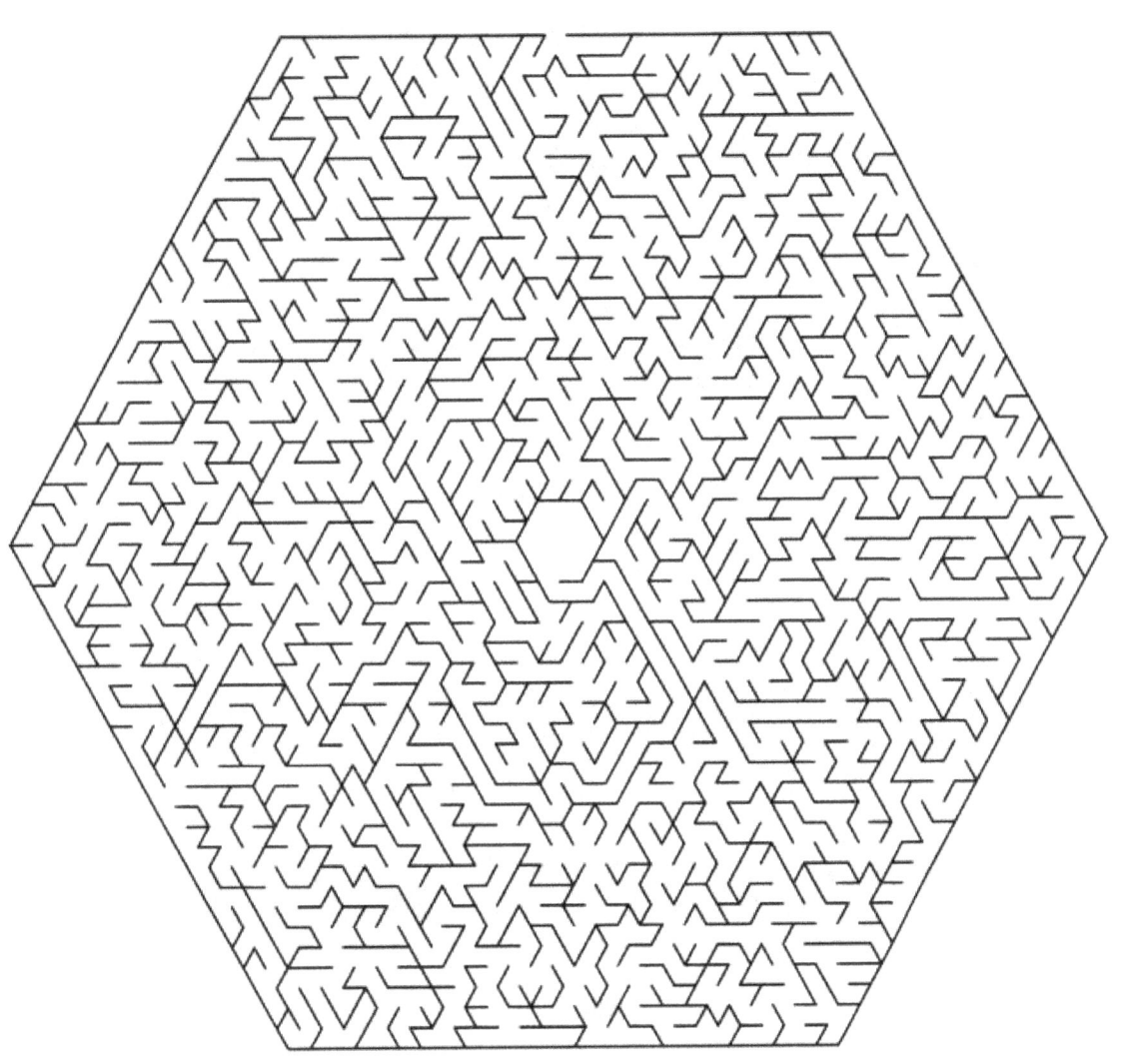

PUT A HEX ON IT #9

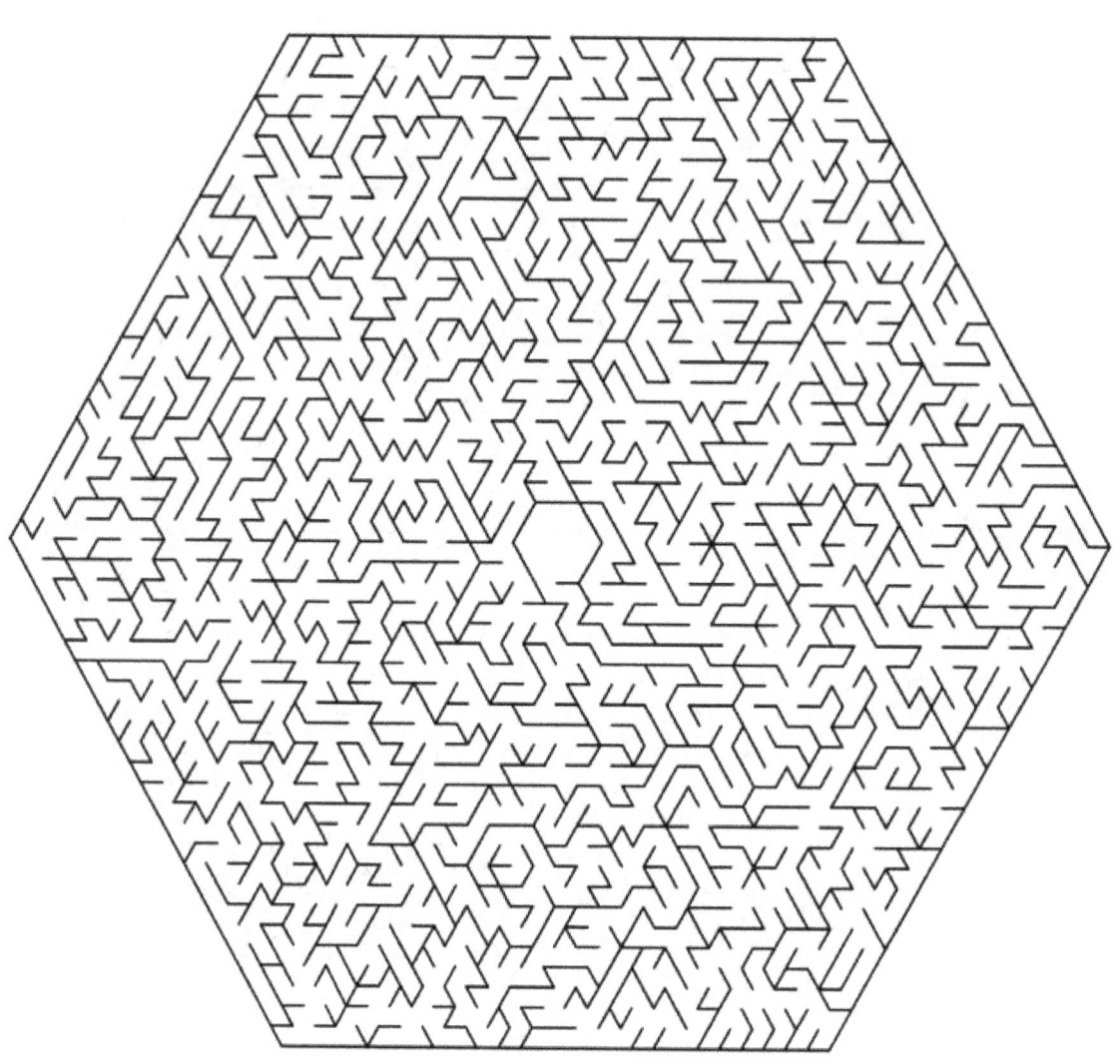

PUT A HEX ON IT #10

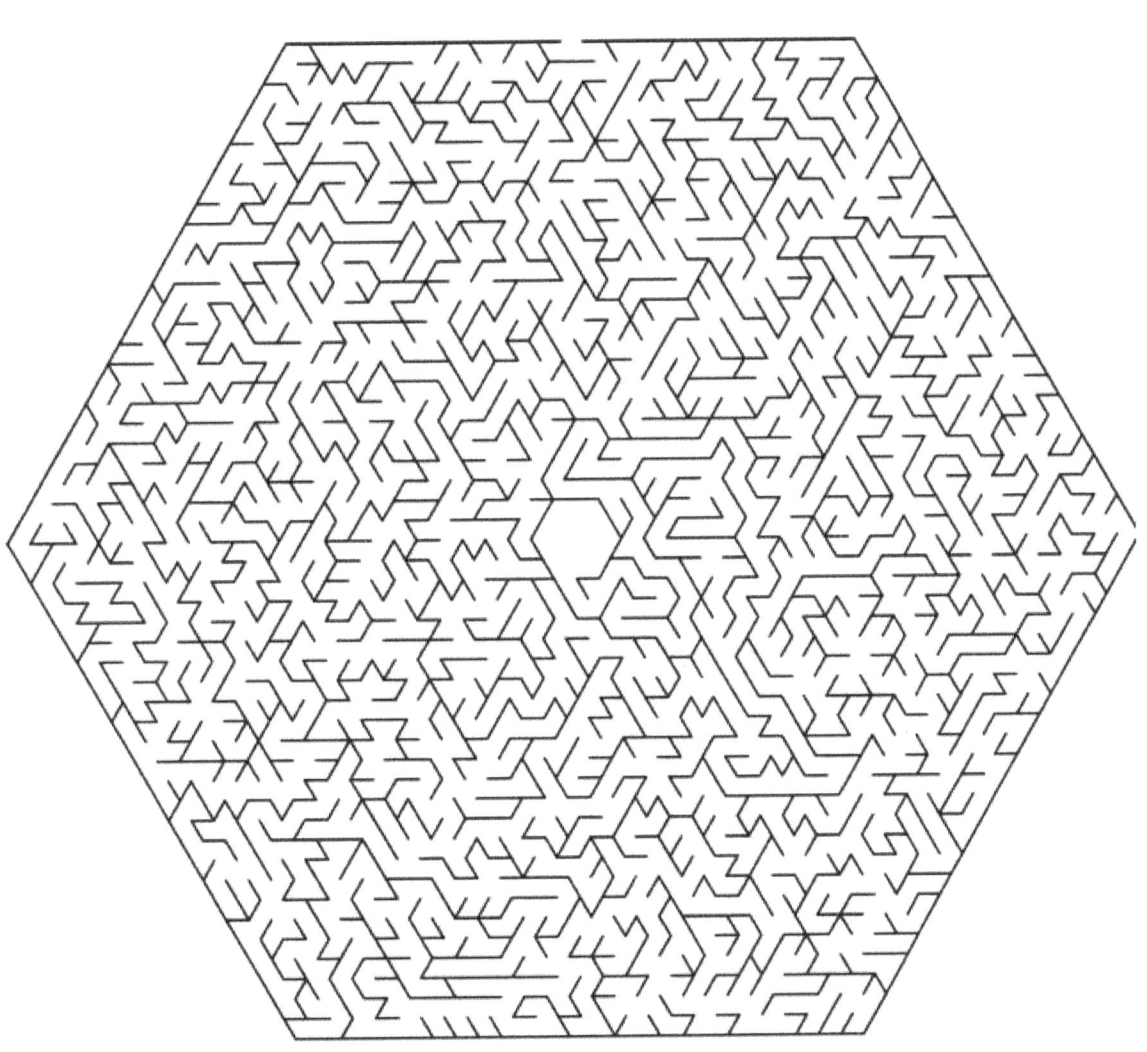

PUT A HEX ON IT #11

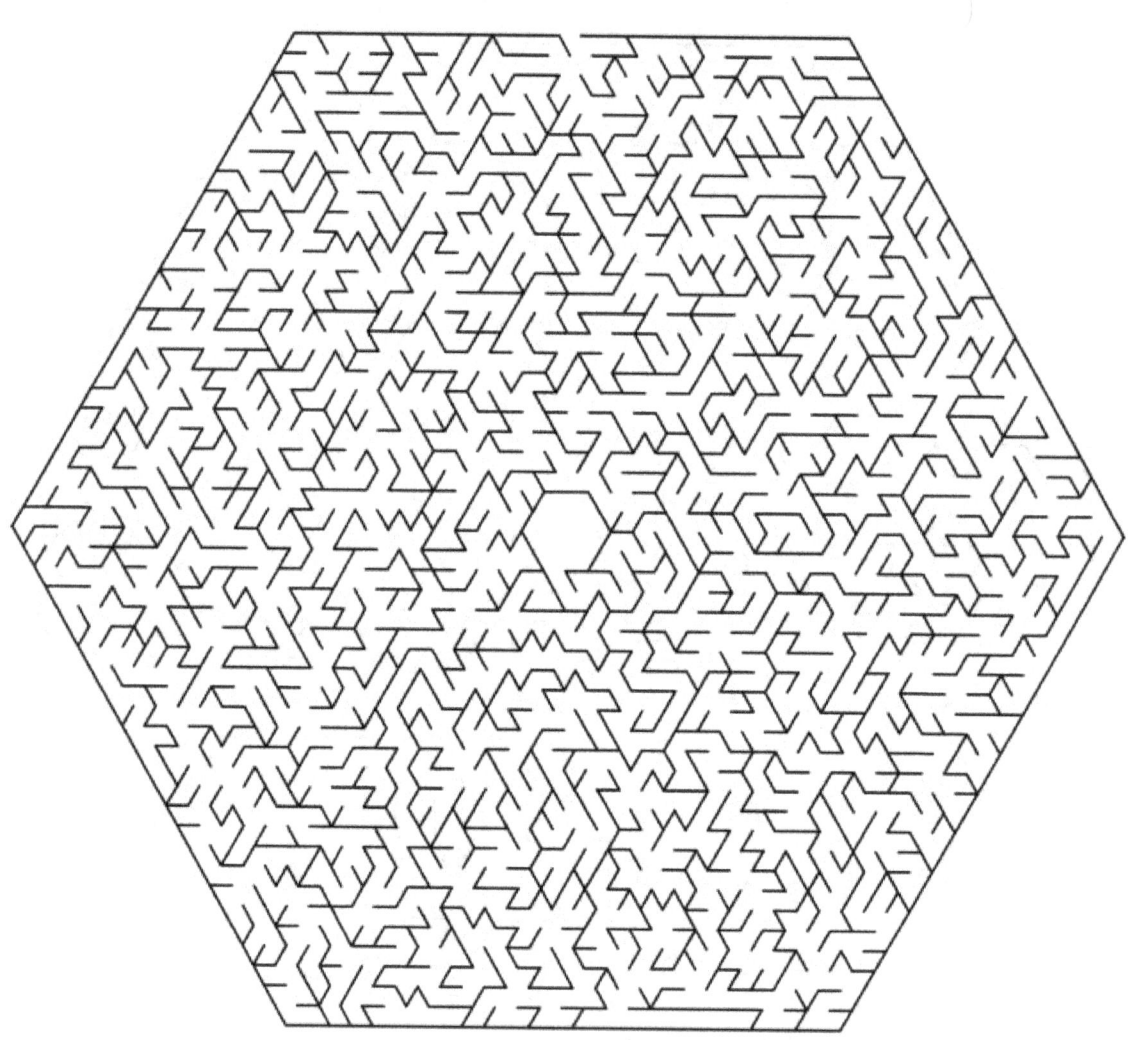

PUT A HEX ON IT #12

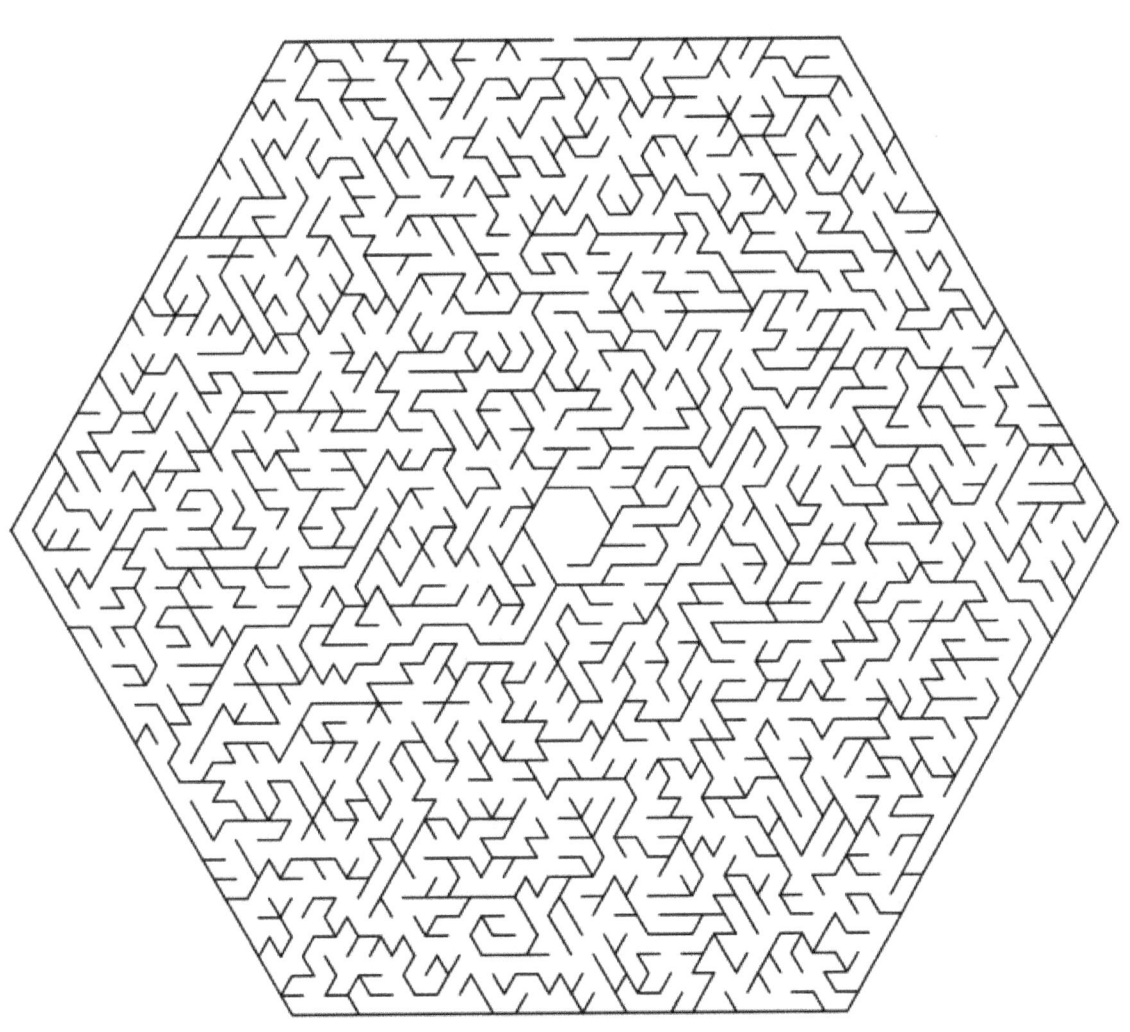

PUT A HEX ON IT #13

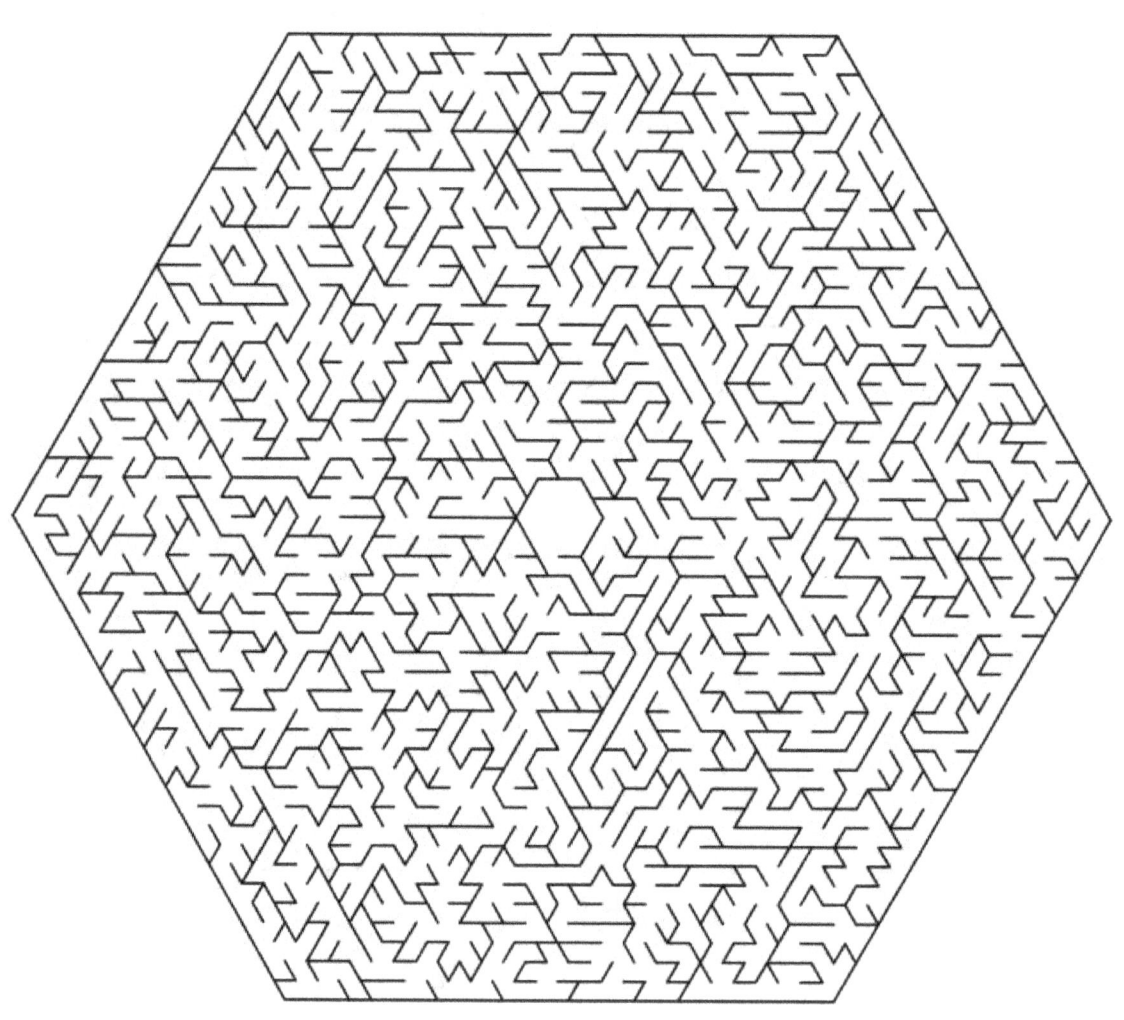

PUT A HEX ON IT #14

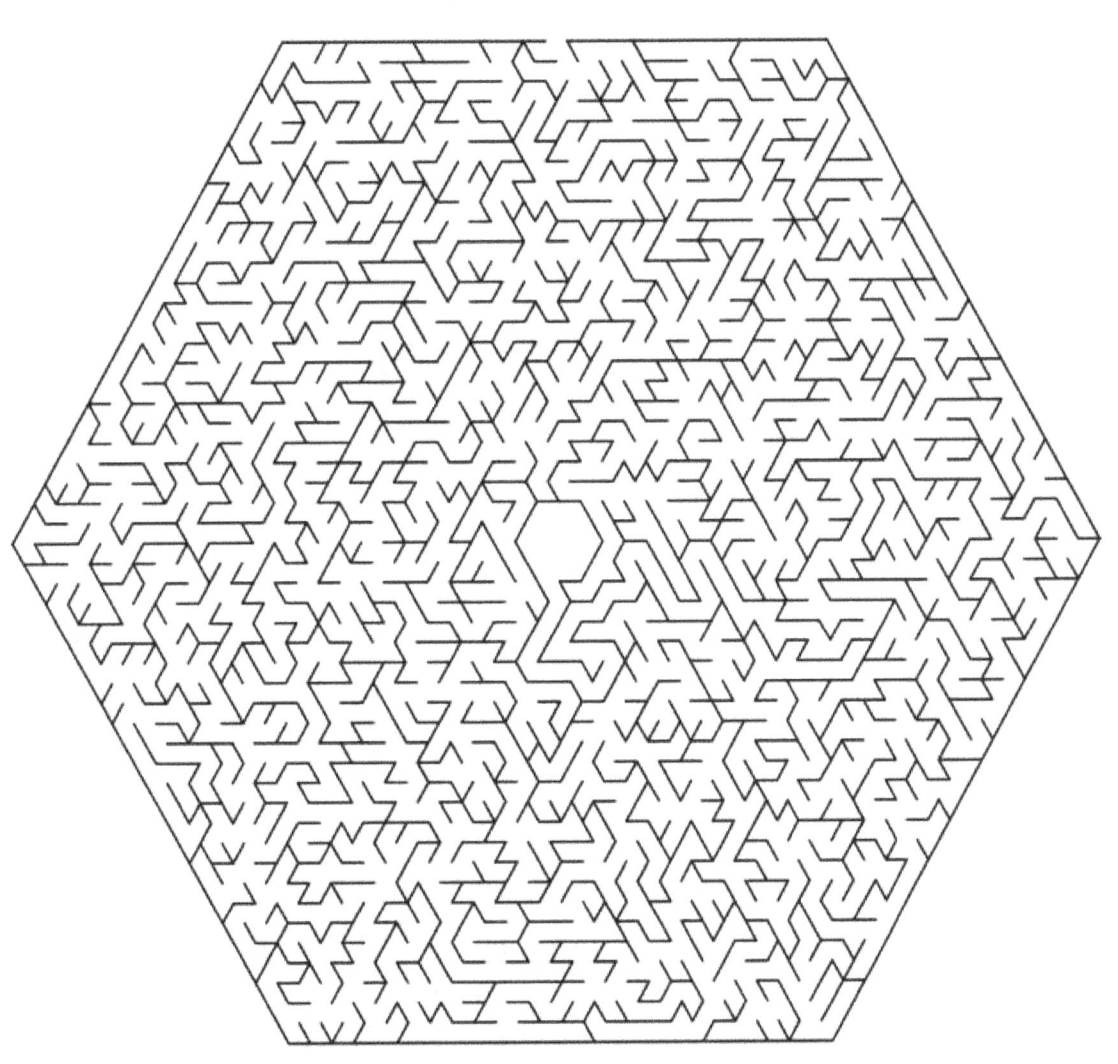

PUT A HEX ON IT #15

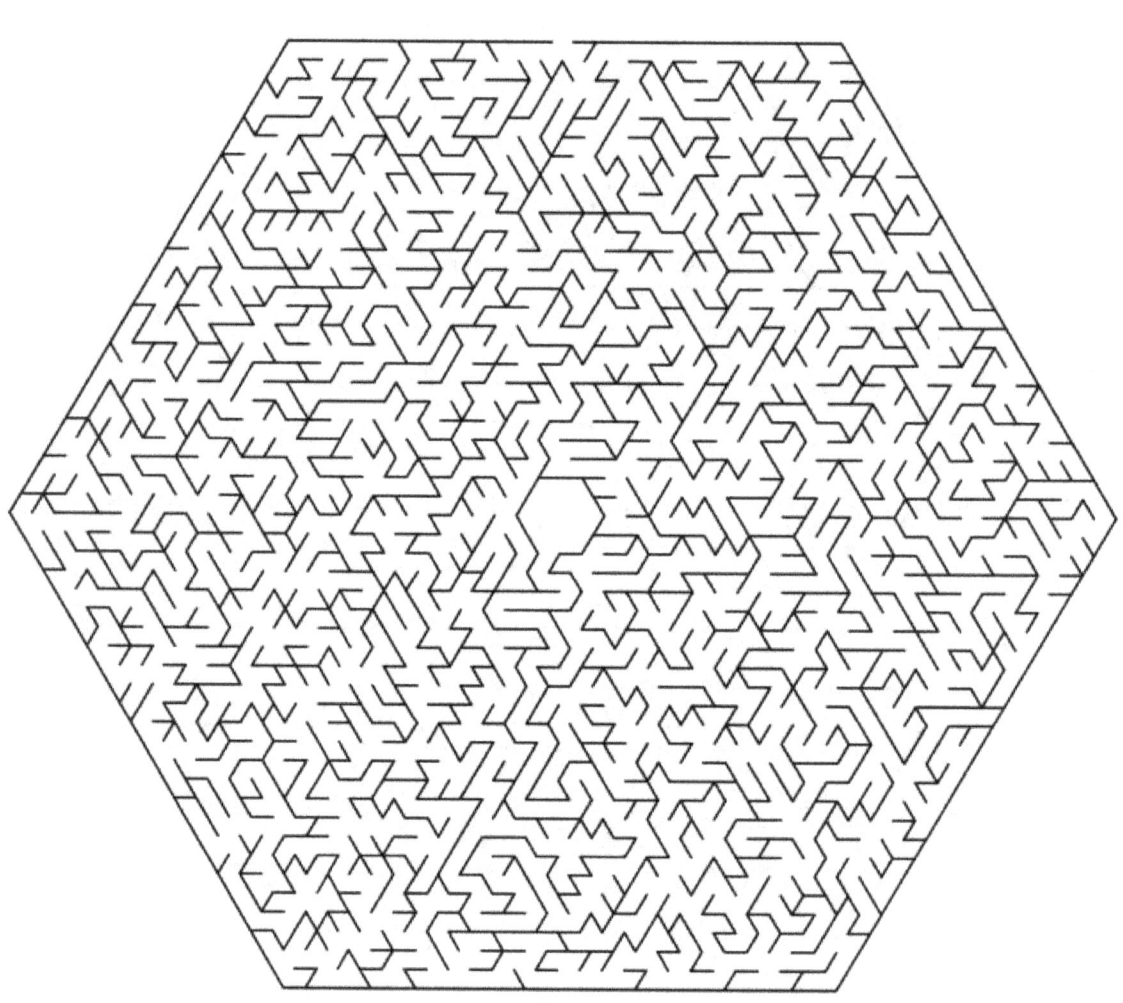

PUT A HEX ON IT #16

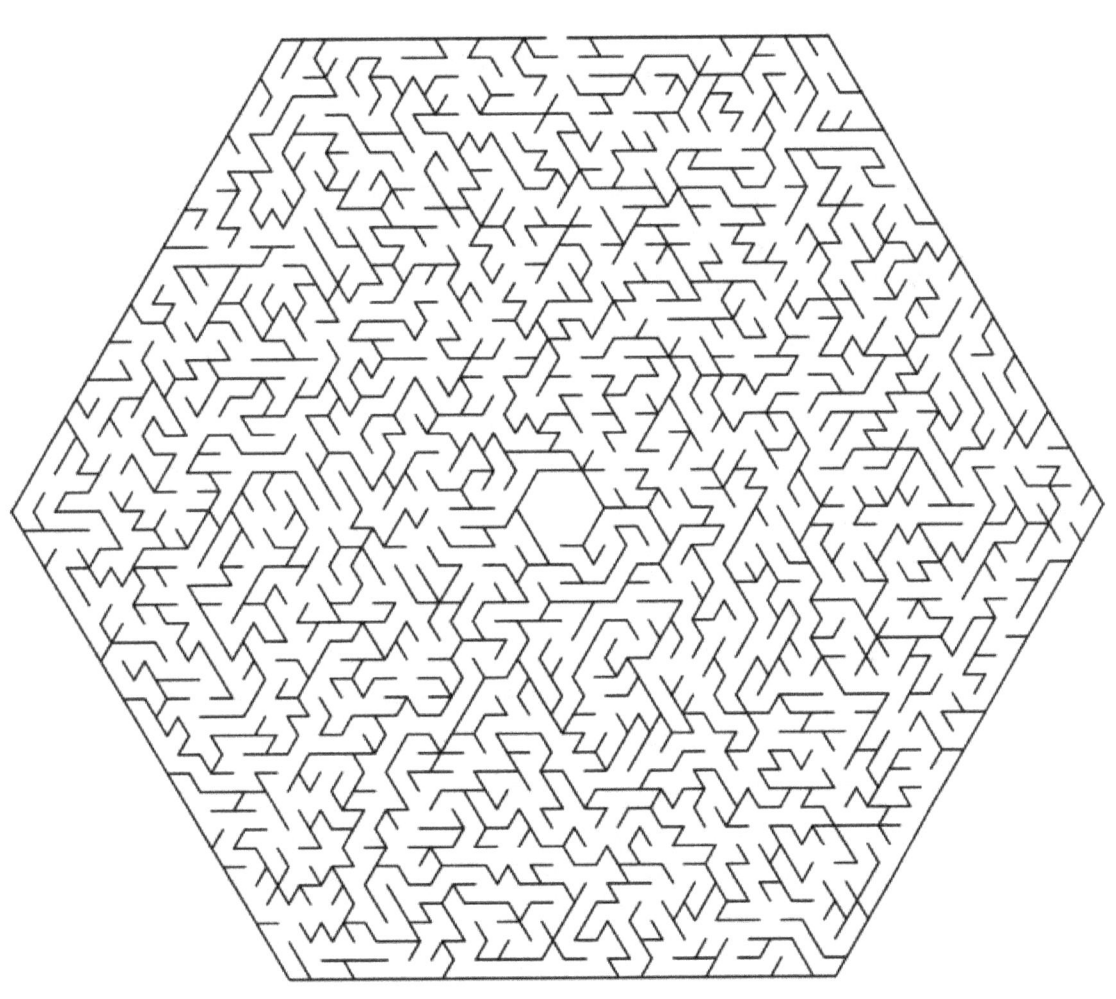

PUT A HEX ON IT #17

PUT A HEX ON IT #18

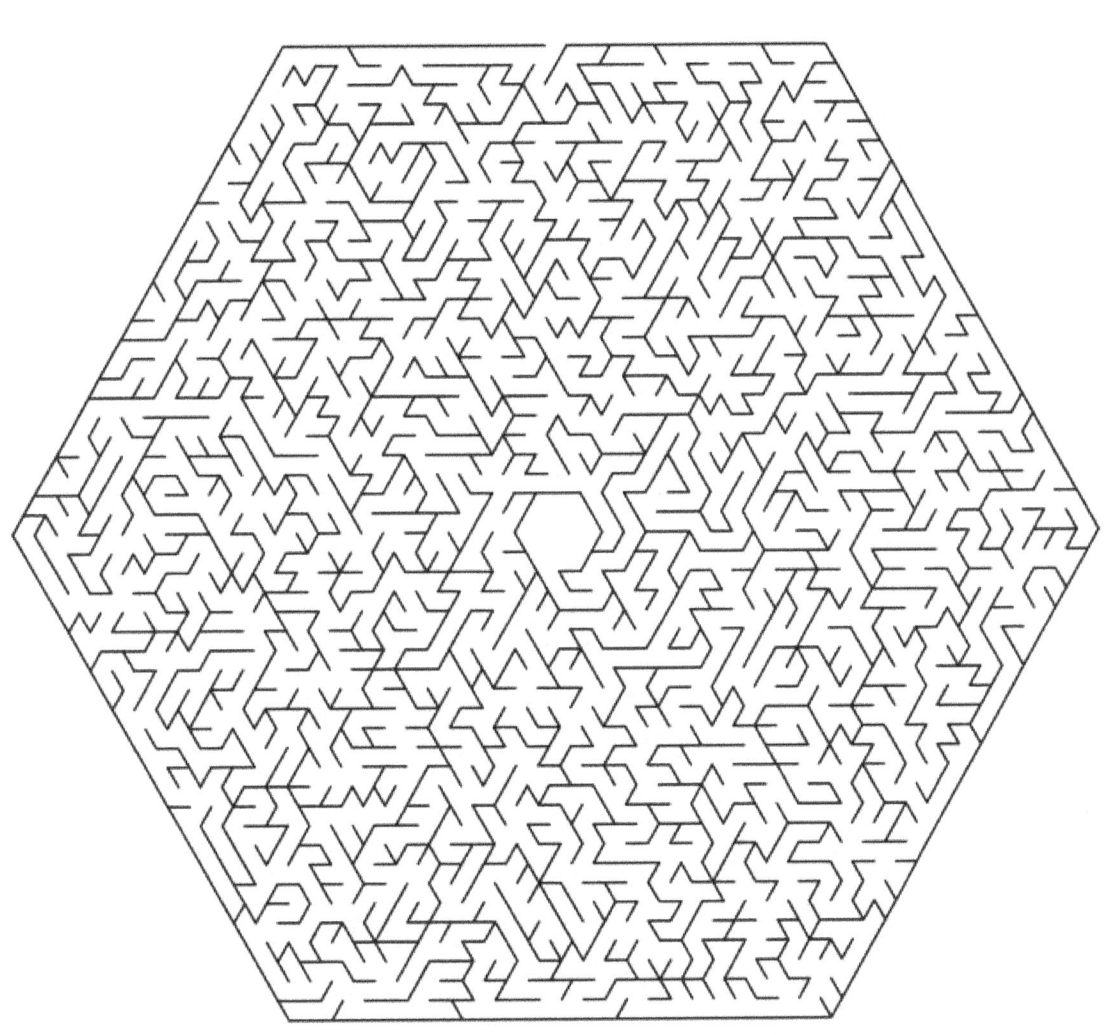

PUT A HEX ON IT #19

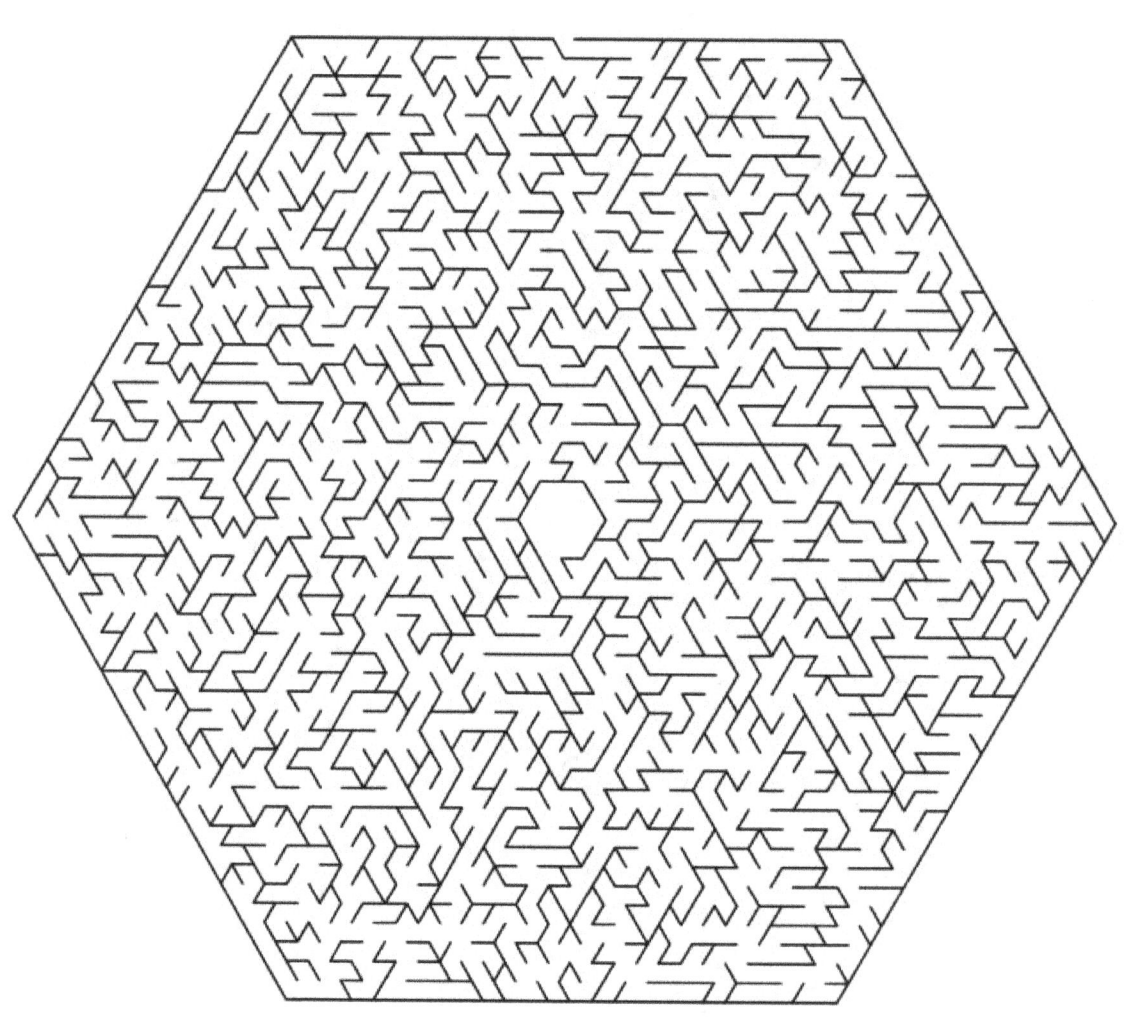

PUT A HEX ON IT #20

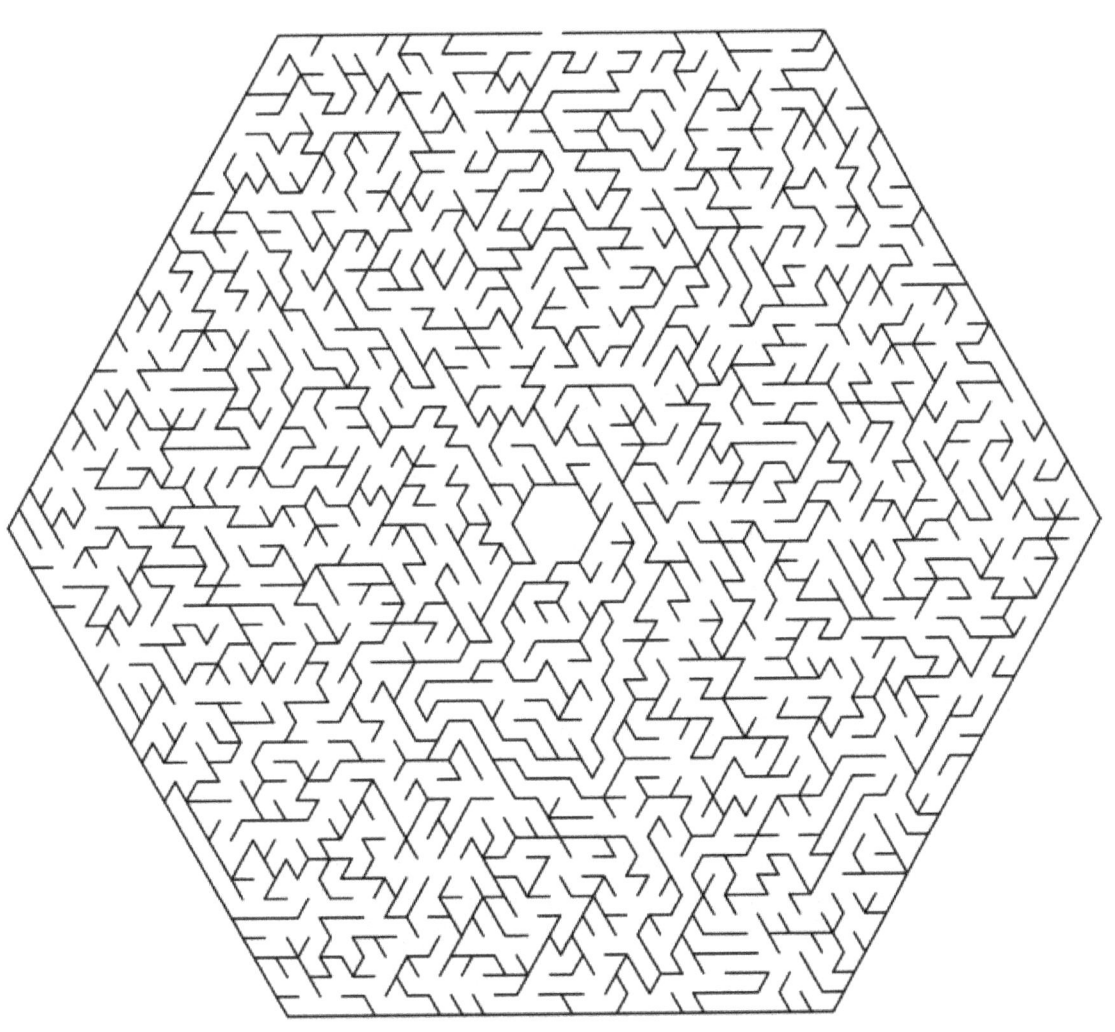

PUT A HEX ON IT #21

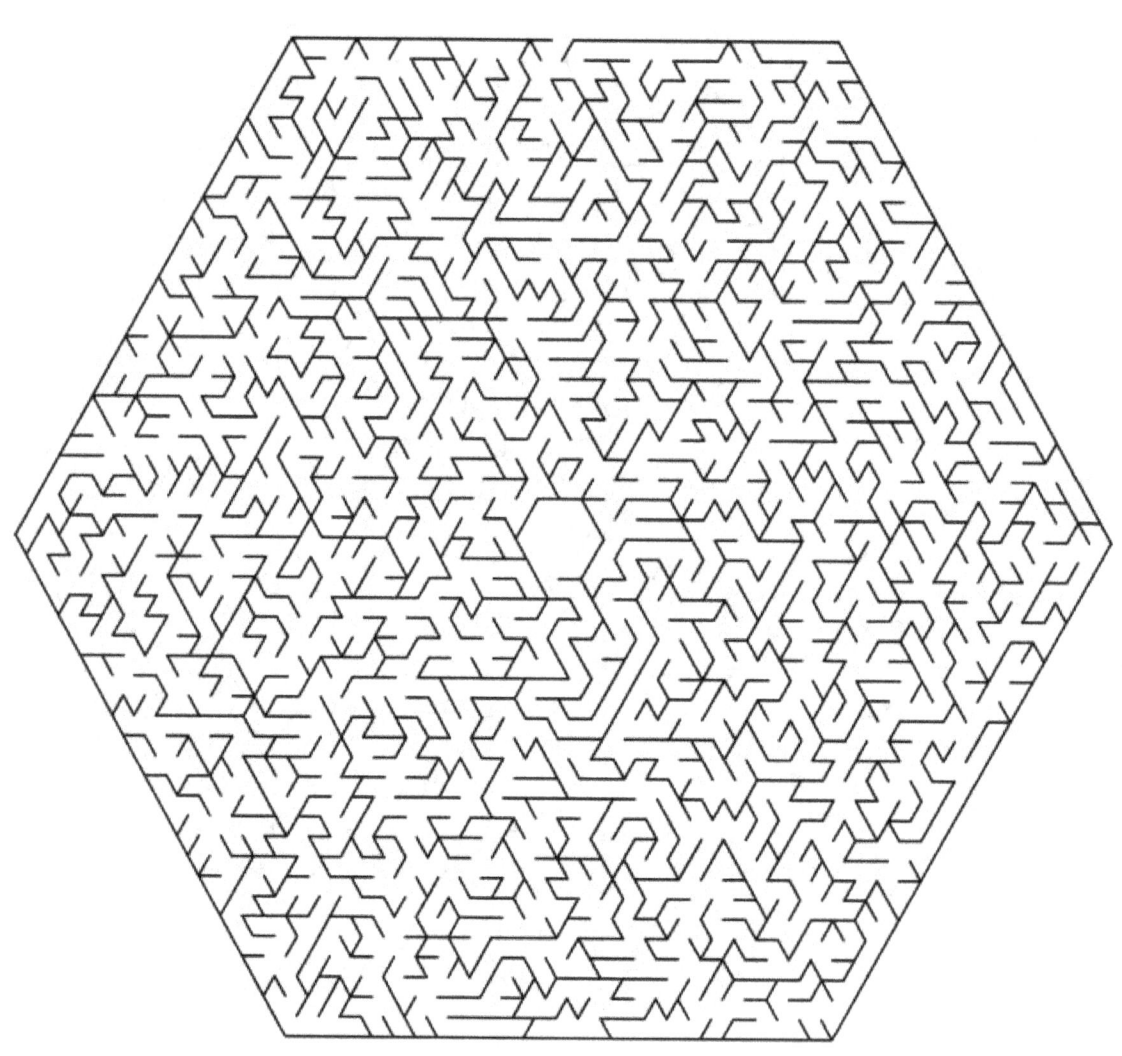

PUT A HEX ON IT #22

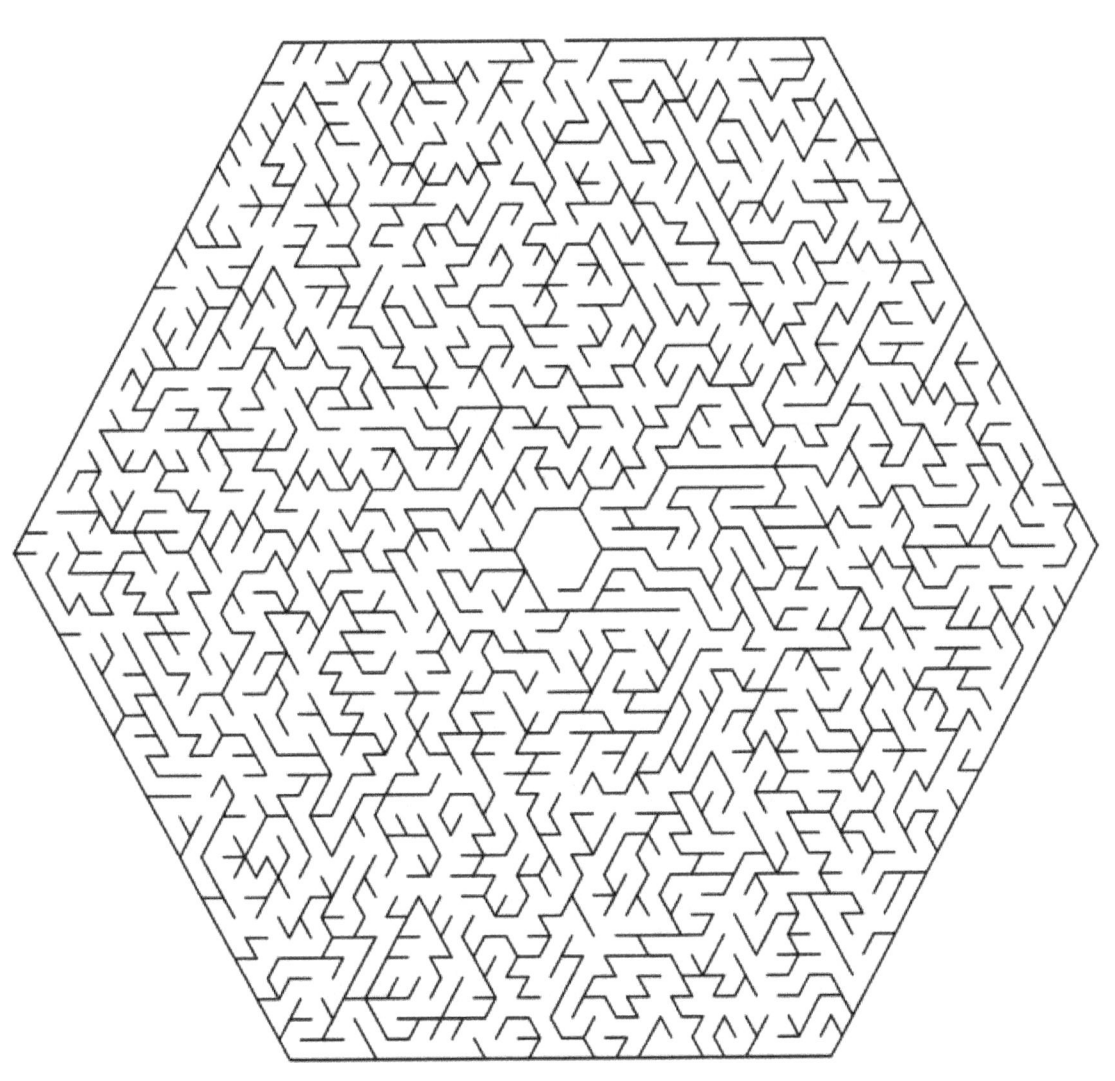

PUT A HEX ON IT #23

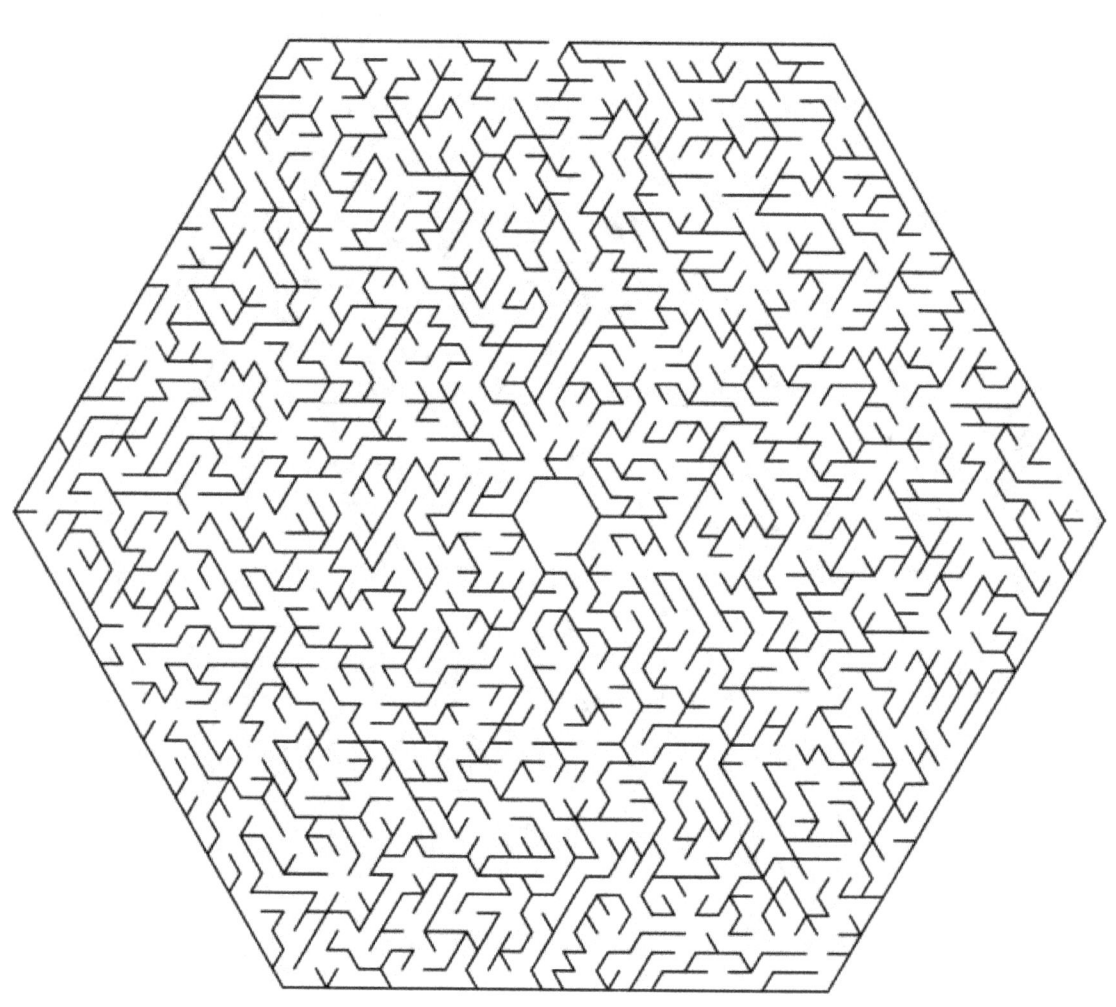

PUT A HEX ON IT #24

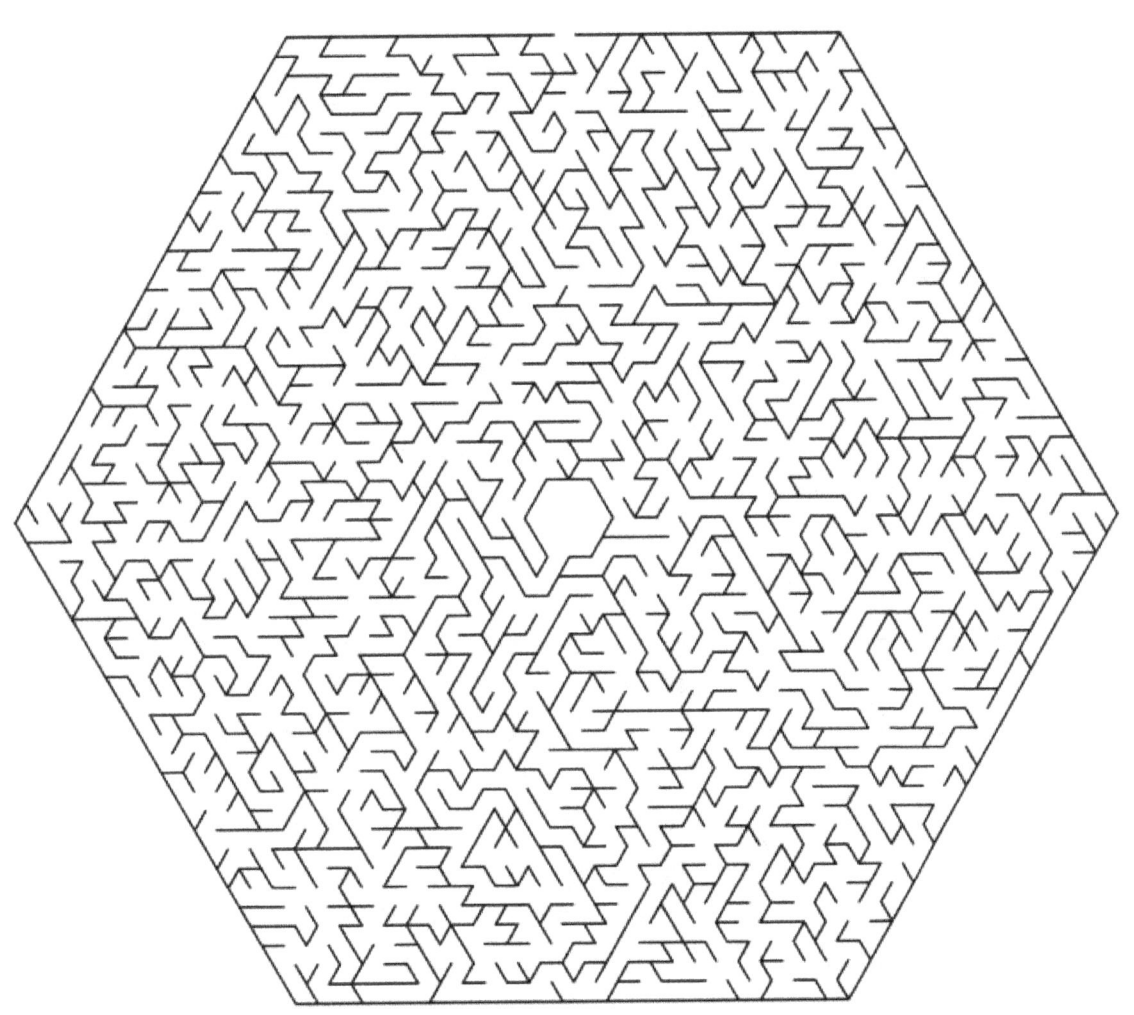

PUT A HEX ON IT #25

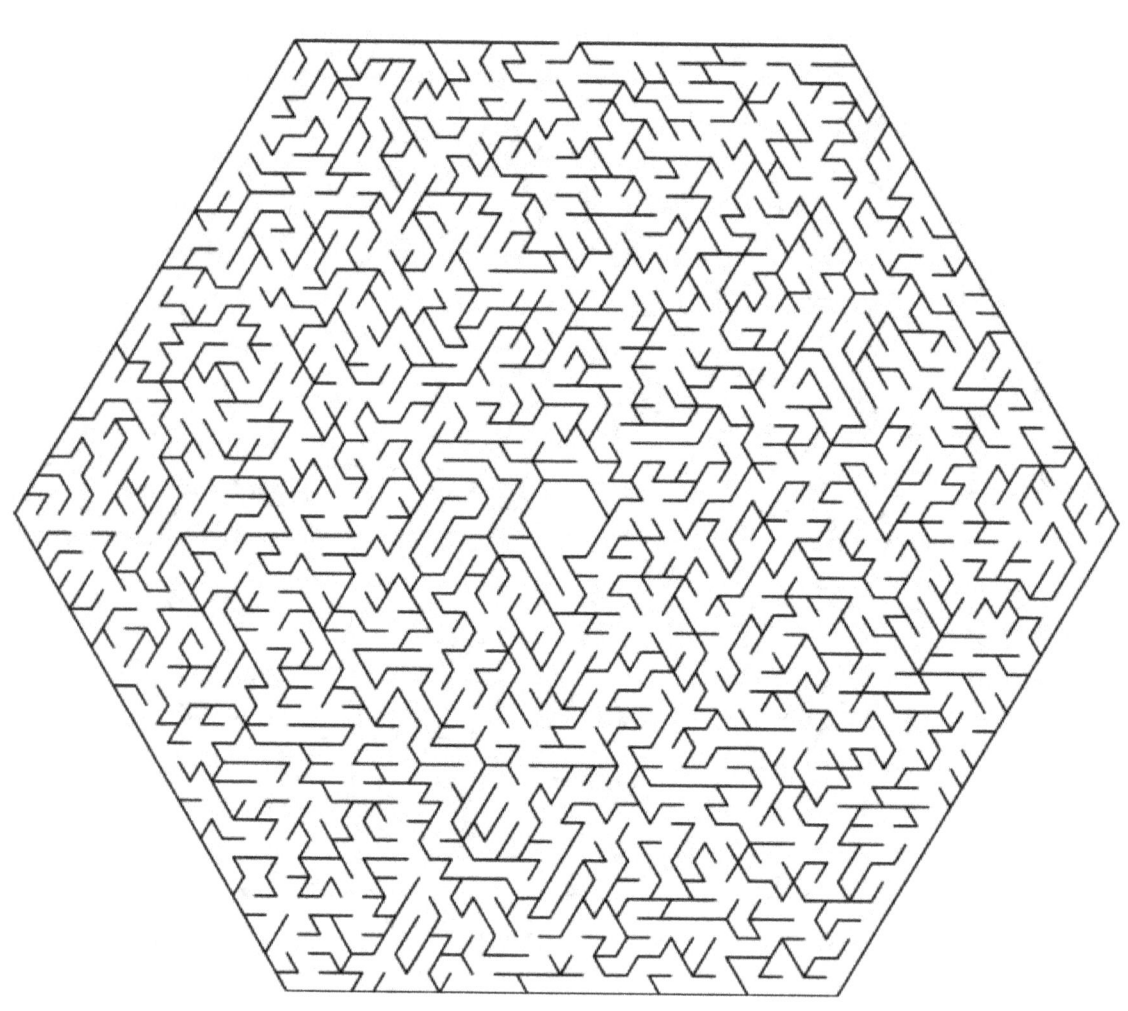

PUT A HEX ON IT #26

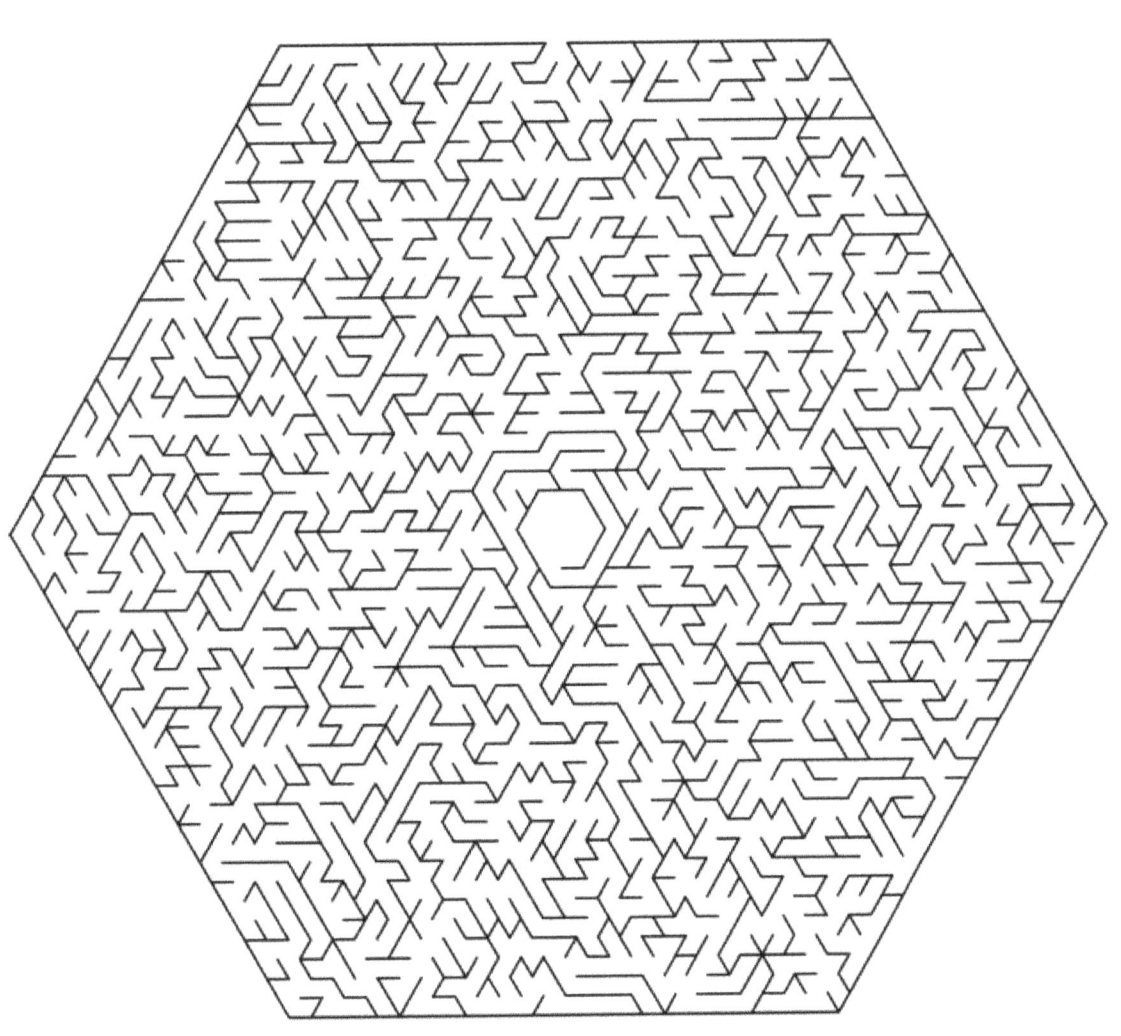

PUT A HEX ON IT #27

PUT A HEX ON IT #28

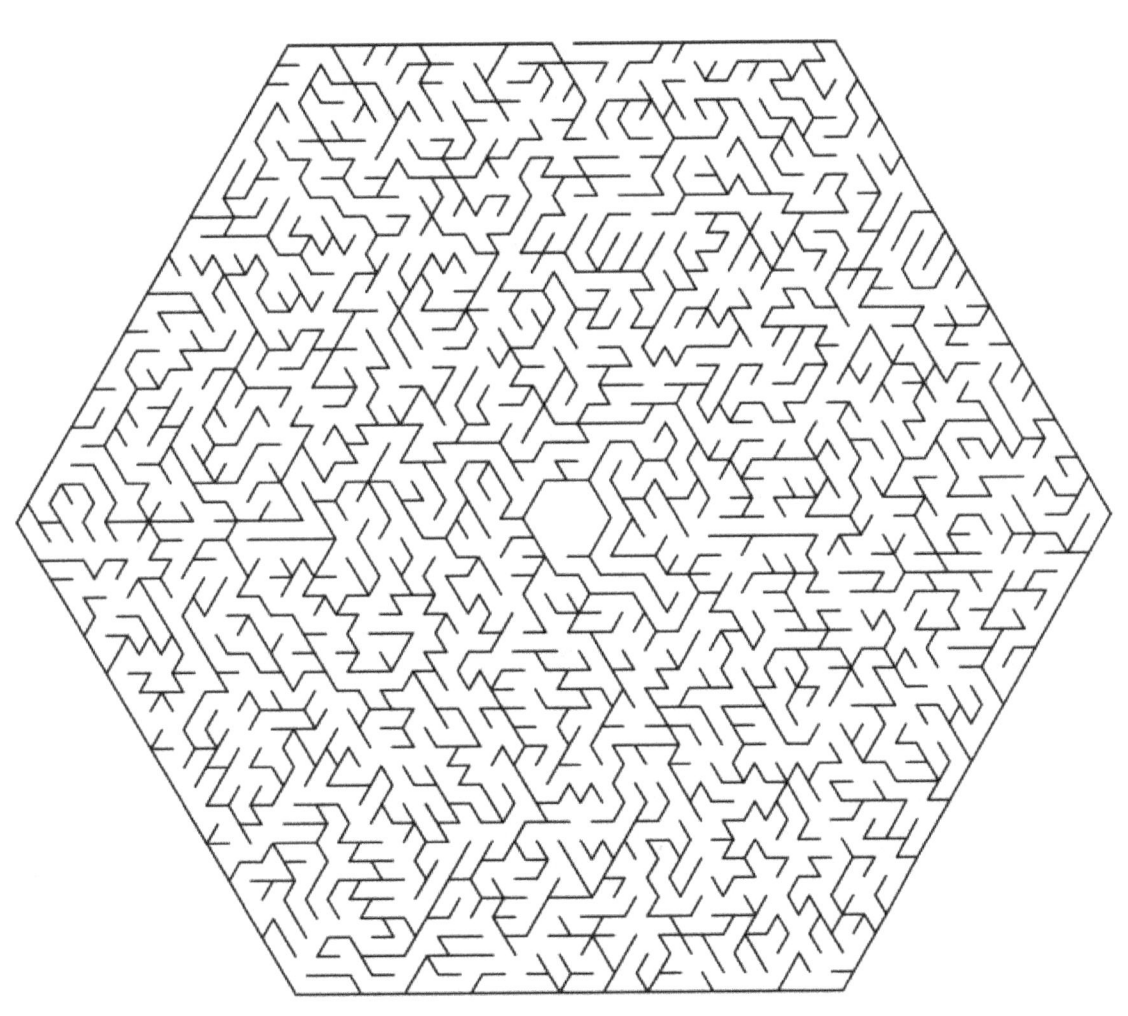

PUT A HEX ON IT #29

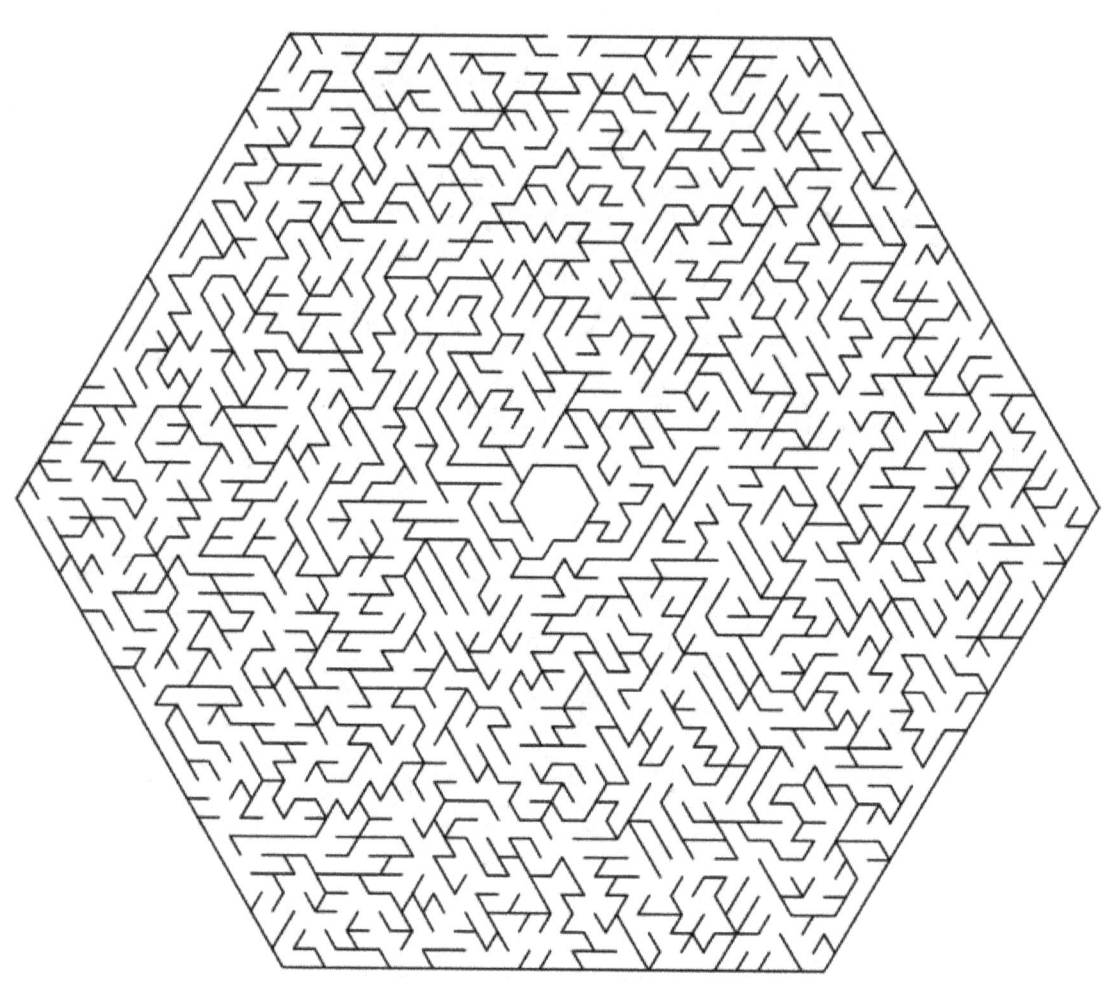

PUT A HEX ON IT #30

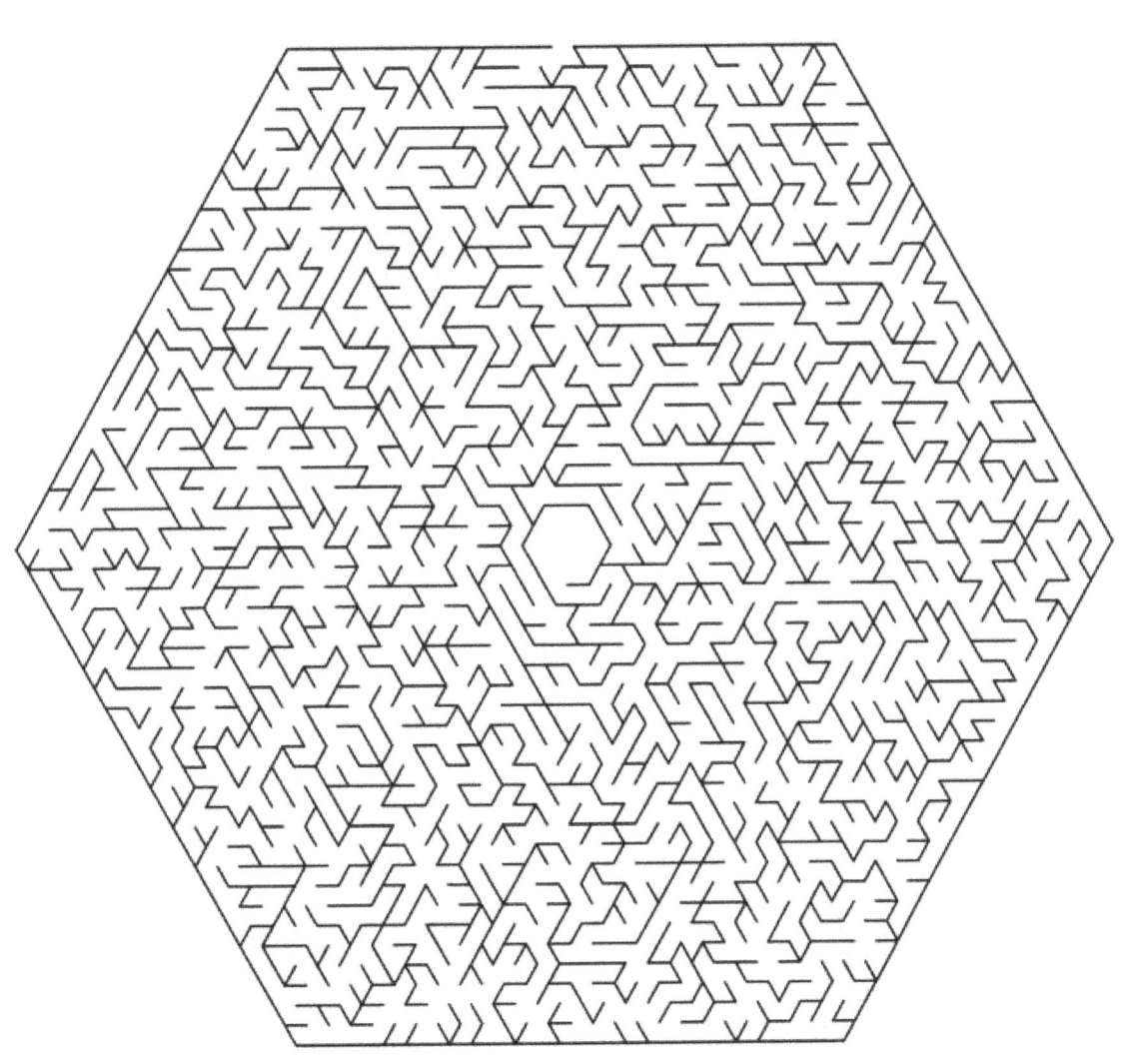

PUT A HEX ON IT #31

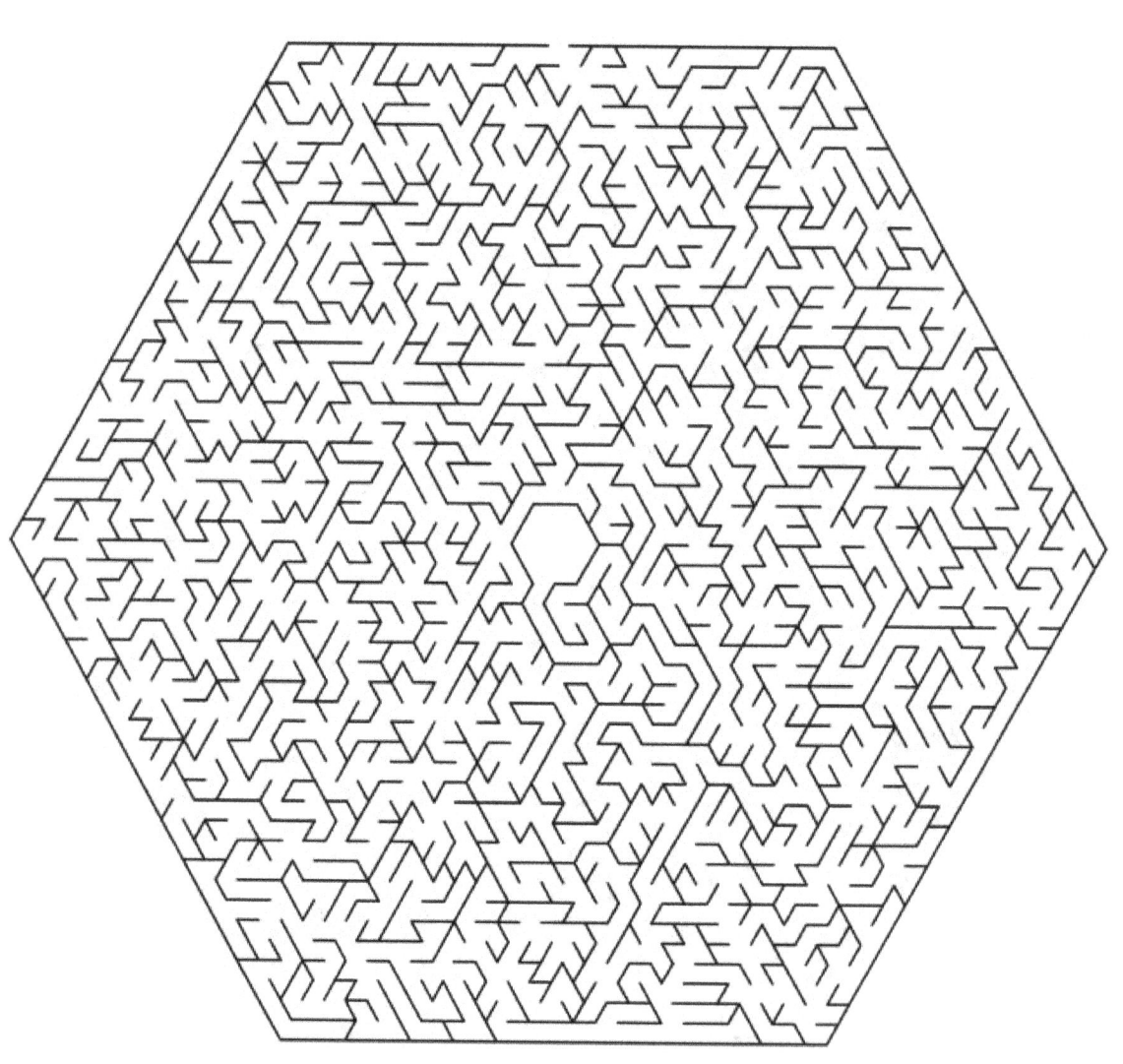

PUT A HEX ON IT #32

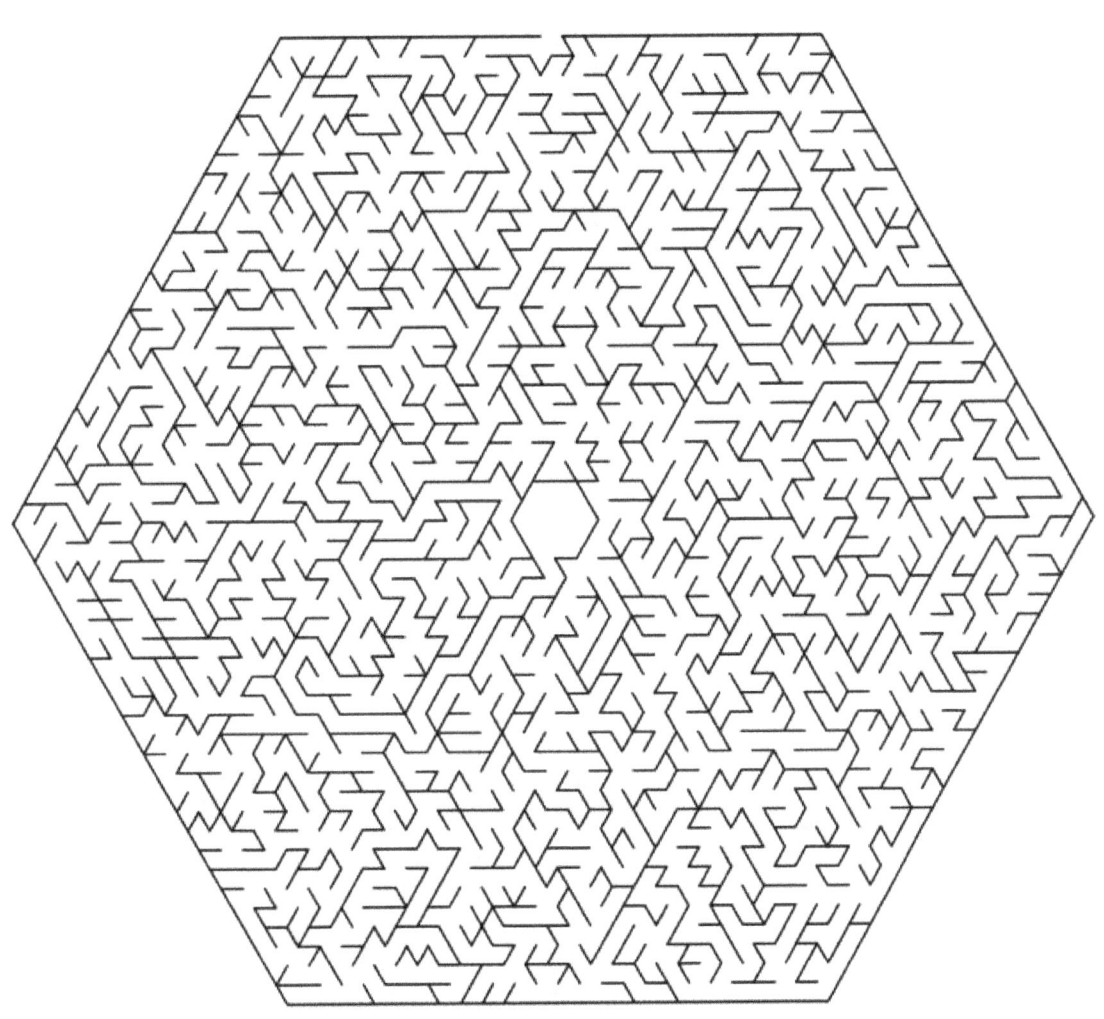

PUT A HEX ON IT #33

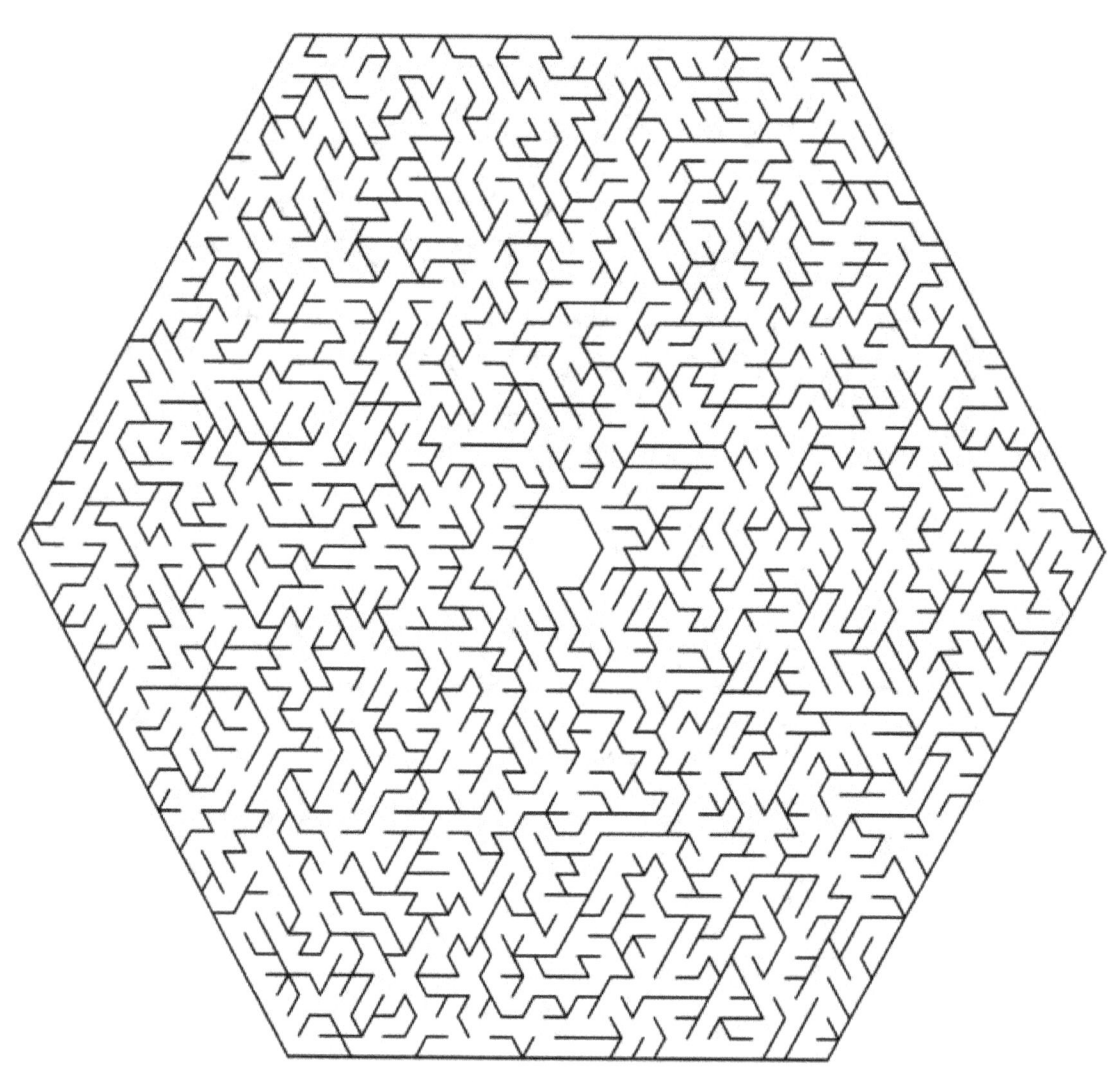

PUT A HEX ON IT #34

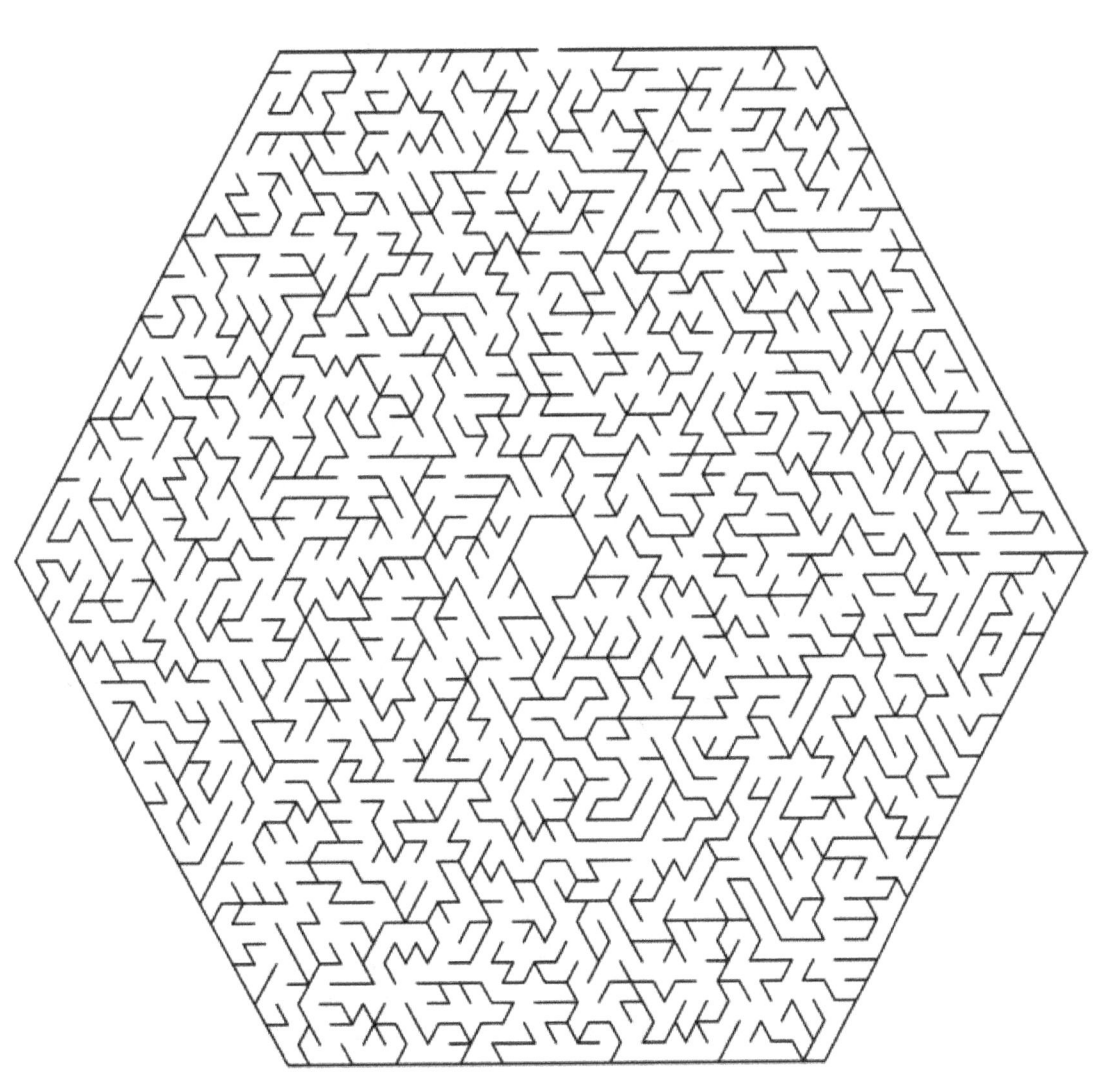

PUT A HEX ON IT #35

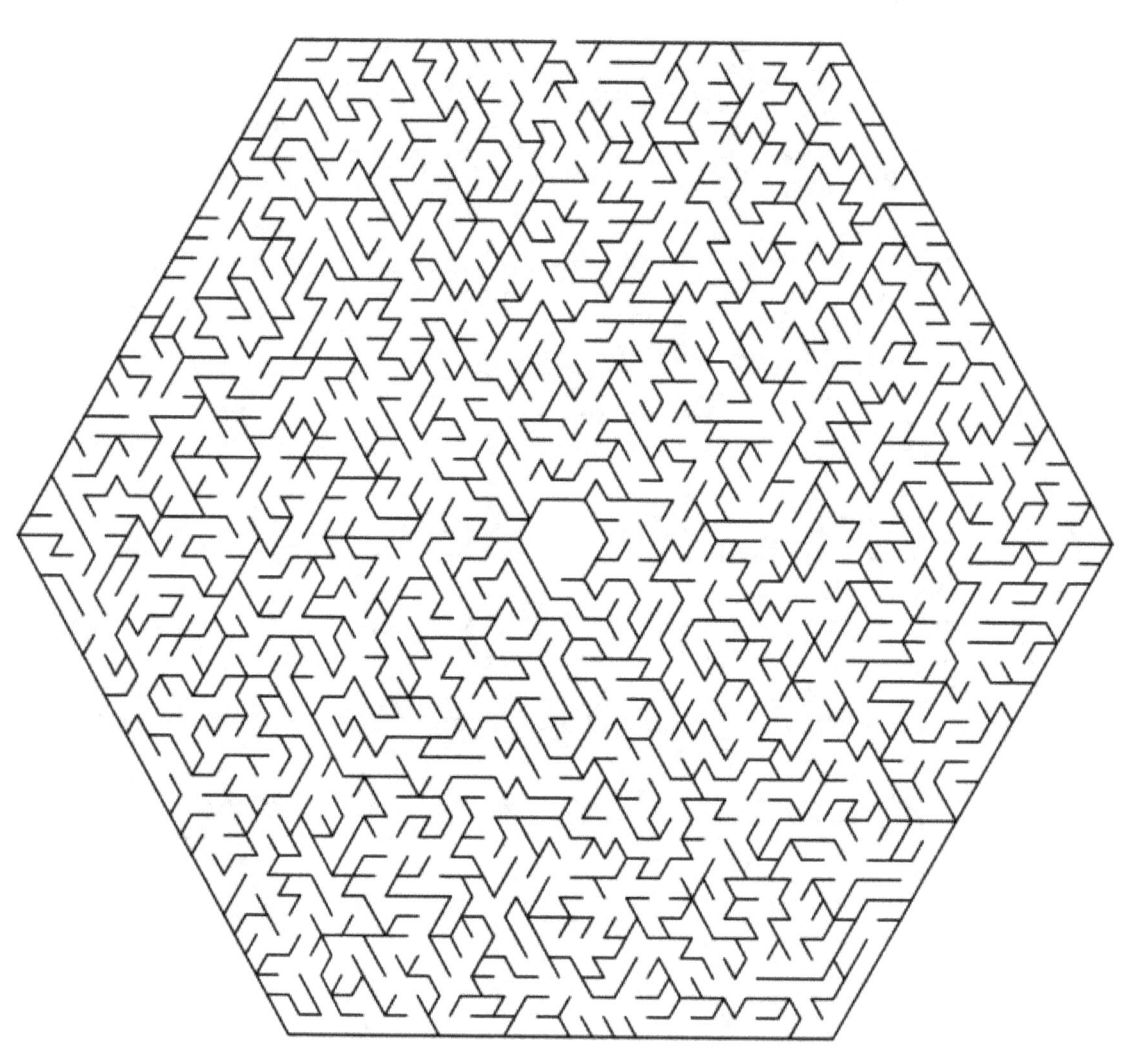

PUT A HEX ON IT #36

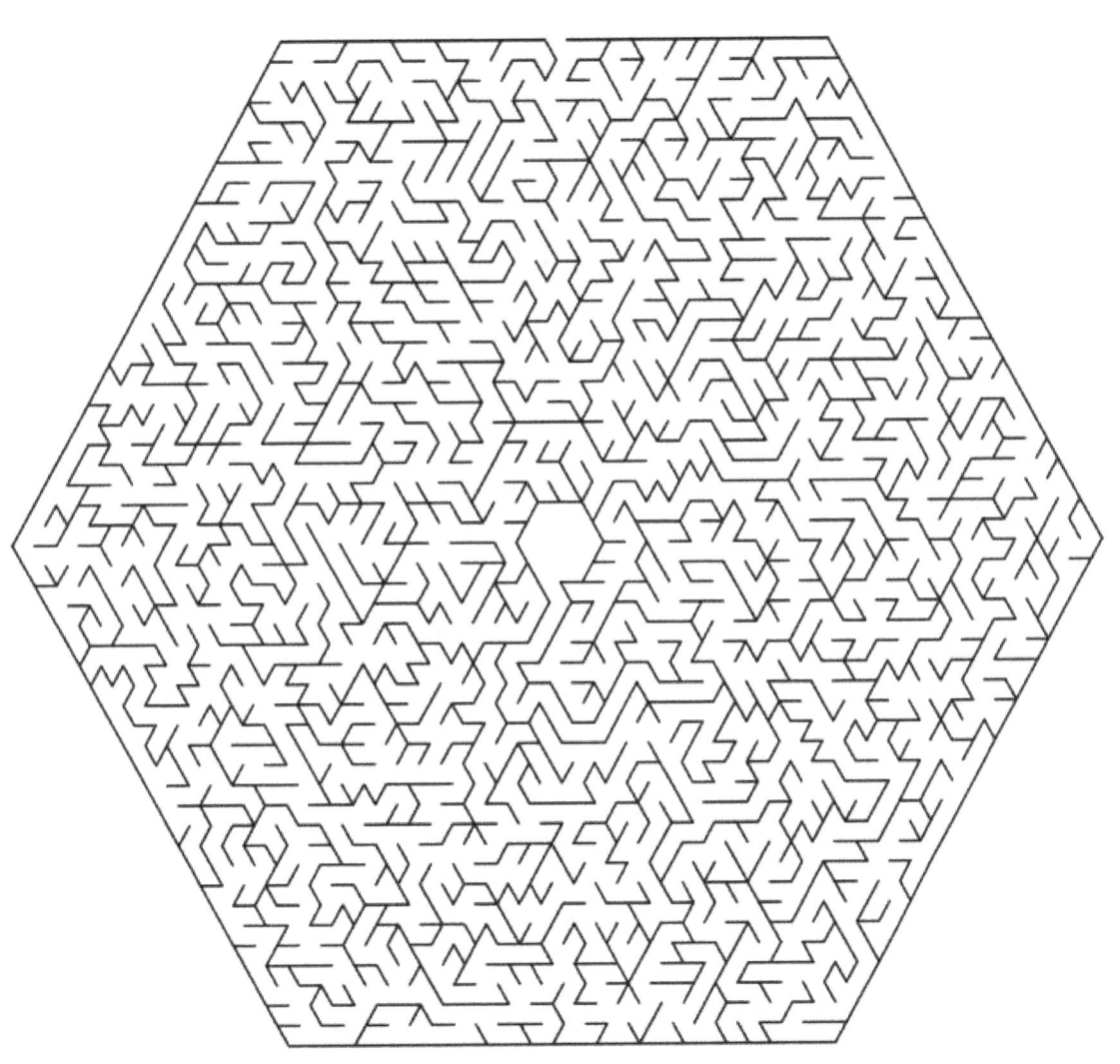

PUT A HEX ON IT #37

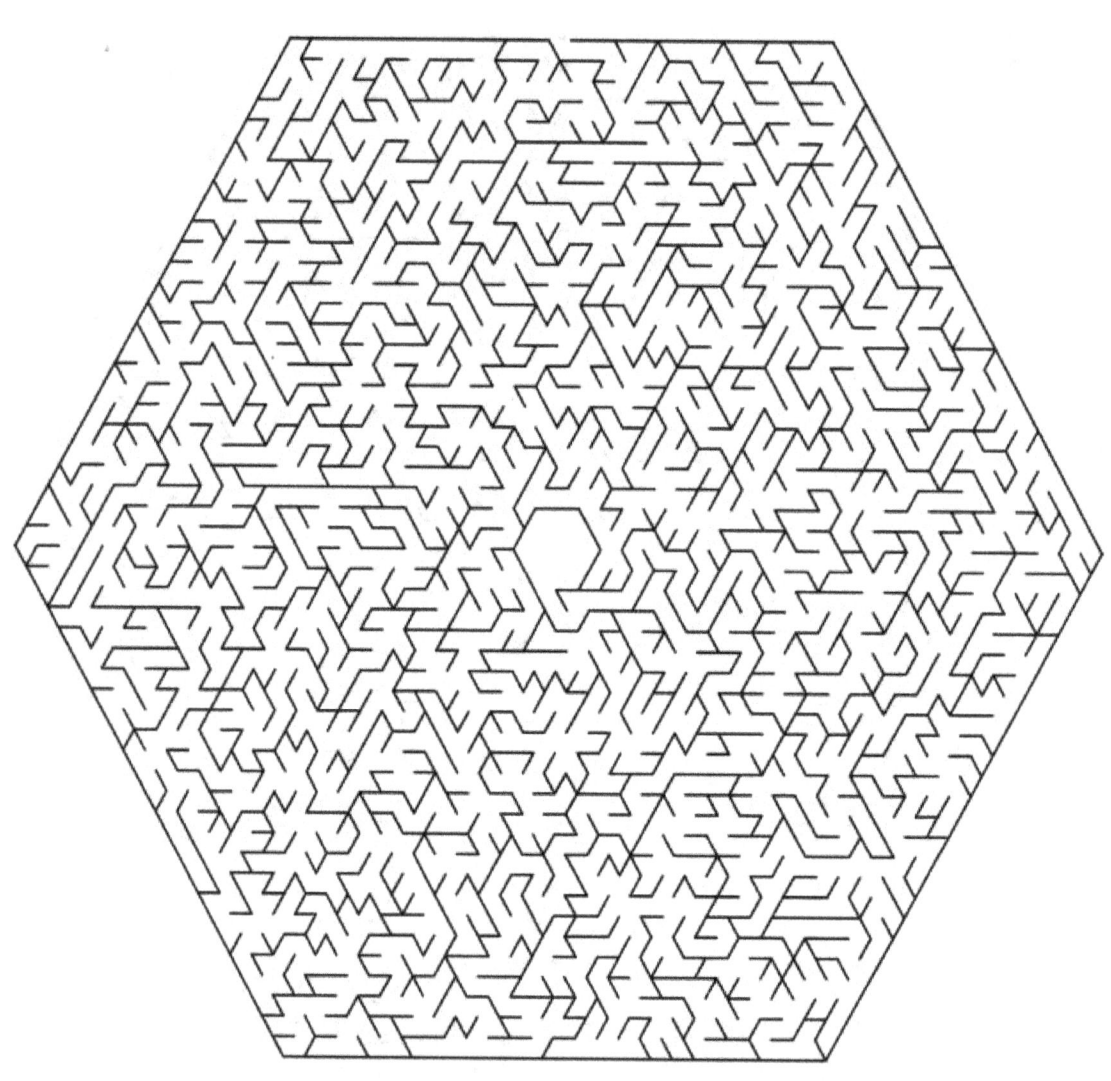

PUT A HEX ON IT #38

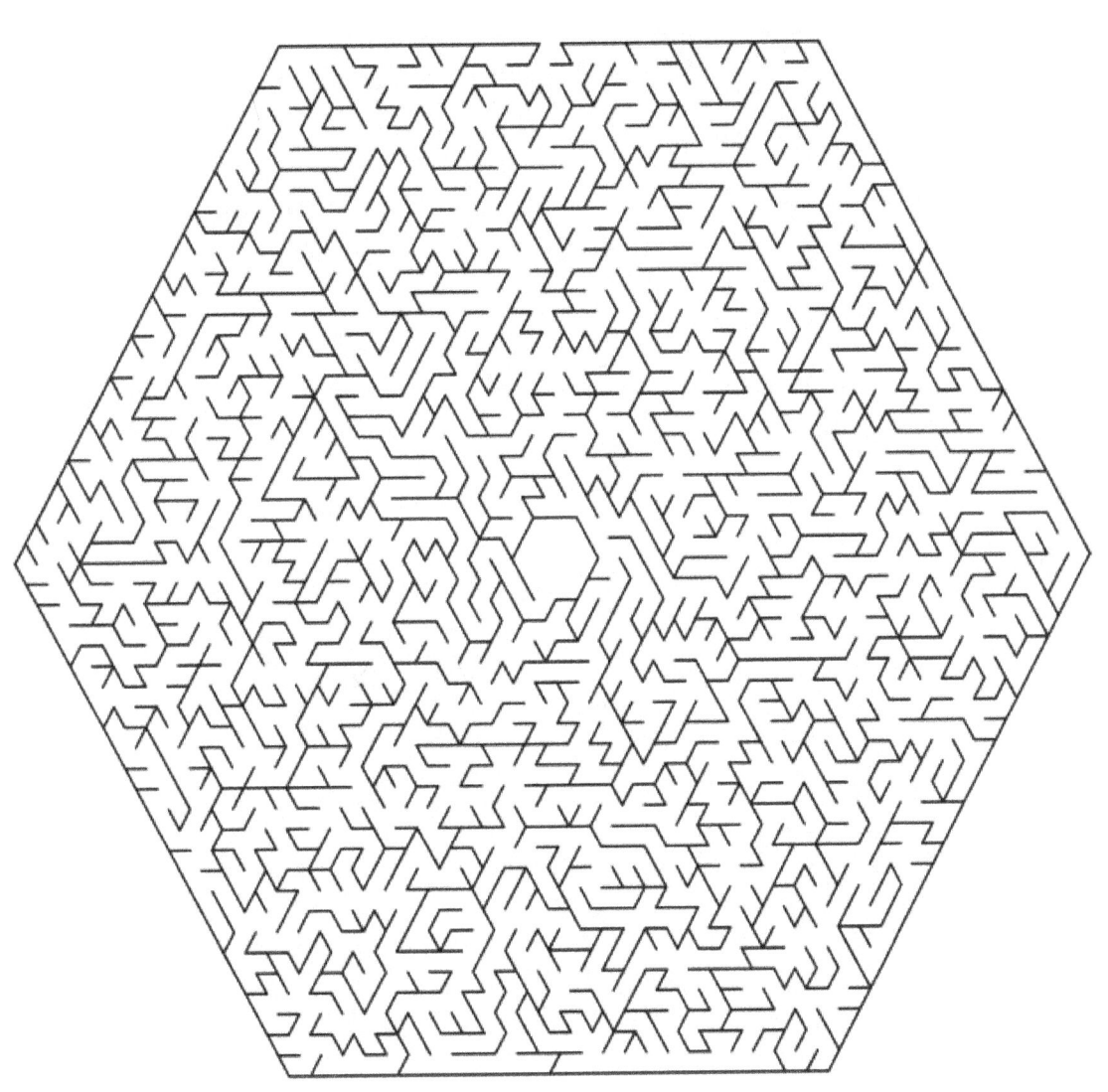

PUT A HEX ON IT #39

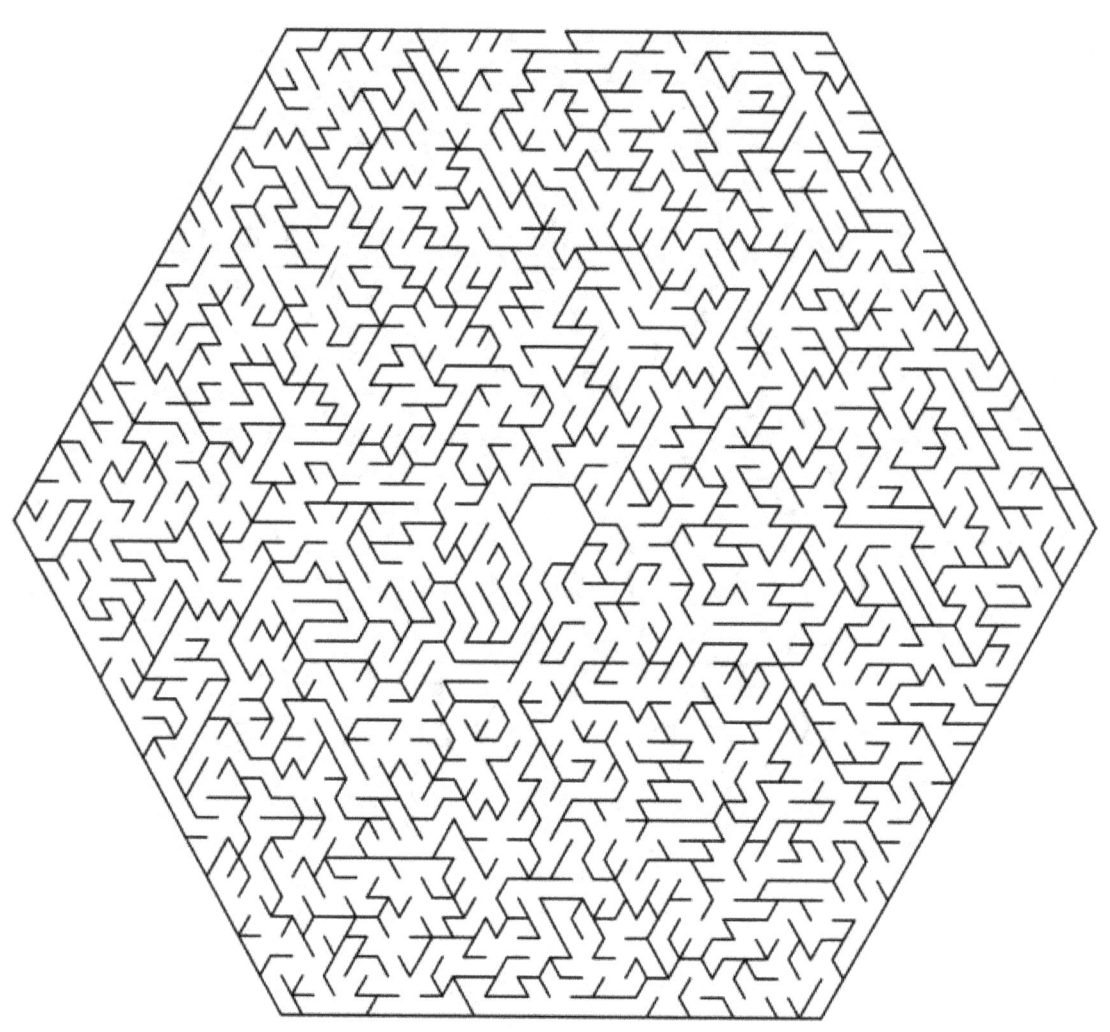

PUT A HEX ON IT #40

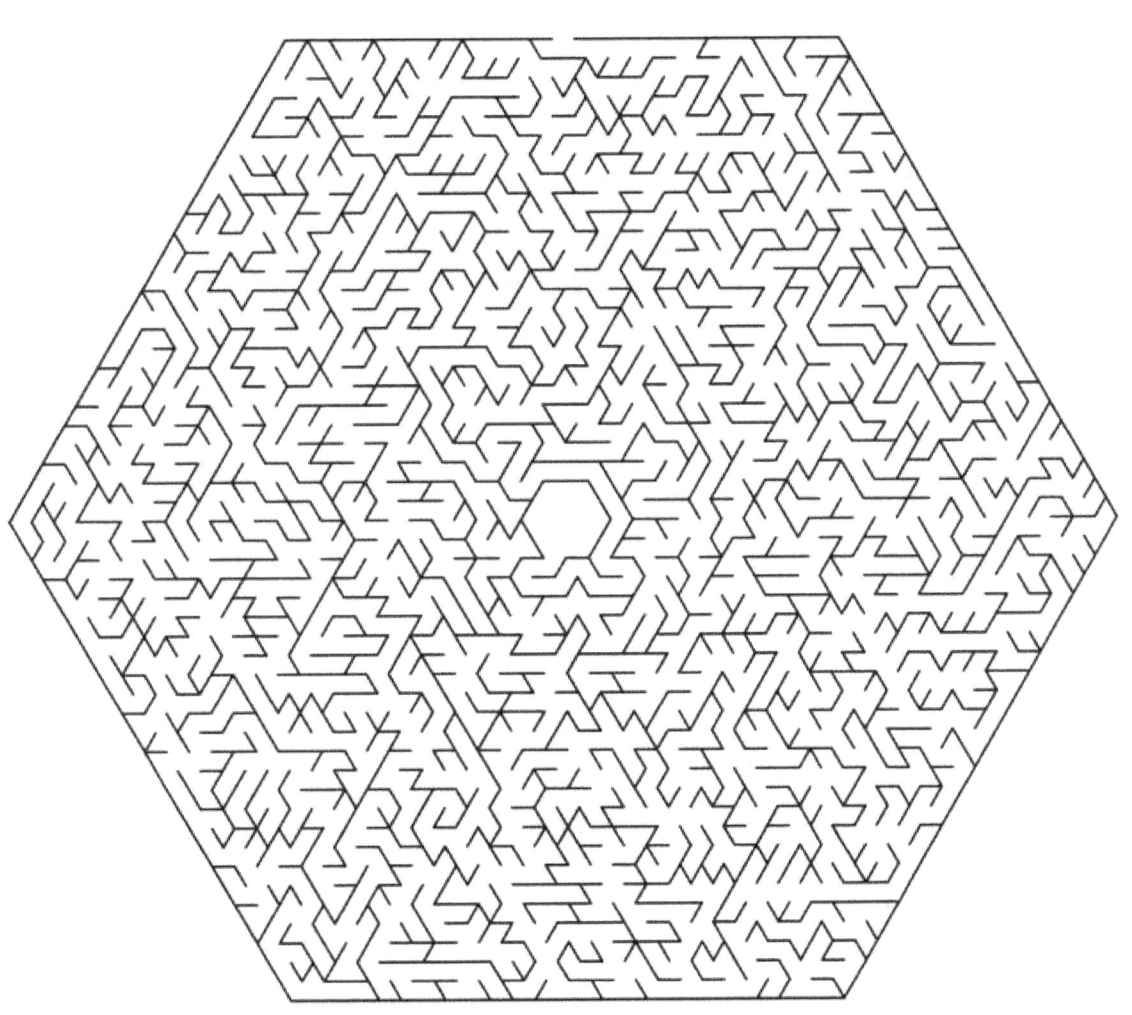

PUT A HEX ON IT #41

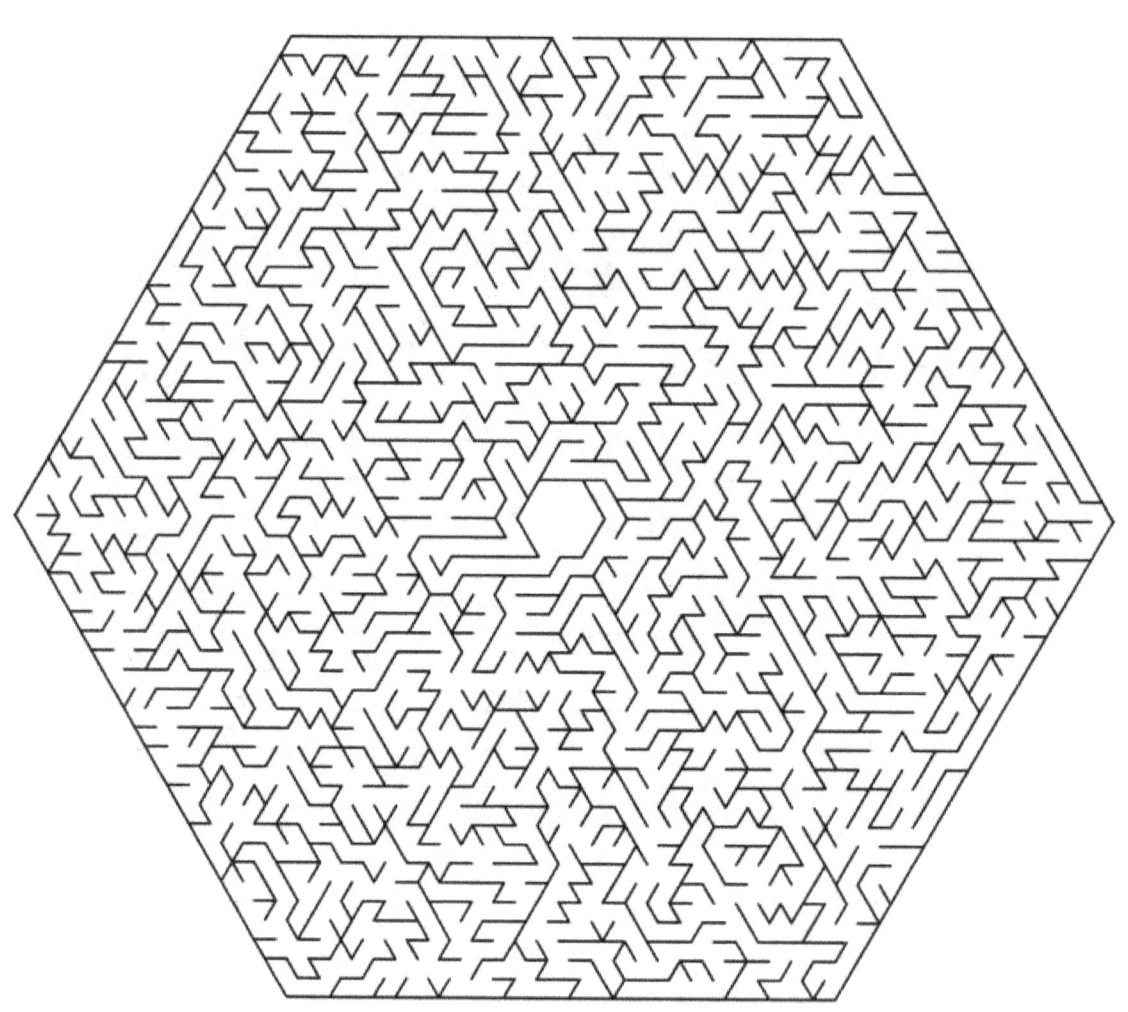

PUT A HEX ON IT #42

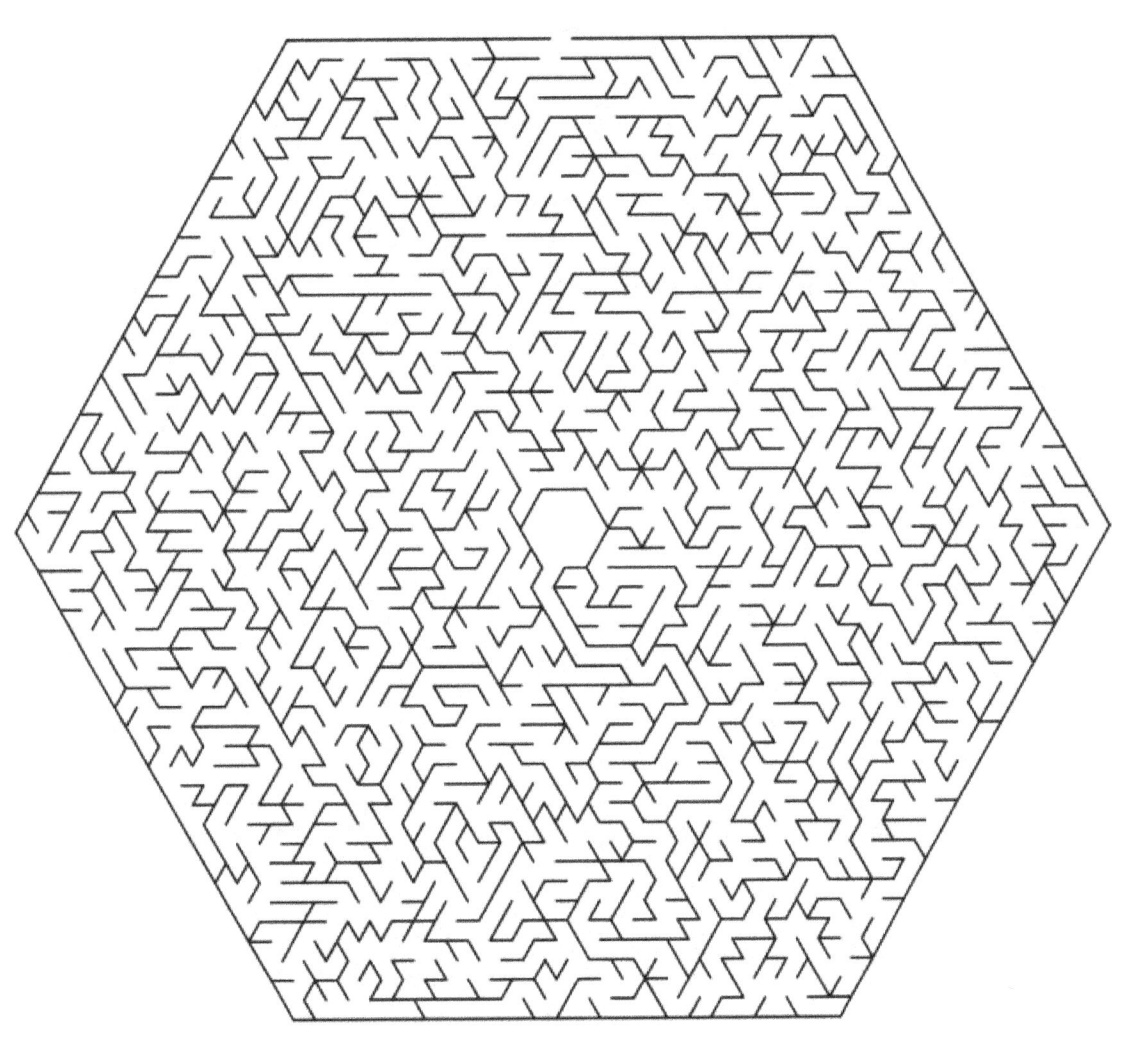

PUT A HEX ON IT #43

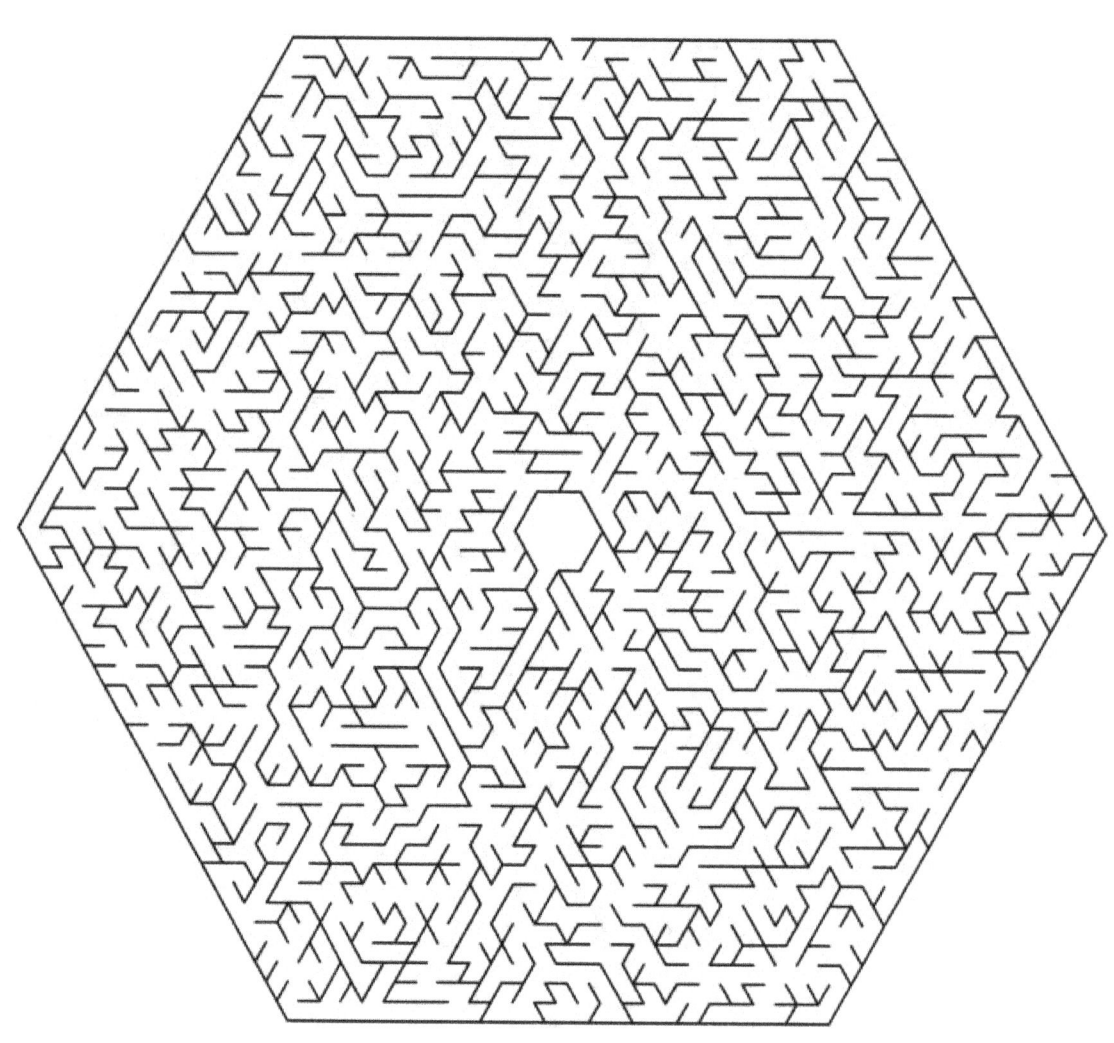

PUT A HEX ON IT #44

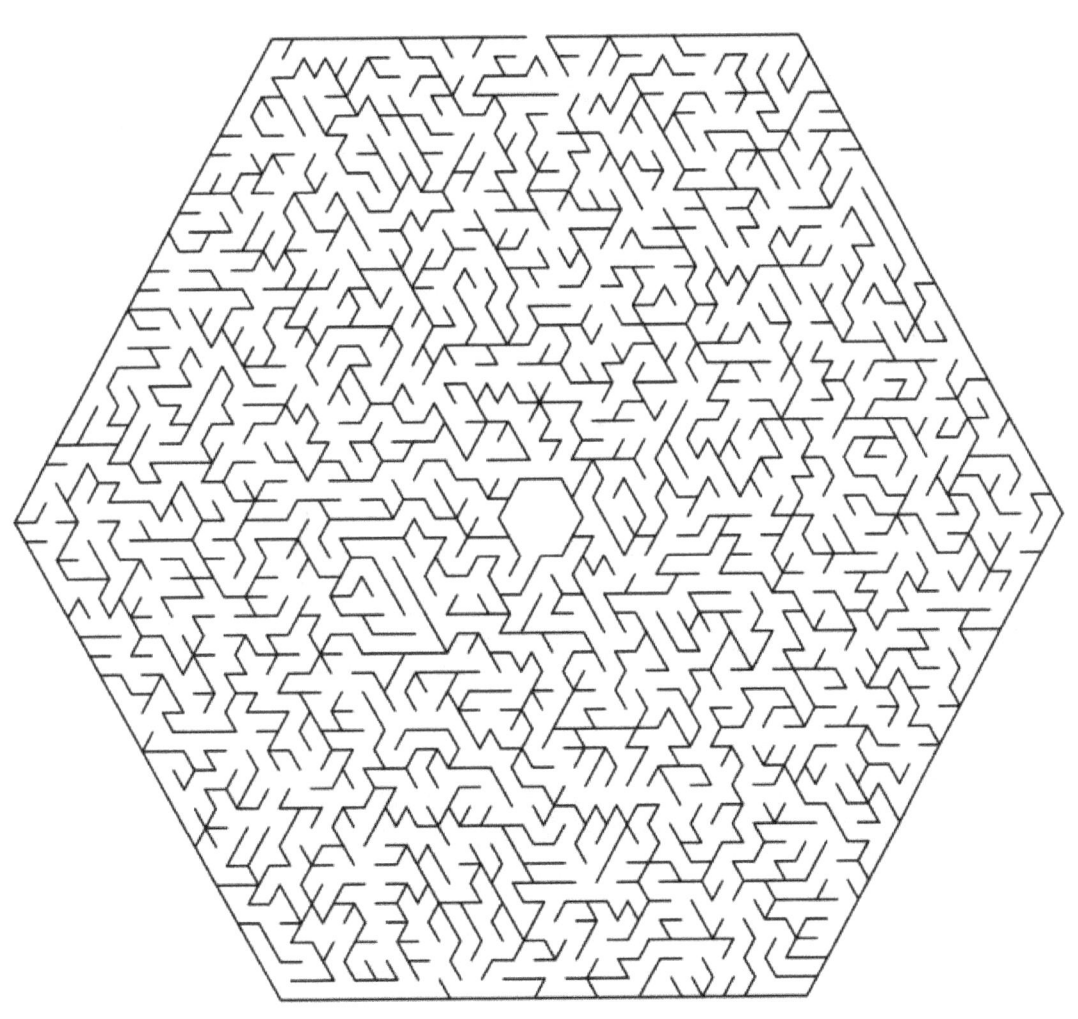

PUT A HEX ON IT #45

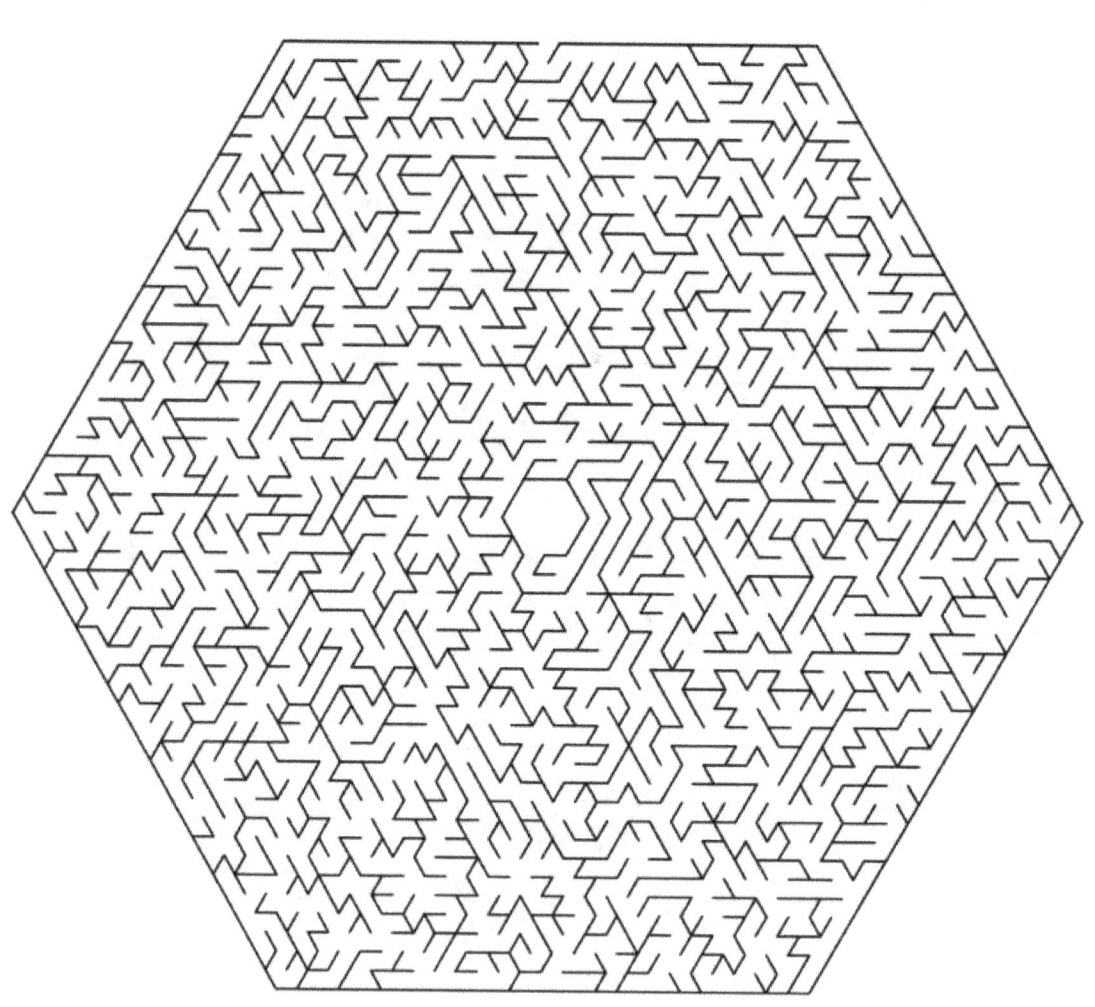

PUT A HEX ON IT #46

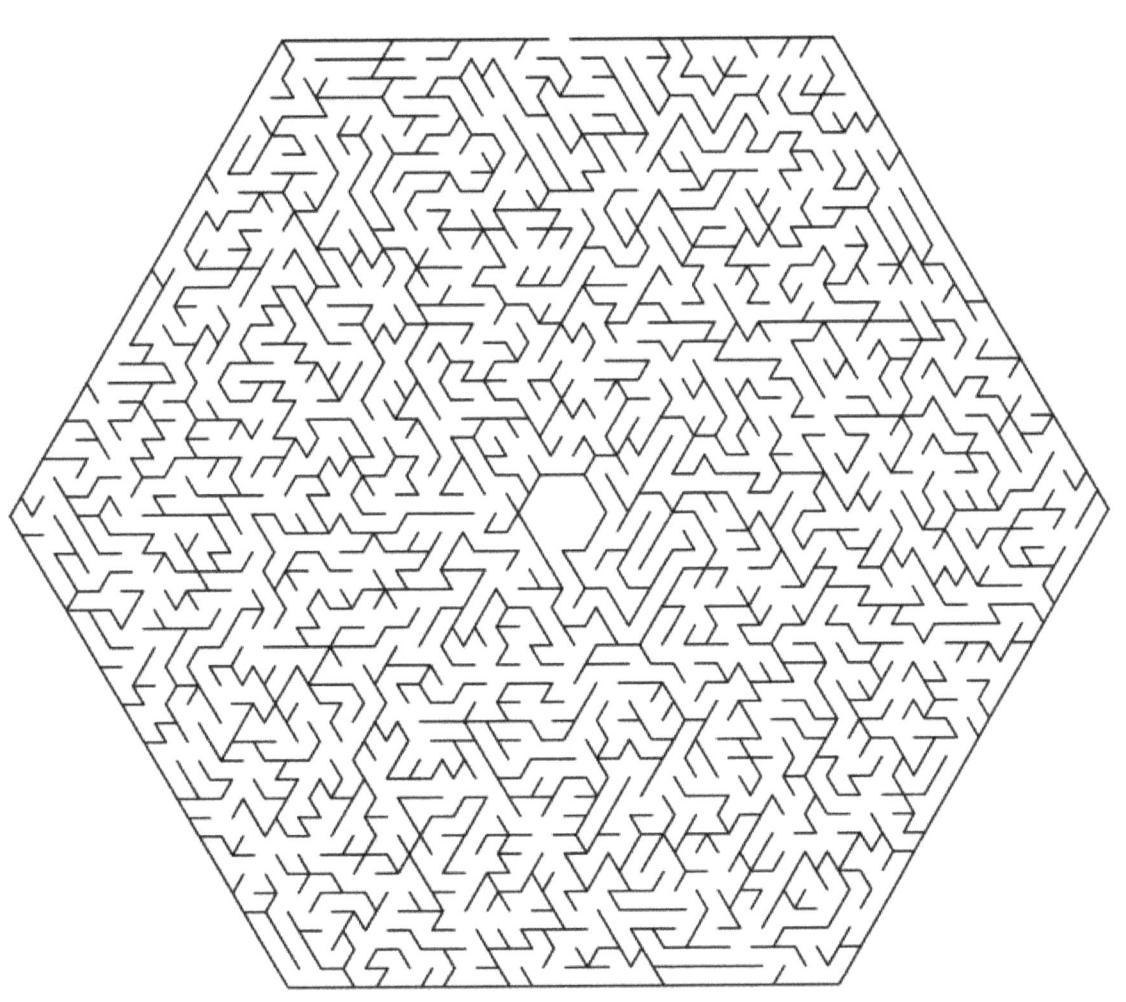

PUT A HEX ON IT #47

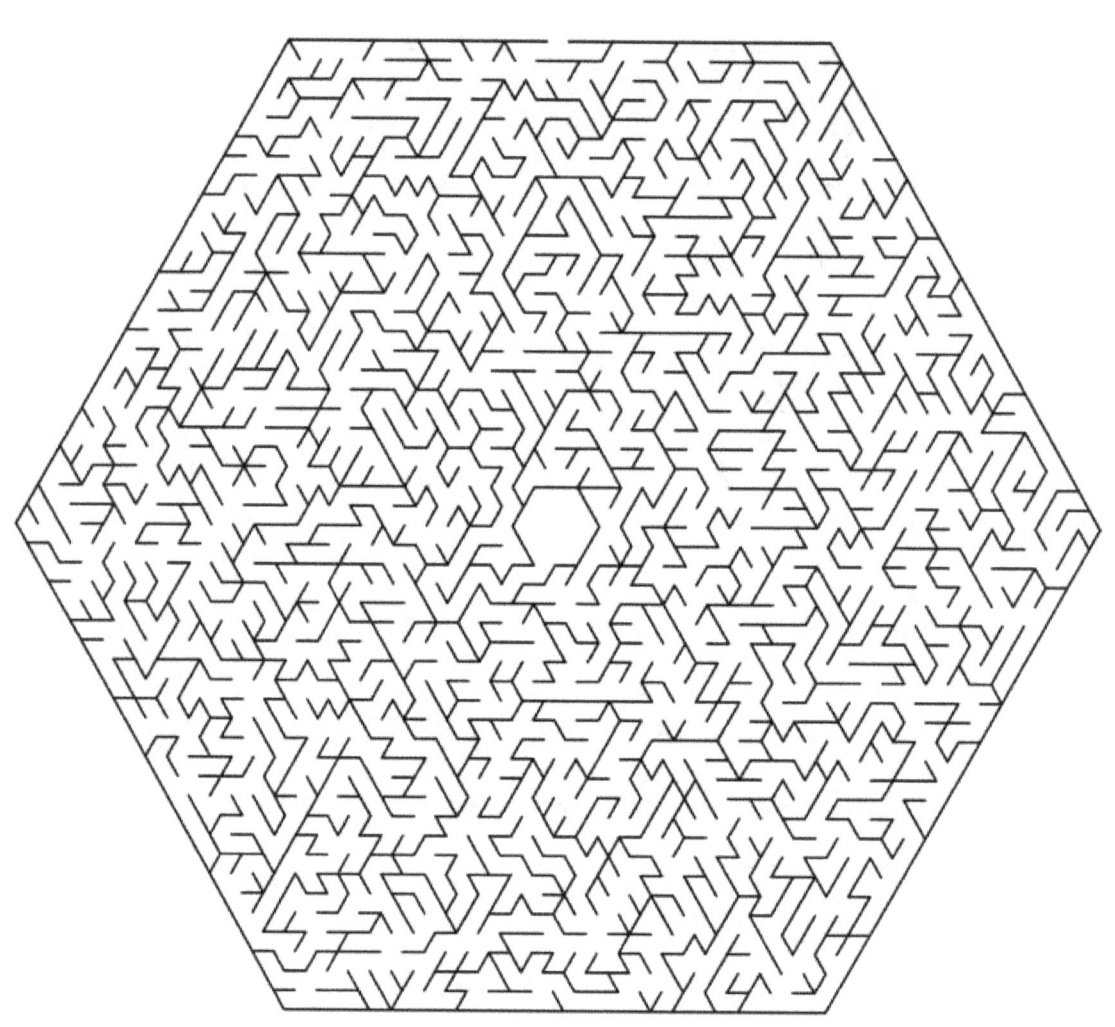

PUT A HEX ON IT #48

PUT A HEX ON IT #49

PUT A HEX ON IT #50

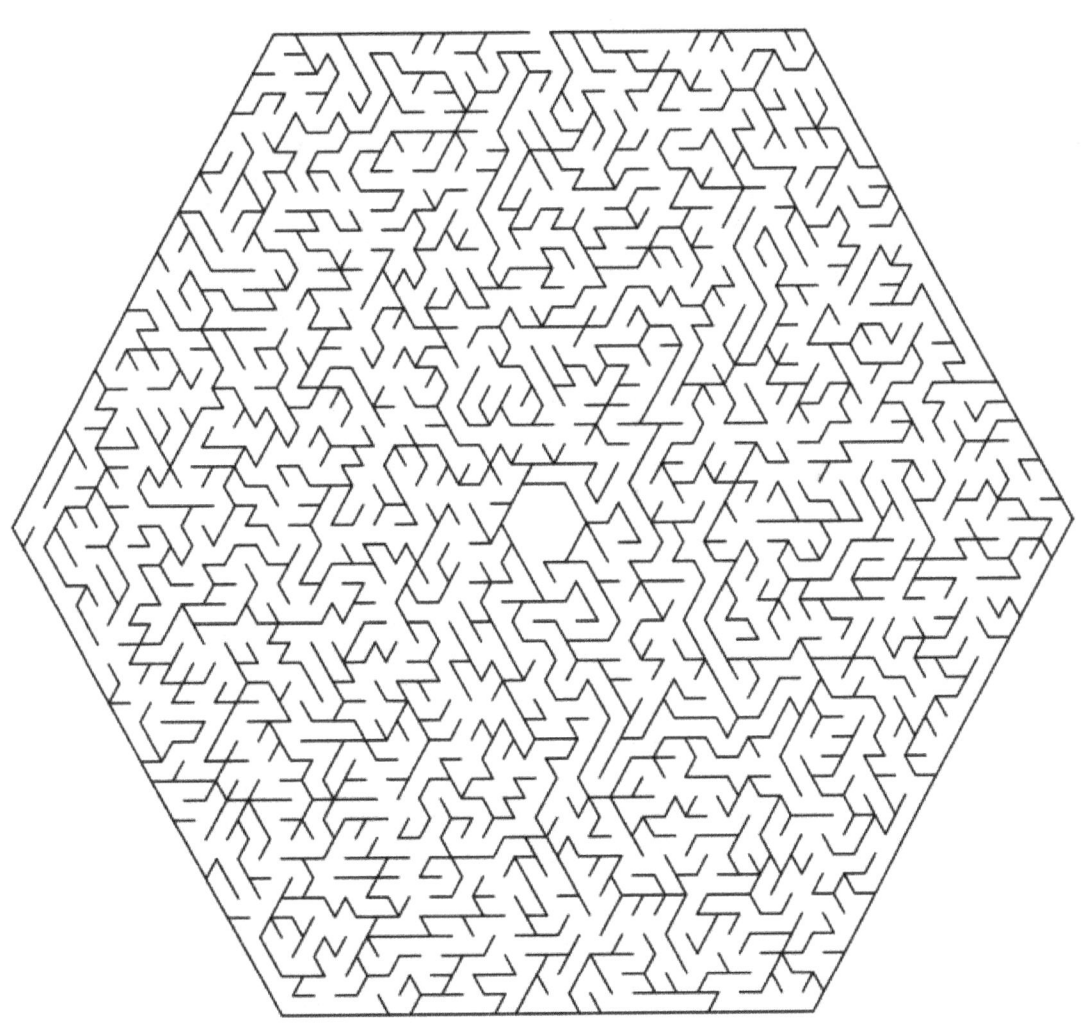

PUT A HEX ON IT #51

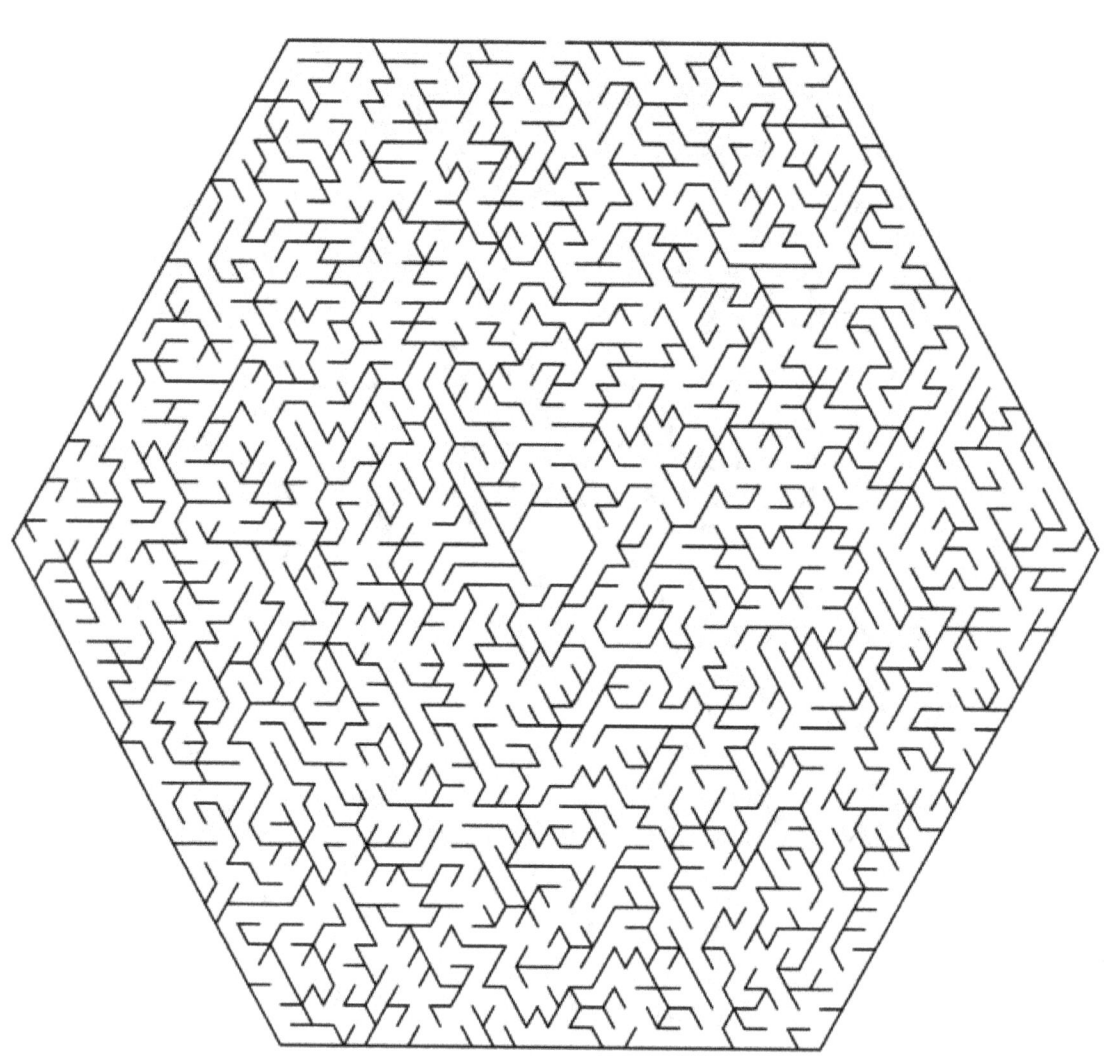

PUT A HEX ON IT #52

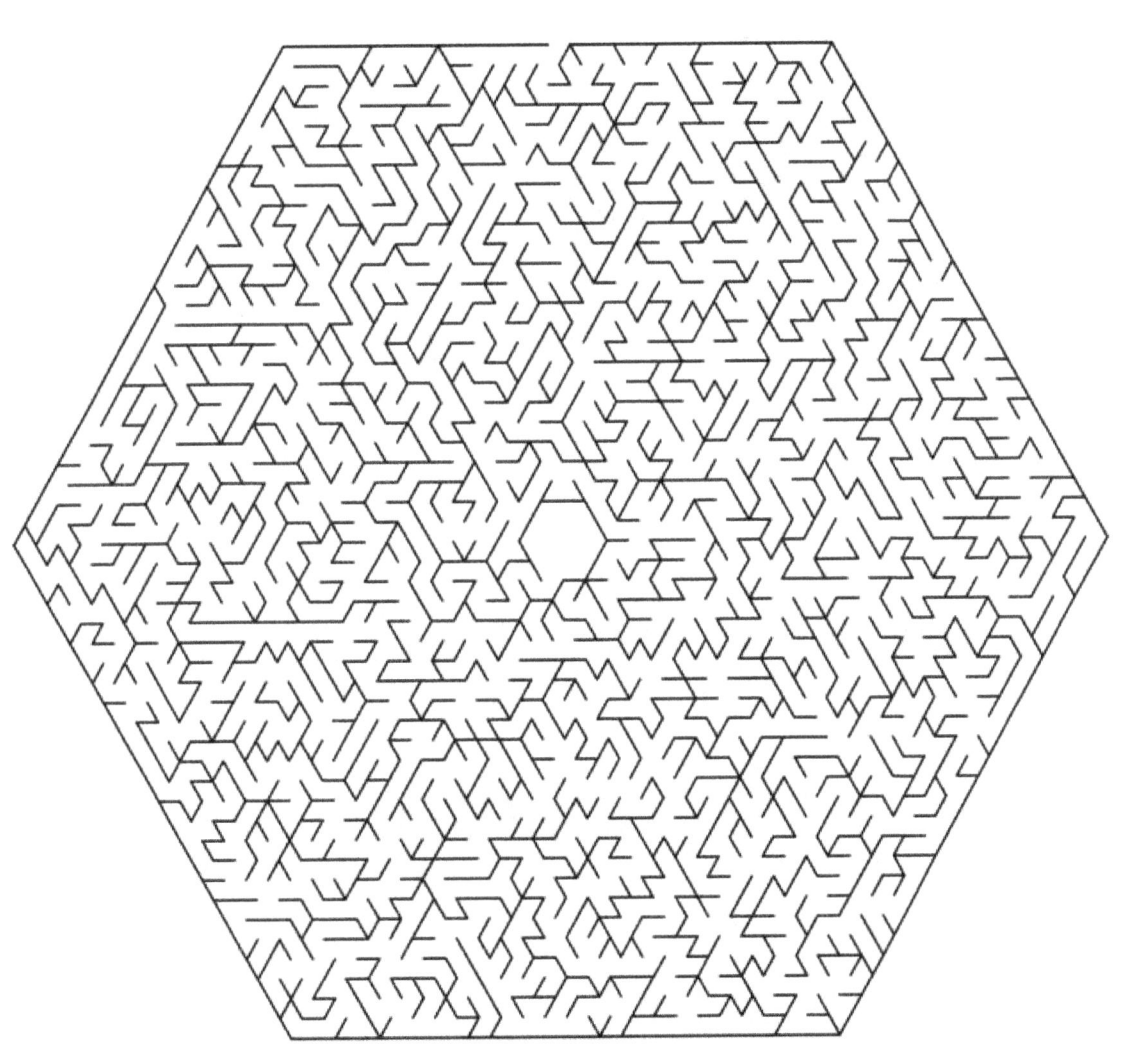

PUT A HEX ON IT #53

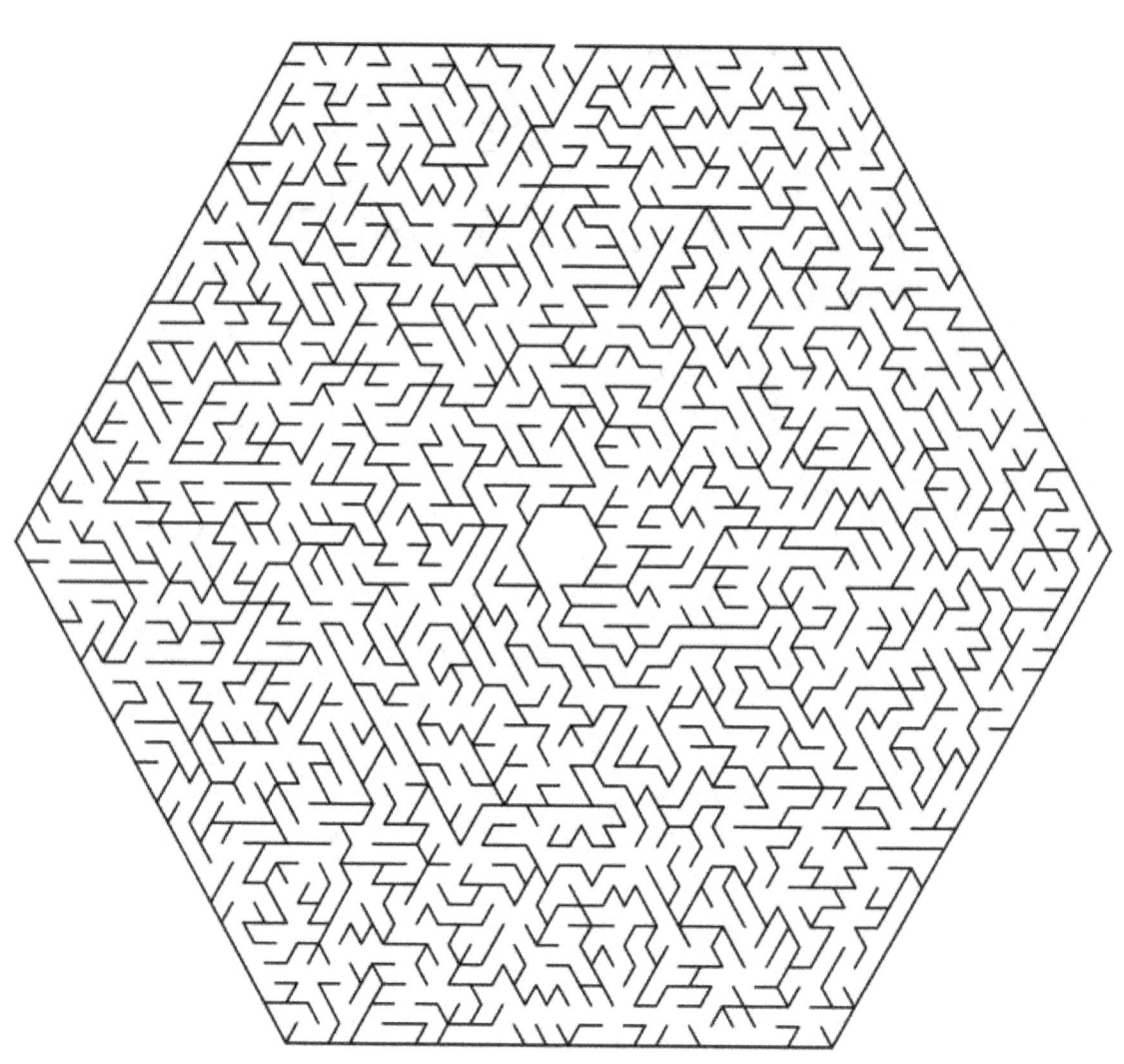

PUT A HEX ON IT #54

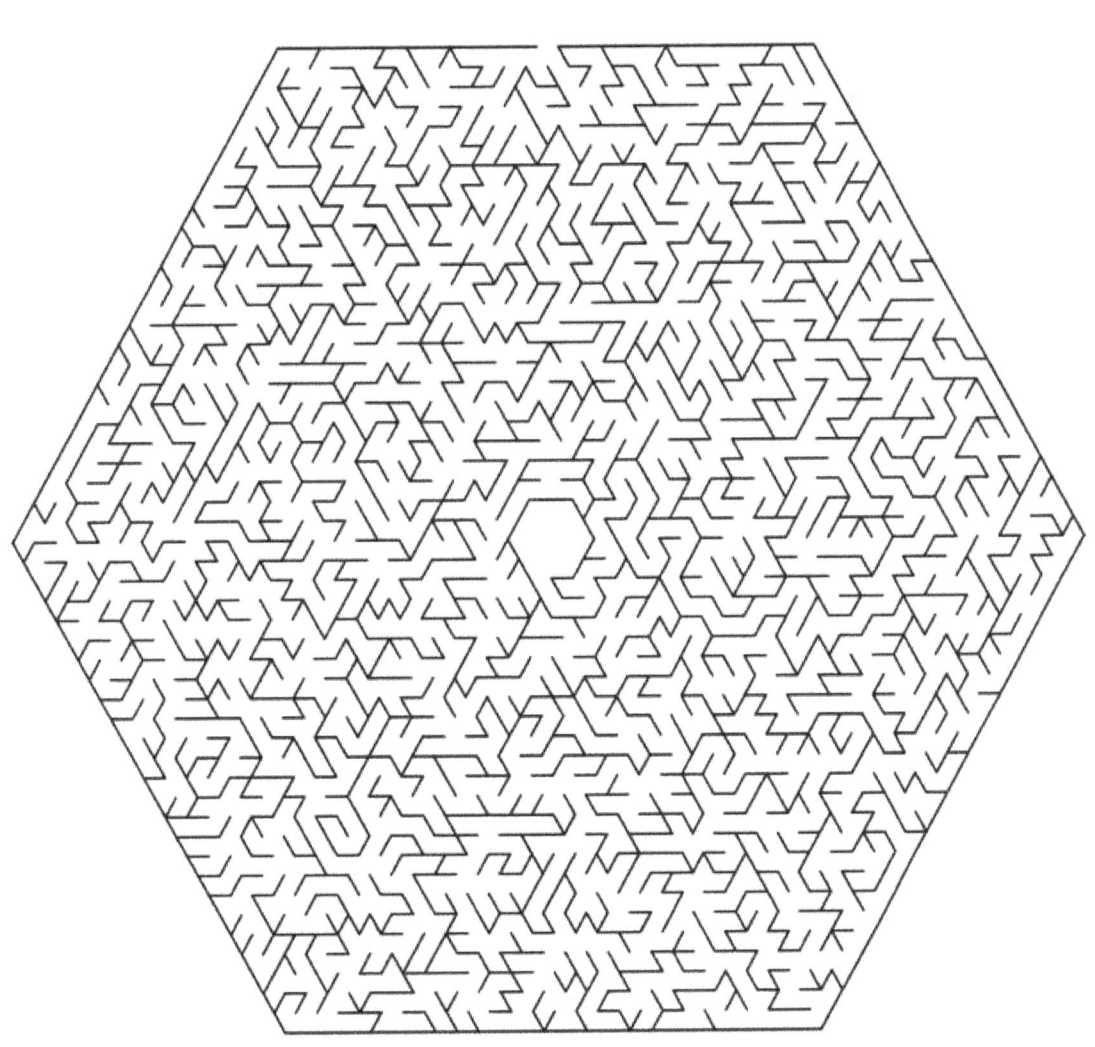

PUT A HEX ON IT #55

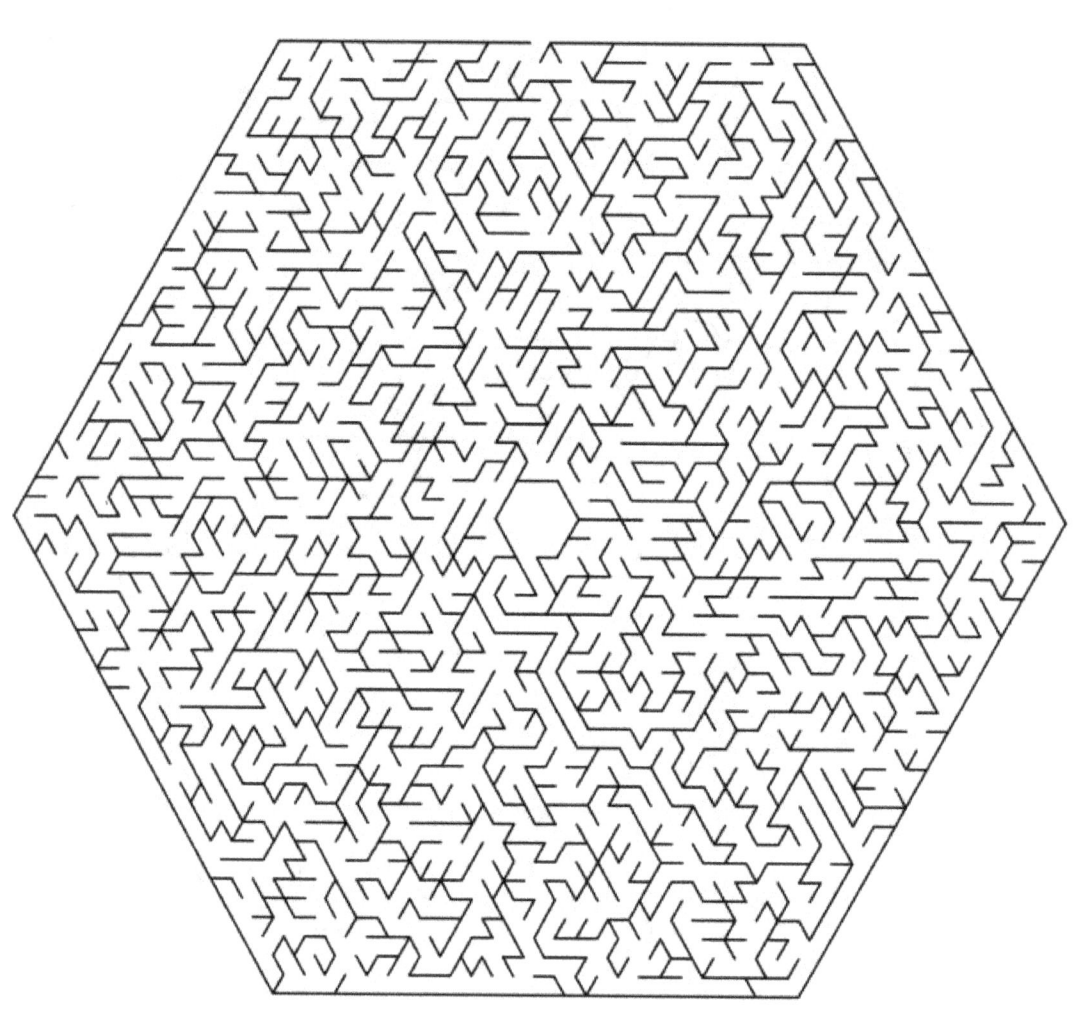

PUT A HEX ON IT #56

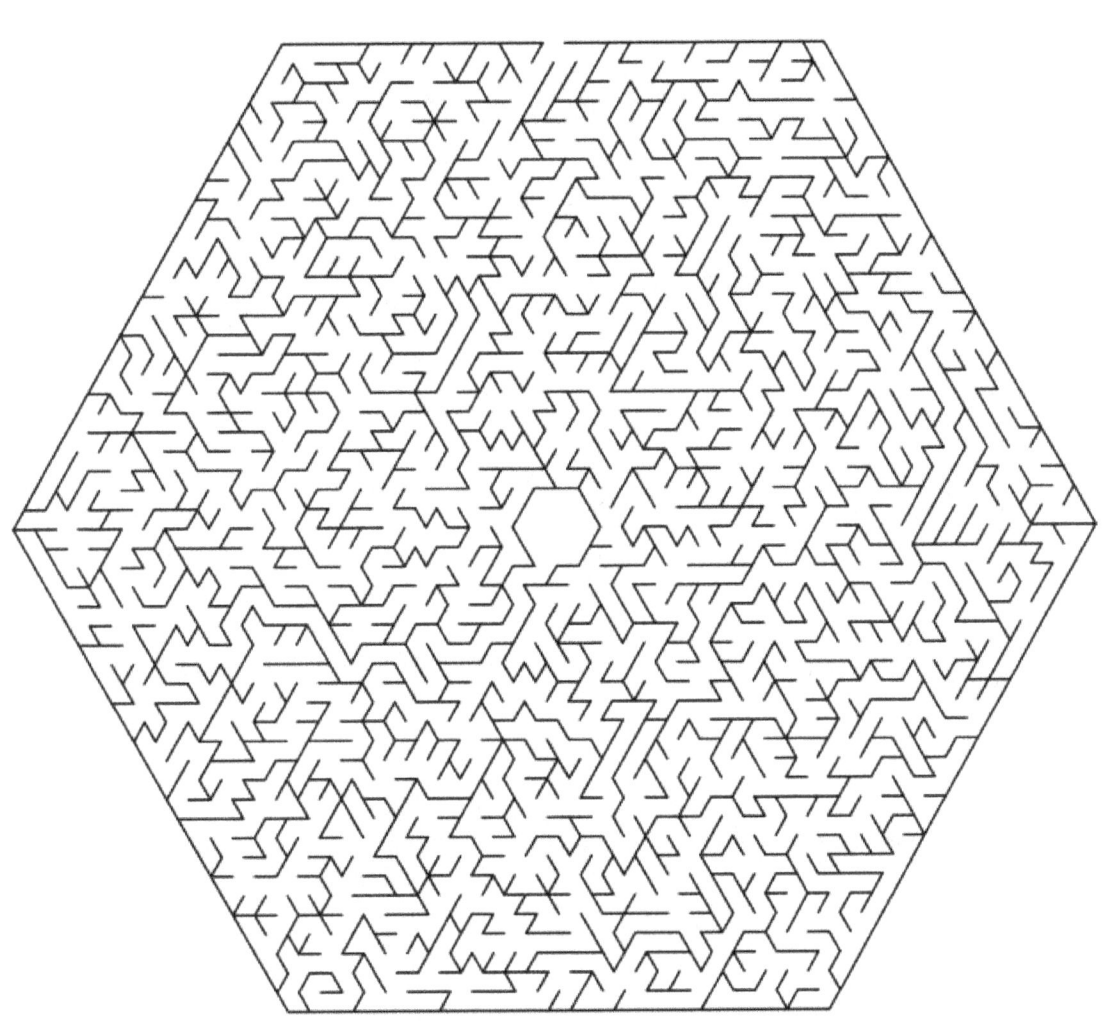

PUT A HEX ON IT #57

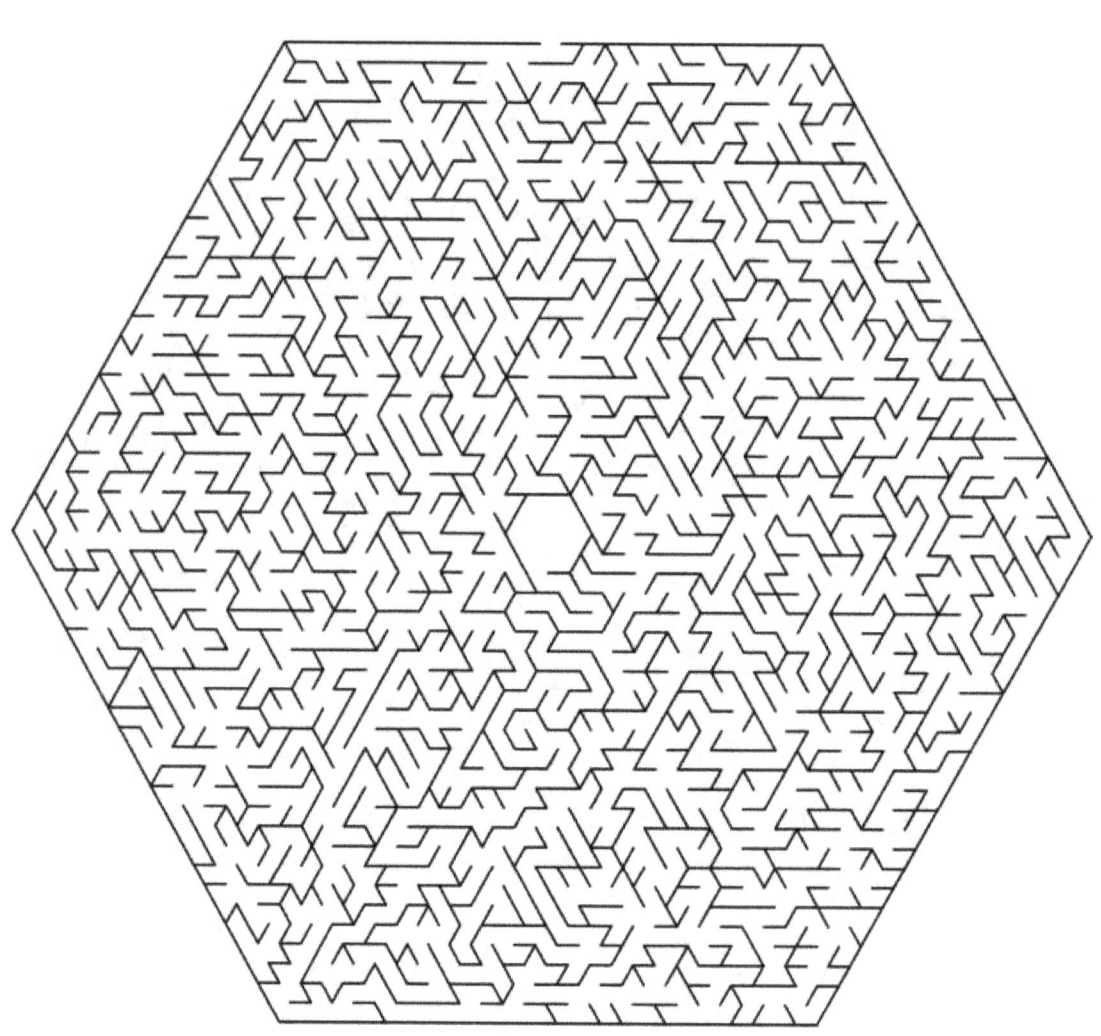

PUT A HEX ON IT #58

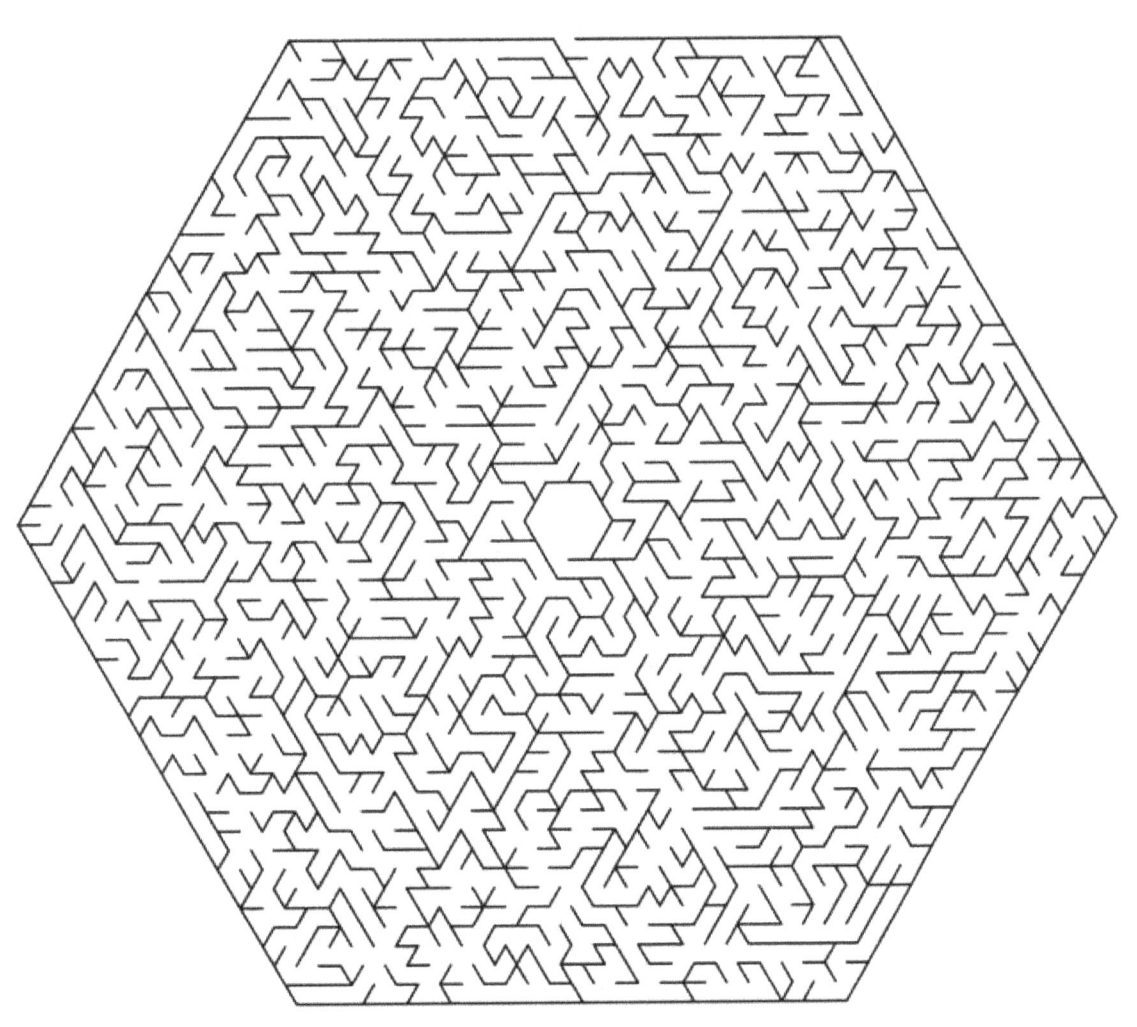

PUT A HEX ON IT #59

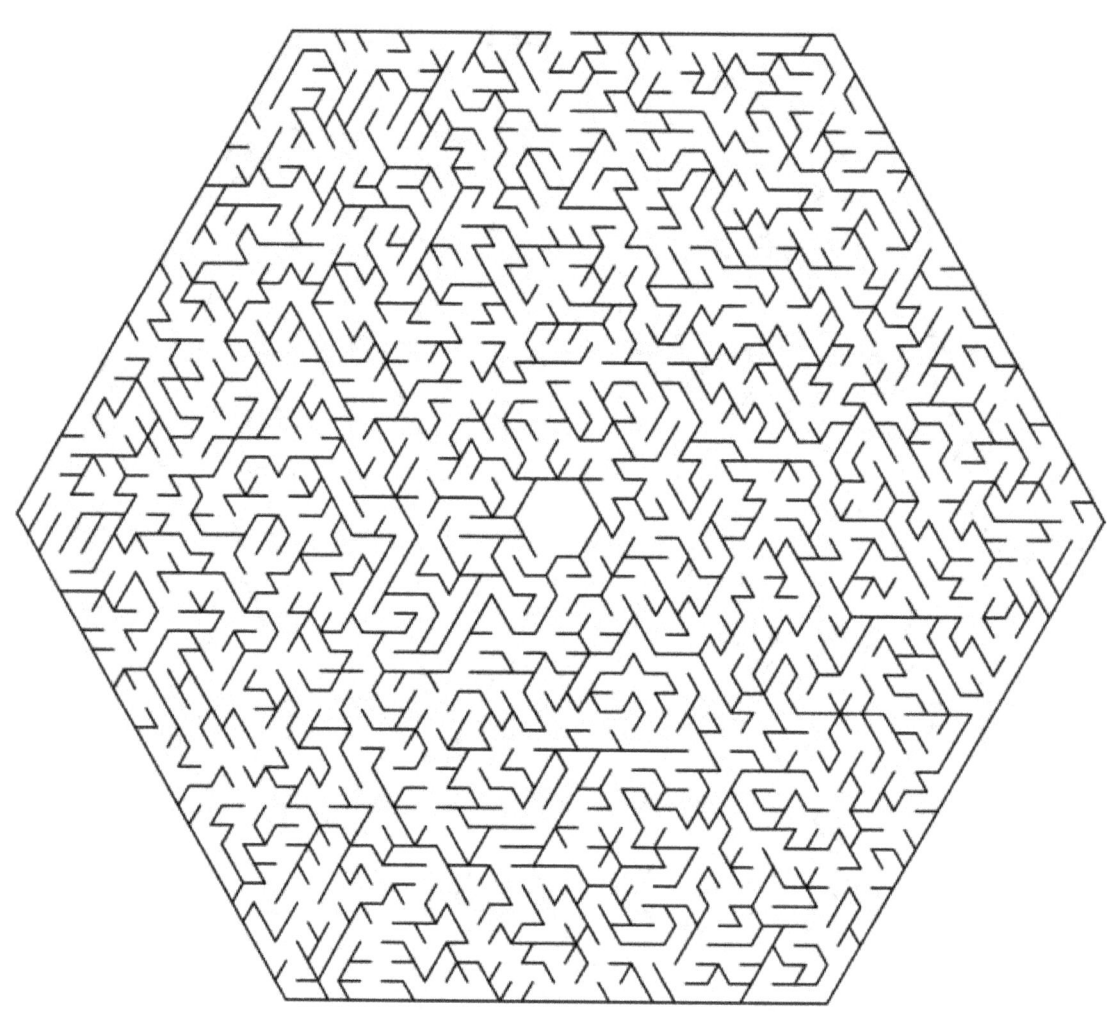

PUT A HEX ON IT #60

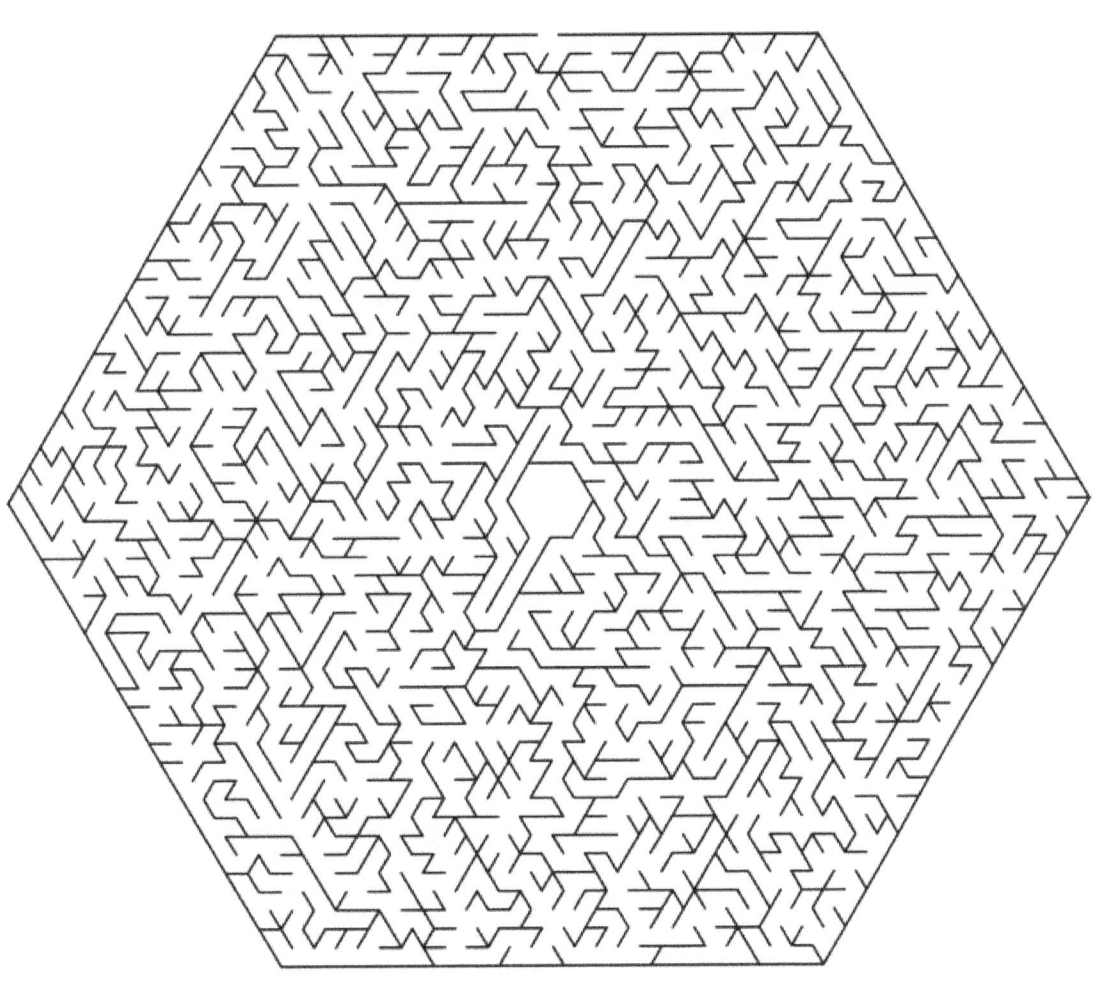

PUT A HEX ON IT #61

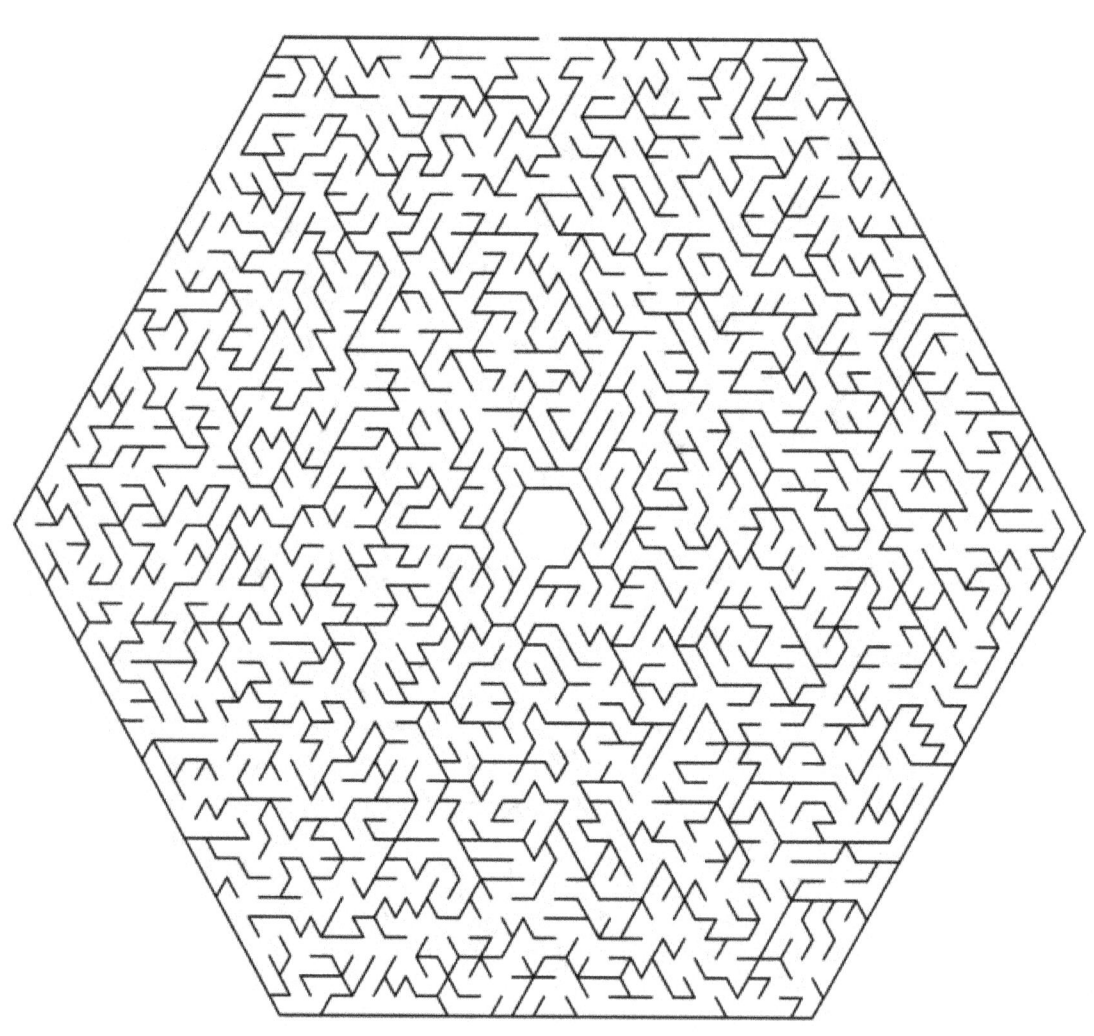

PUT A HEX ON IT #62

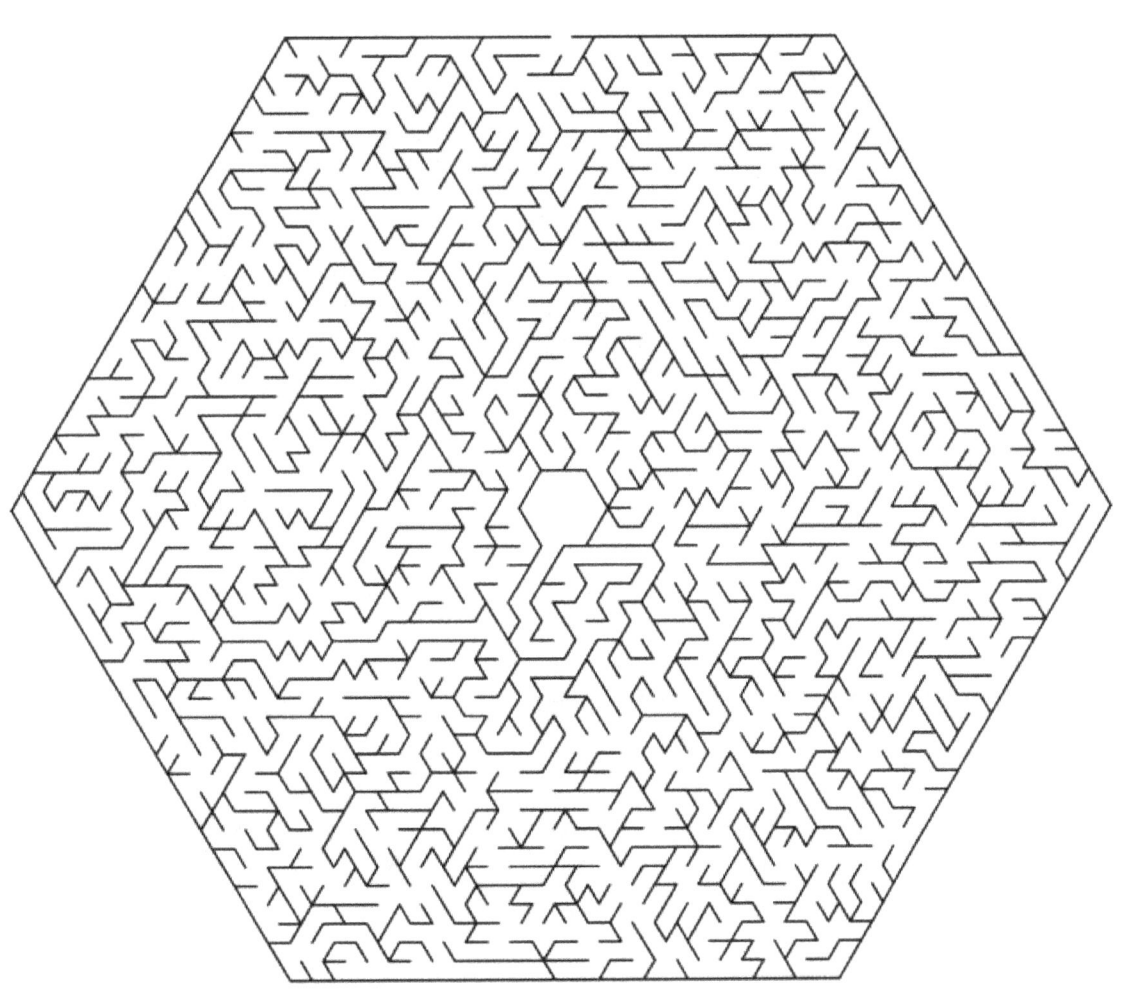

PUT A HEX ON IT #63

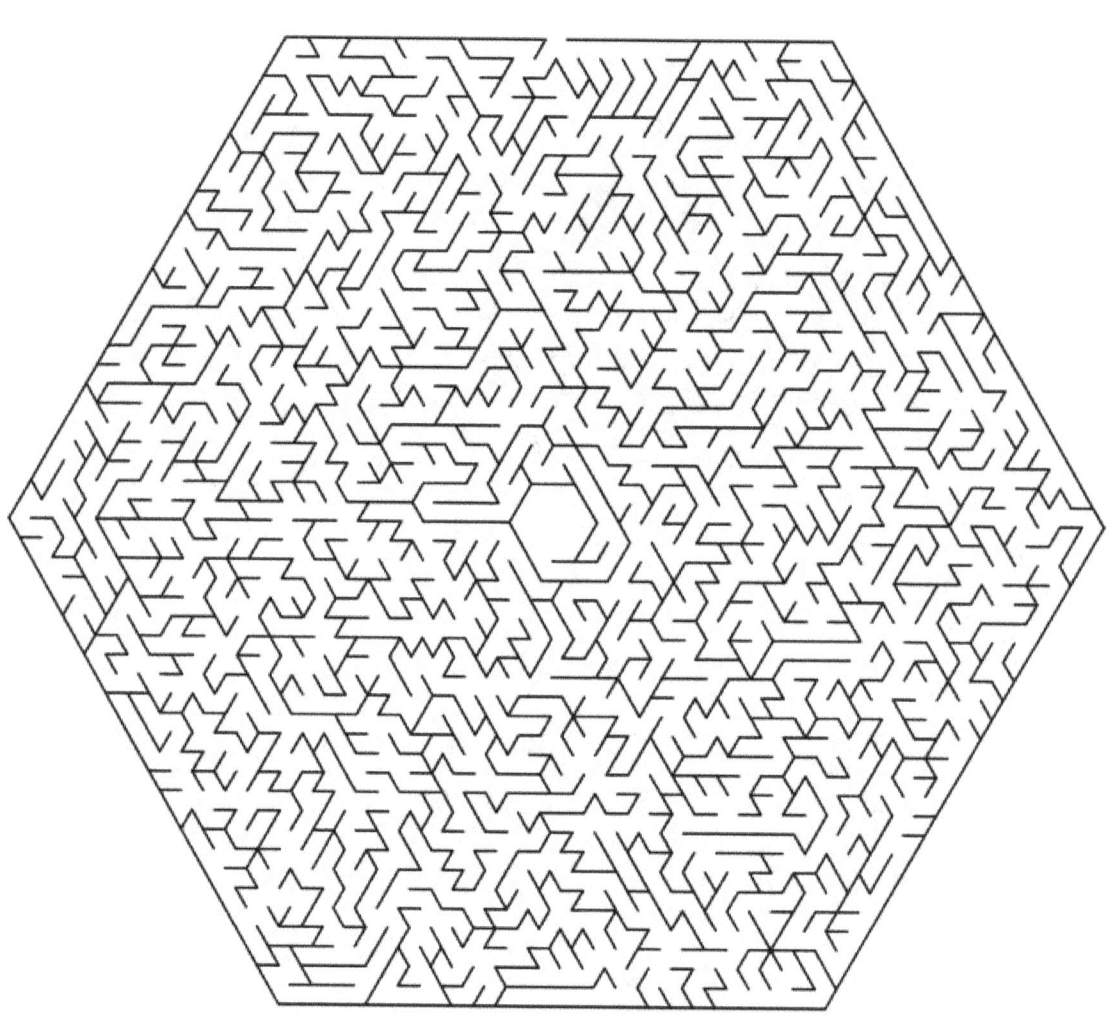

PUT A HEX ON IT #64

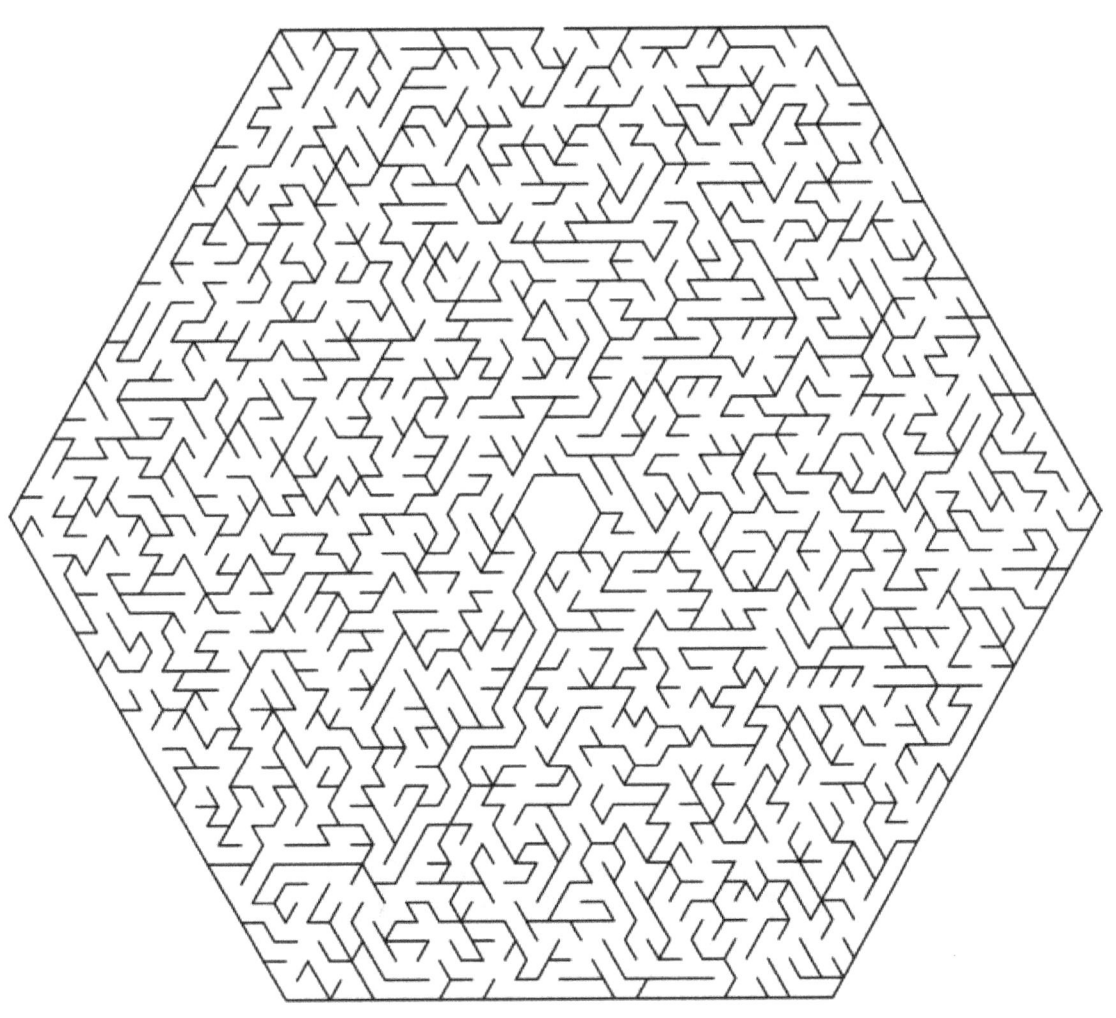

PUT A HEX ON IT #65

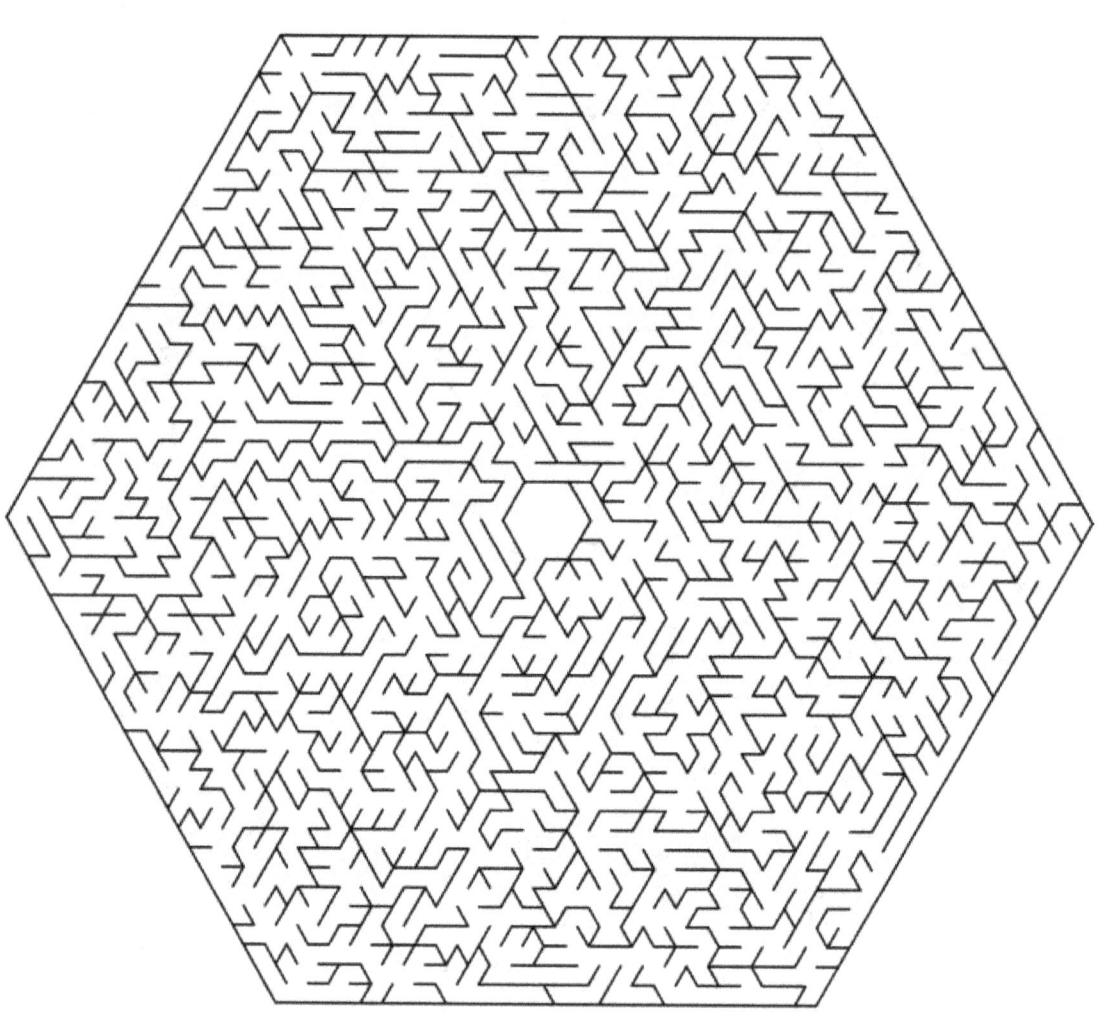

PUT A HEX ON IT #66

PUT A HEX ON IT #67

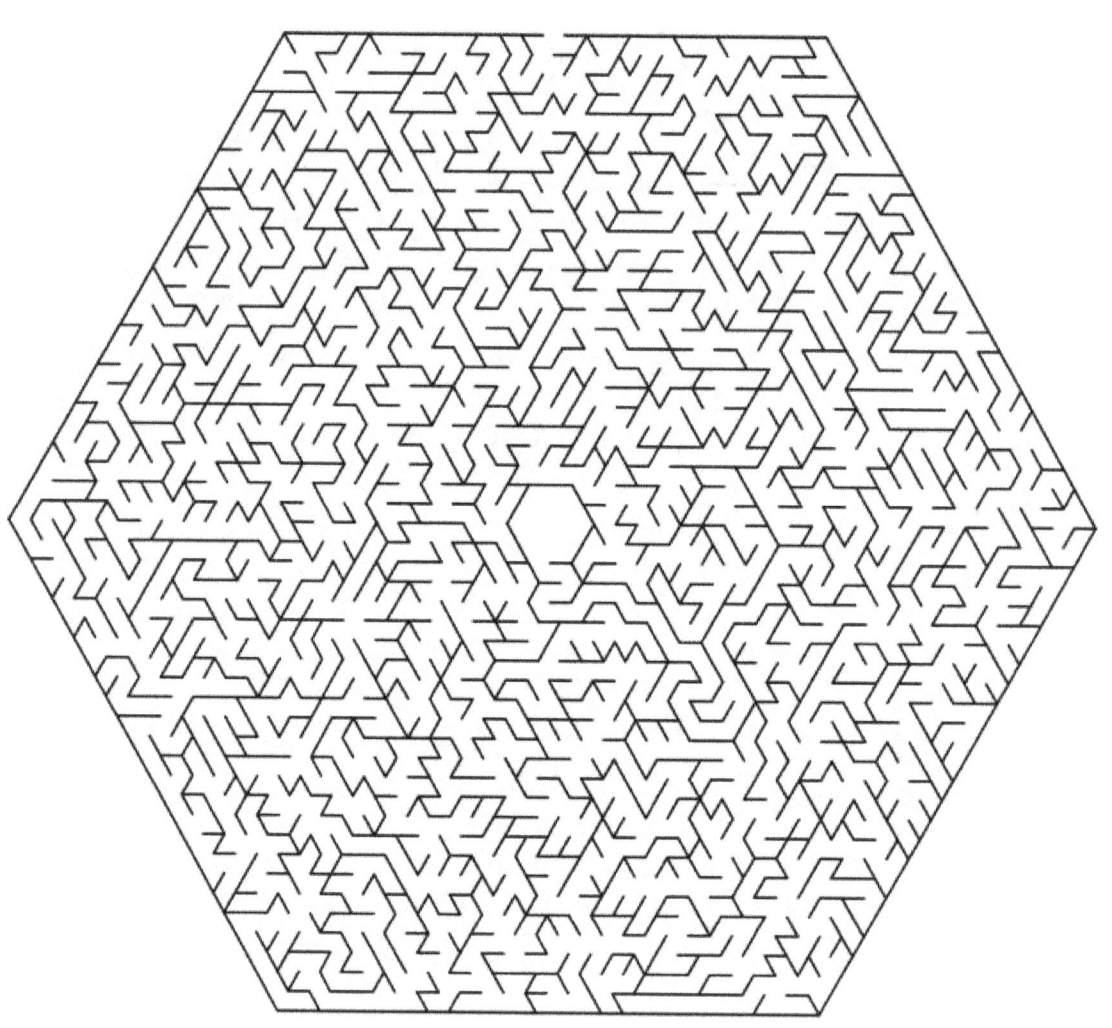

PUT A HEX ON IT #68

PUT A HEX ON IT #69

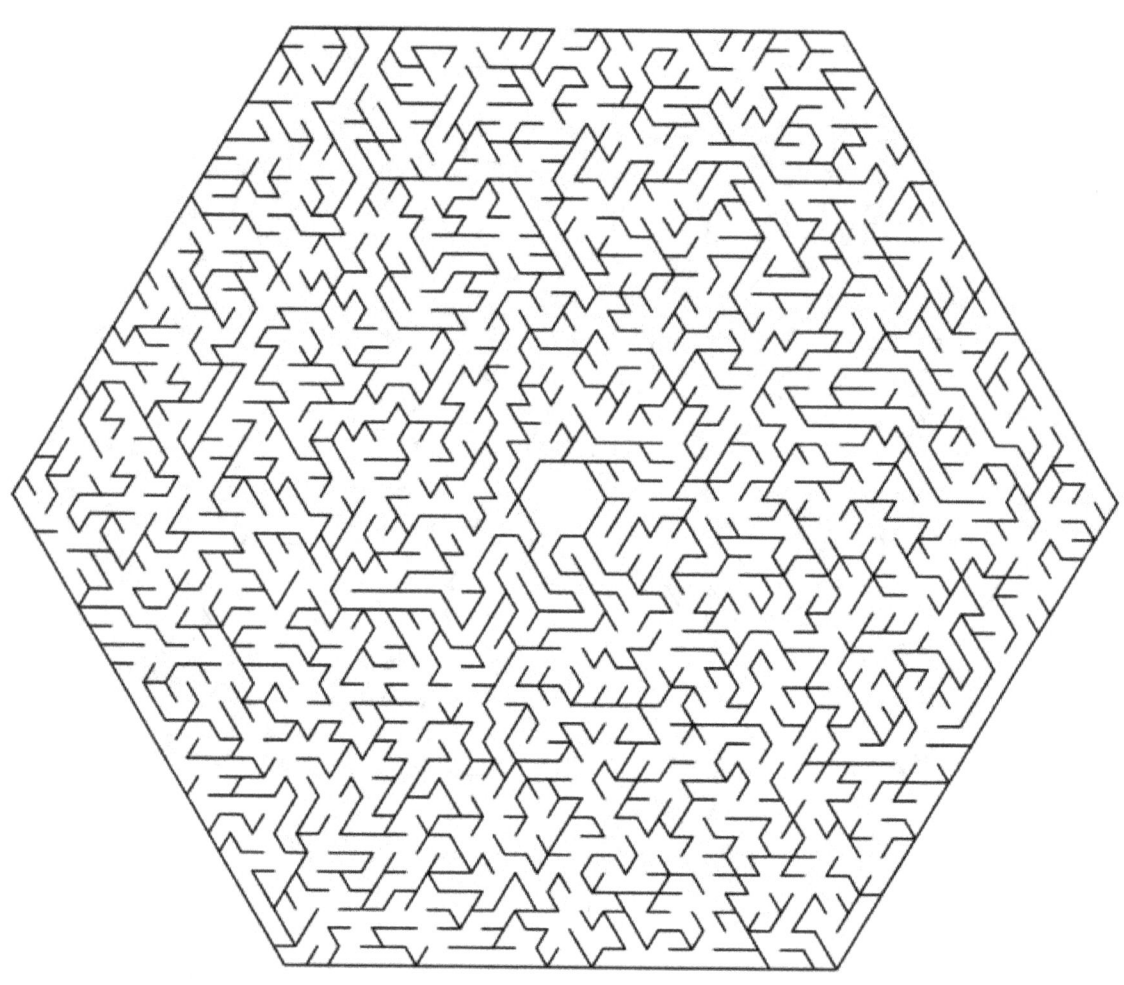

PUT A HEX ON IT #70

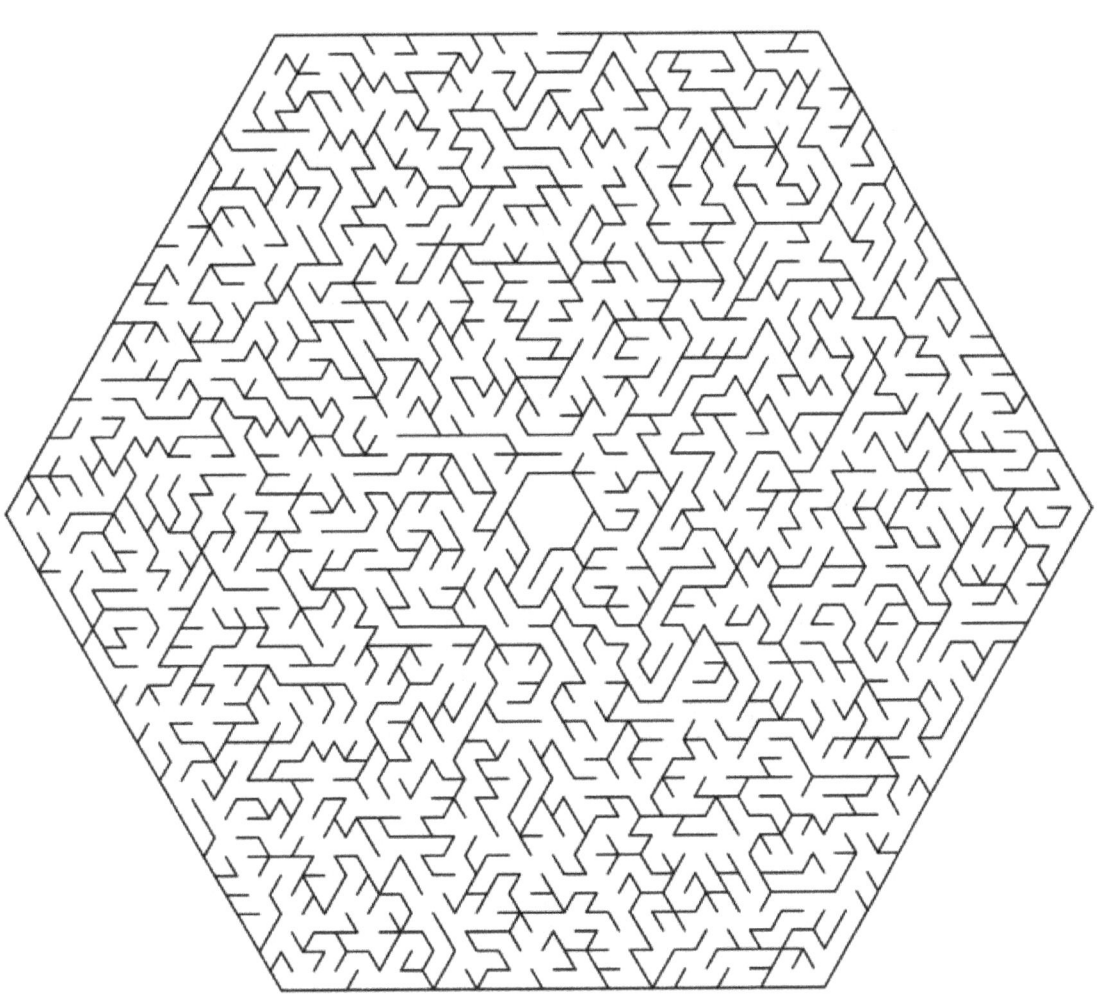

PUT A HEX ON IT #71

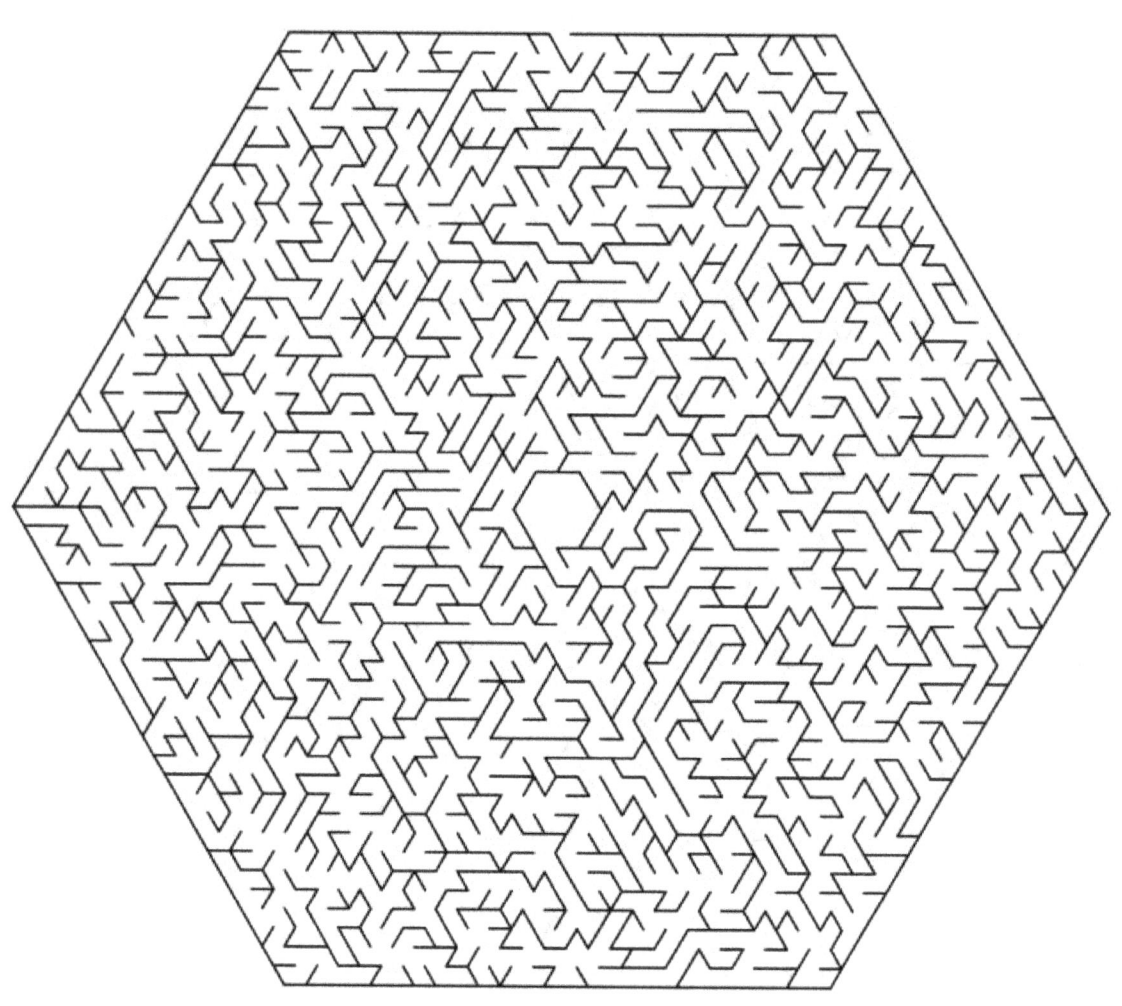

PUT A HEX ON IT #72

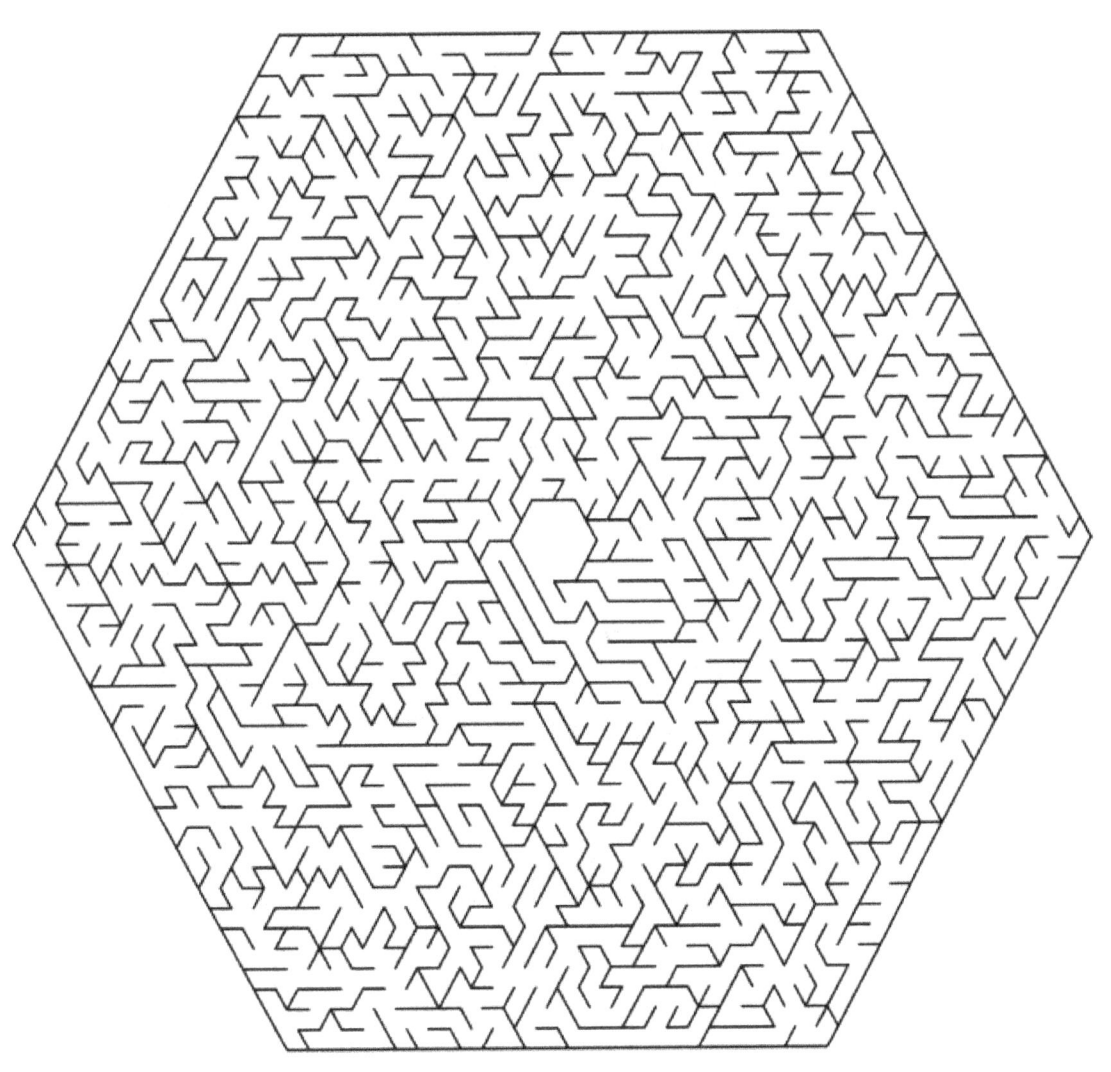

PUT A HEX ON IT #73

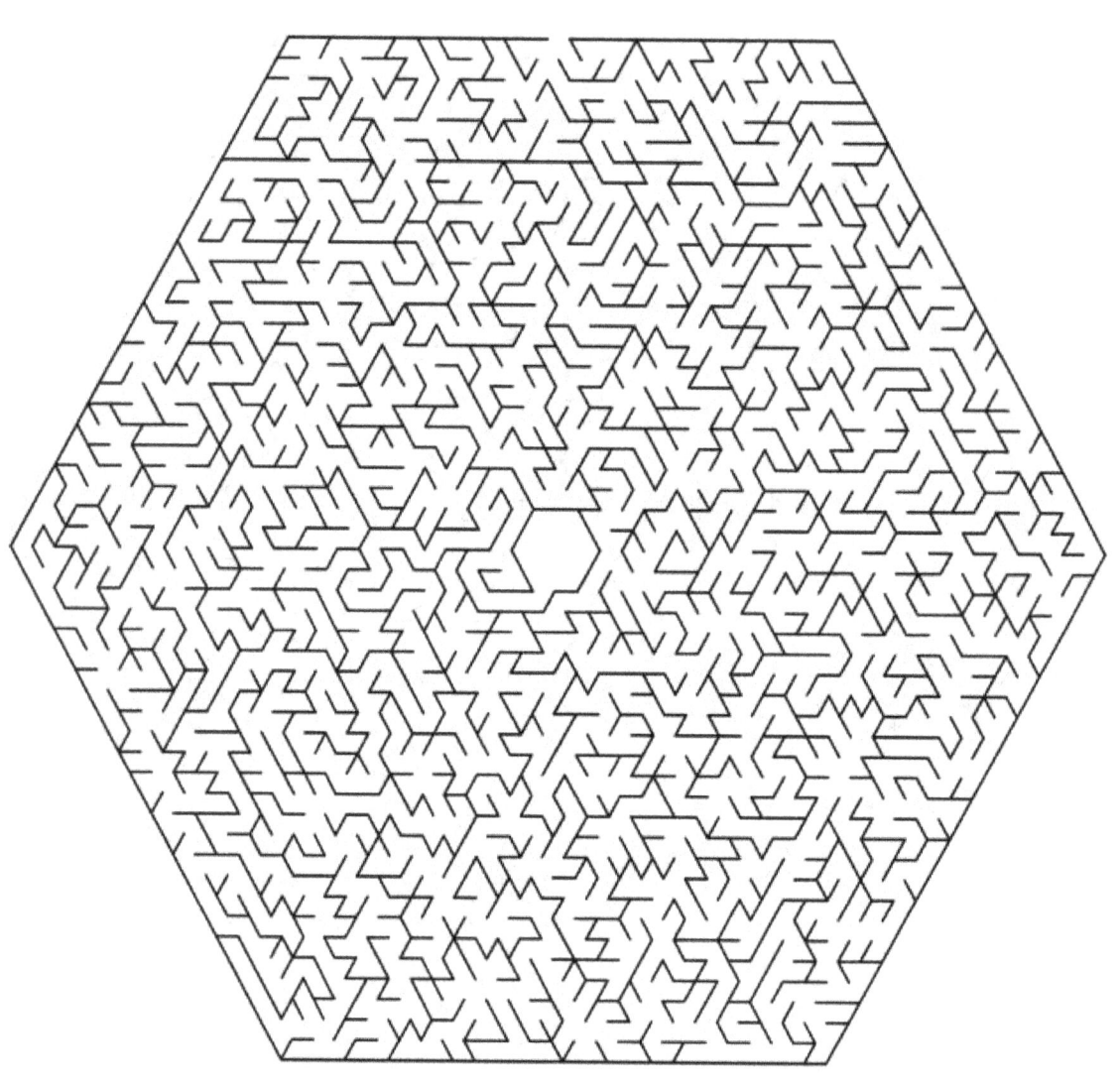

PUT A HEX ON IT #74

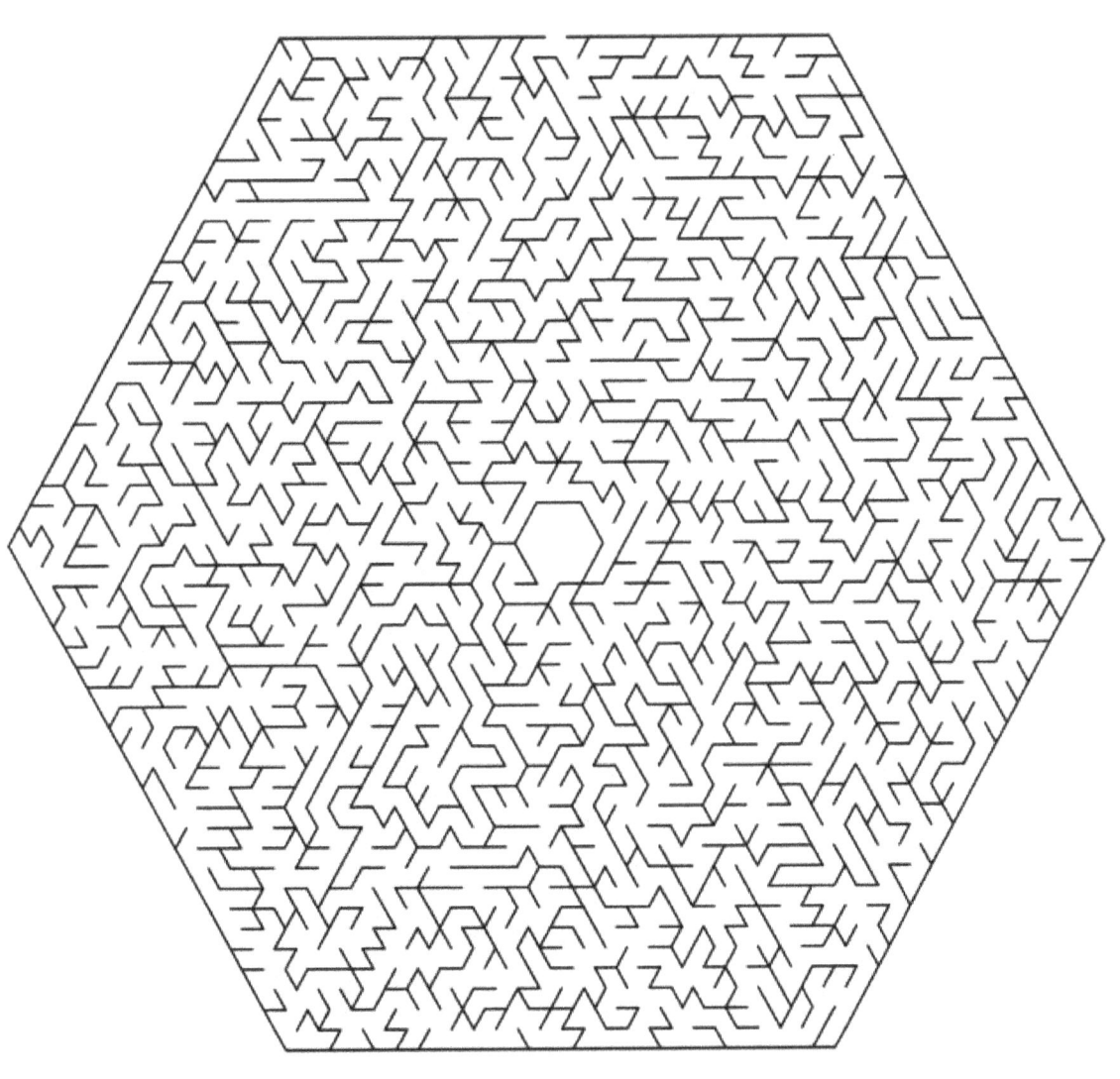

PUT A HEX ON IT #75

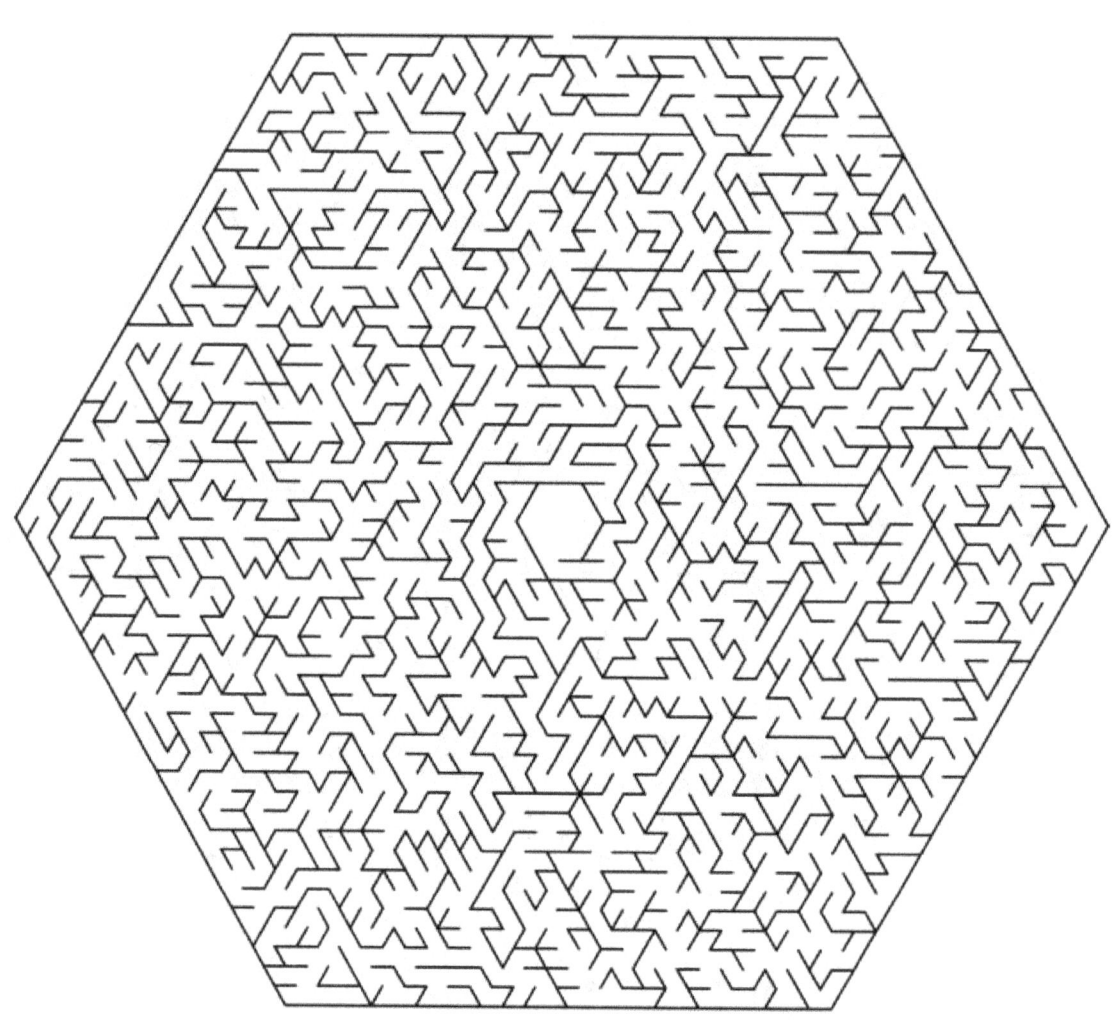

PUT A HEX ON IT #76

PUT A HEX ON IT #77

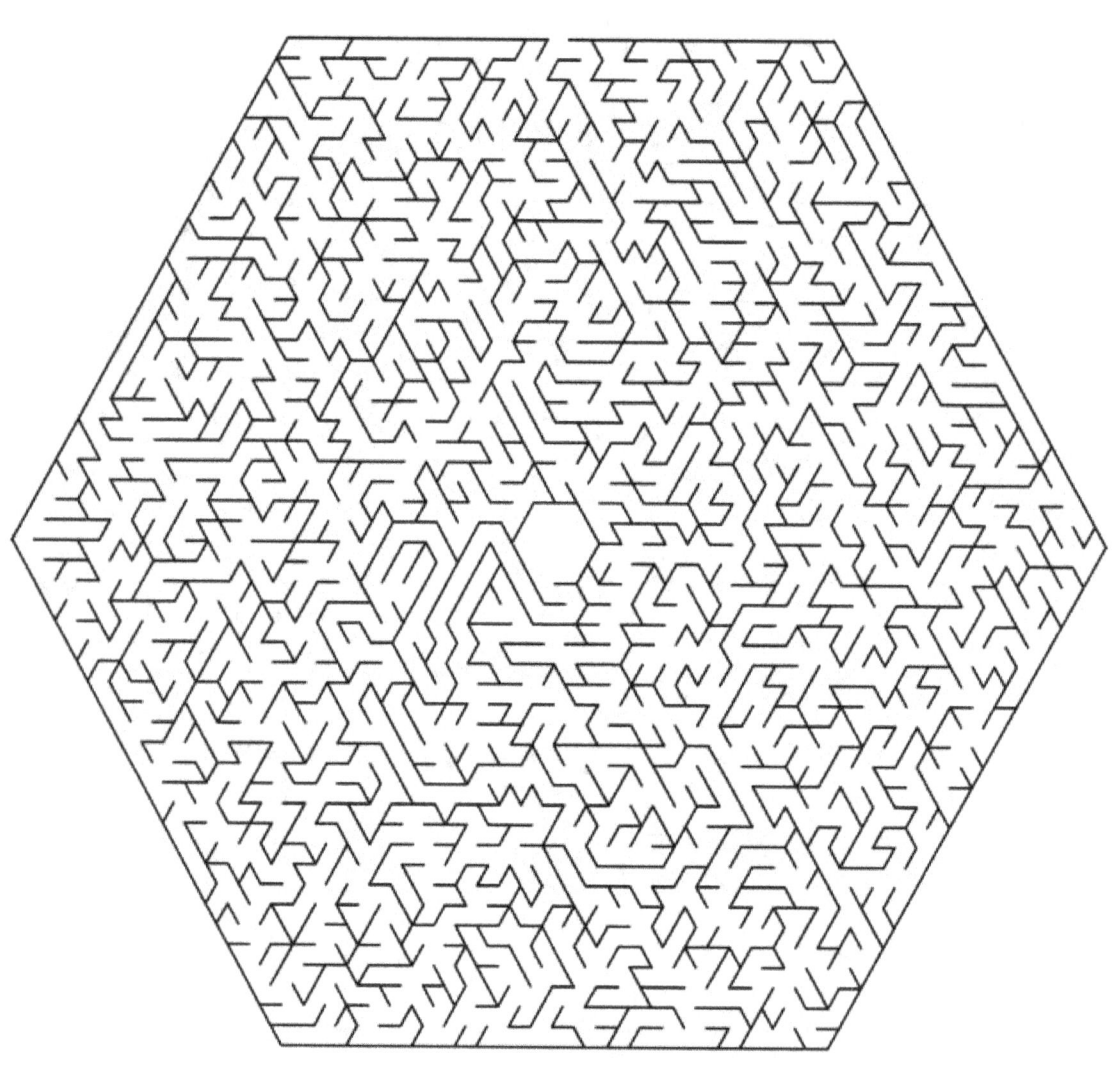

PUT A HEX ON IT #78

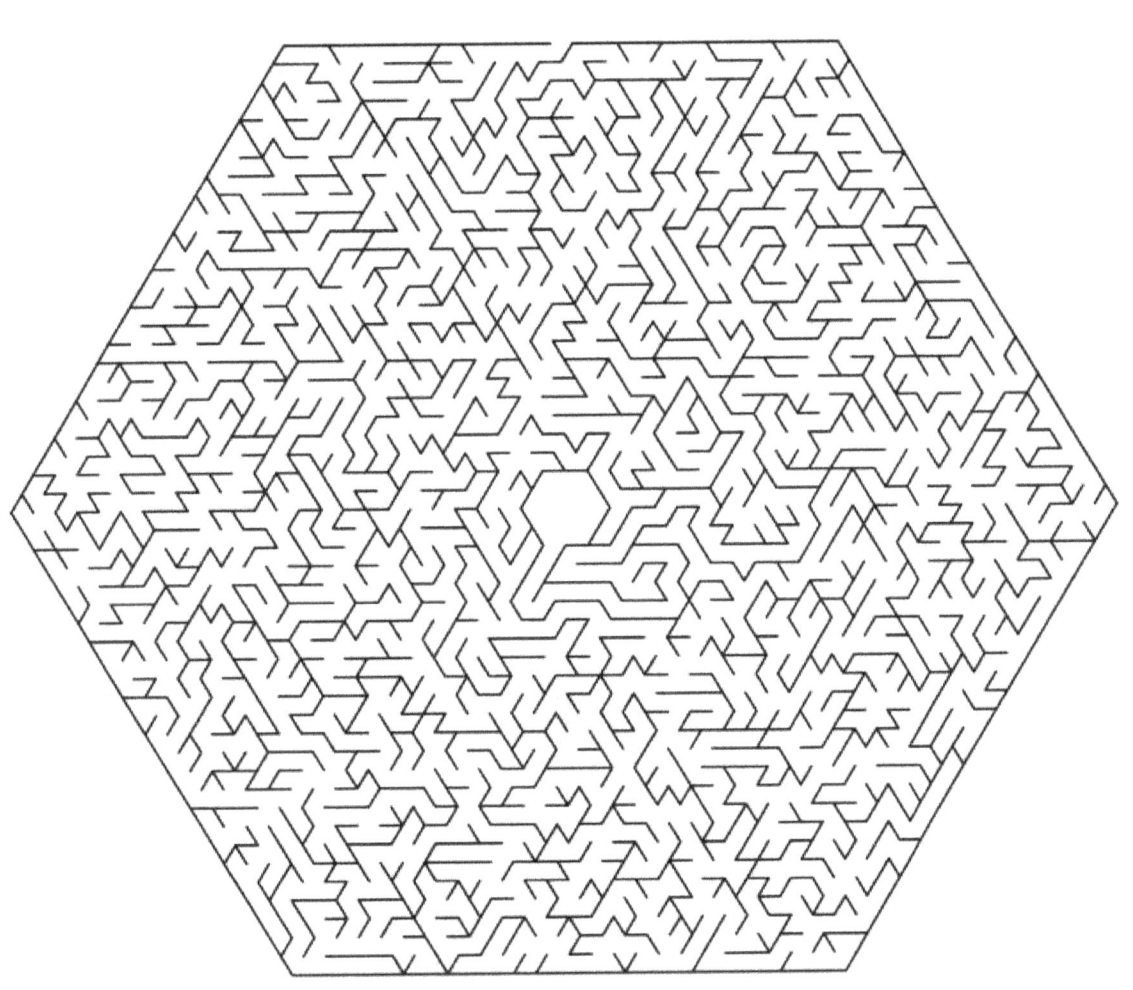

PUT A HEX ON IT #79

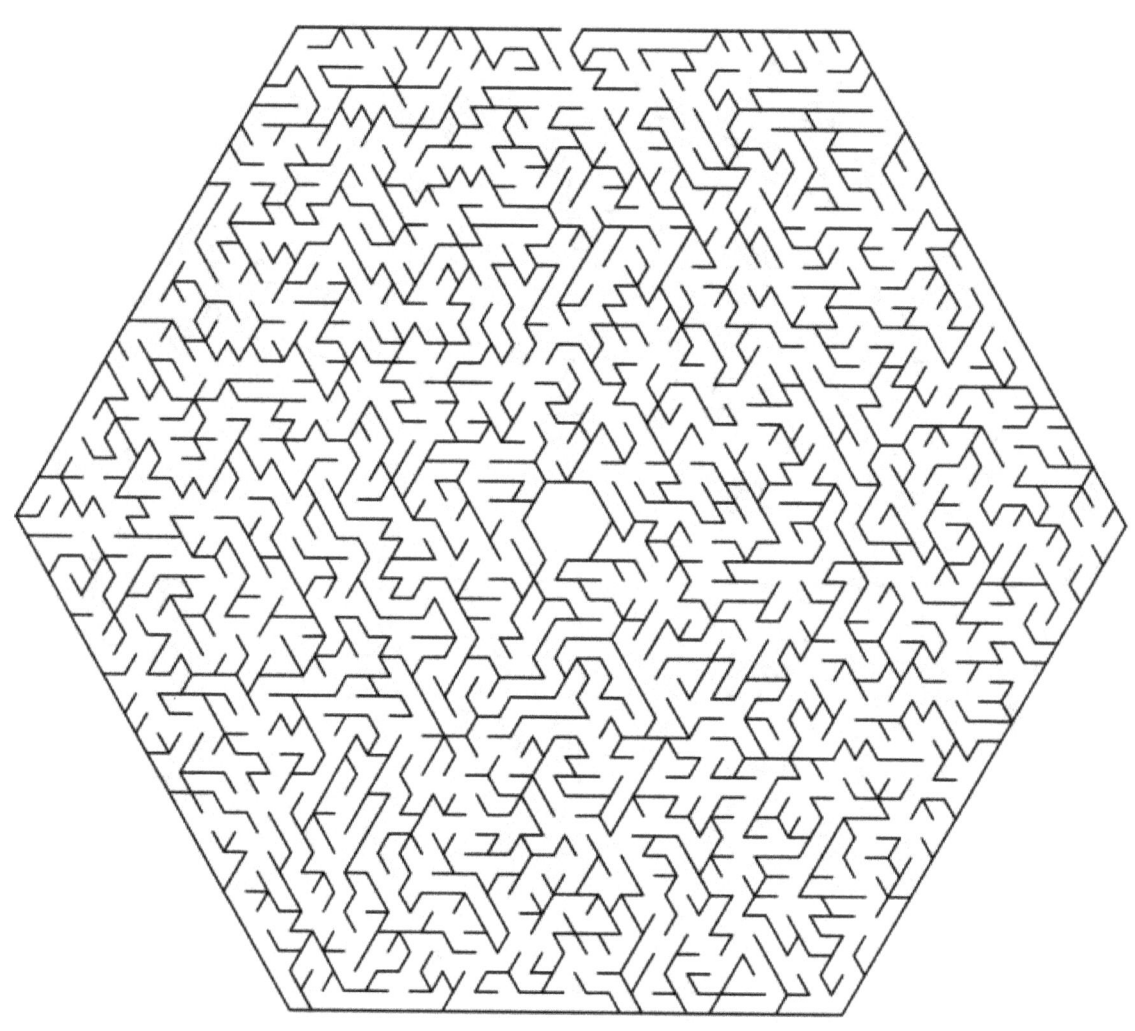

PUT A HEX ON IT #80

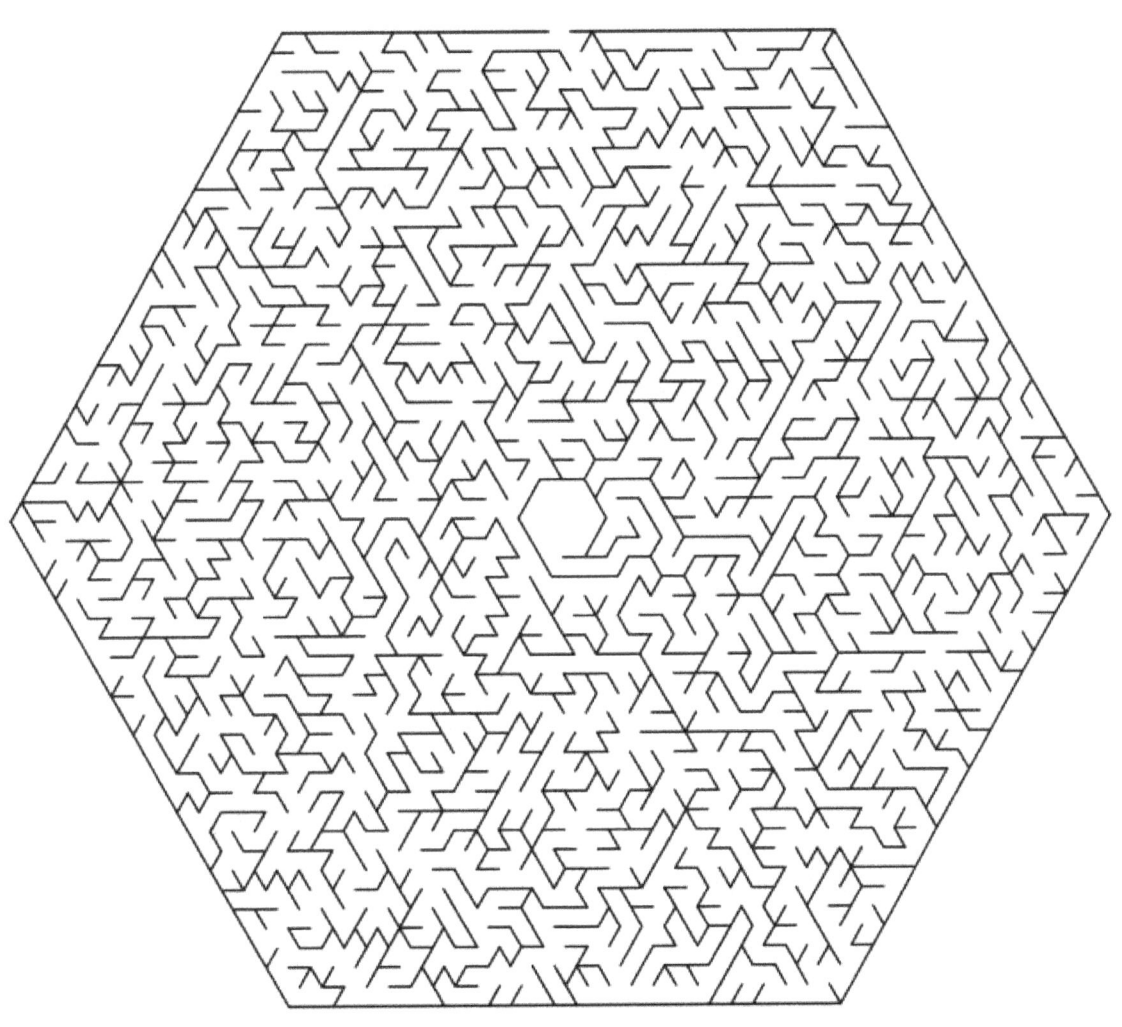

PUT A HEX ON IT #81

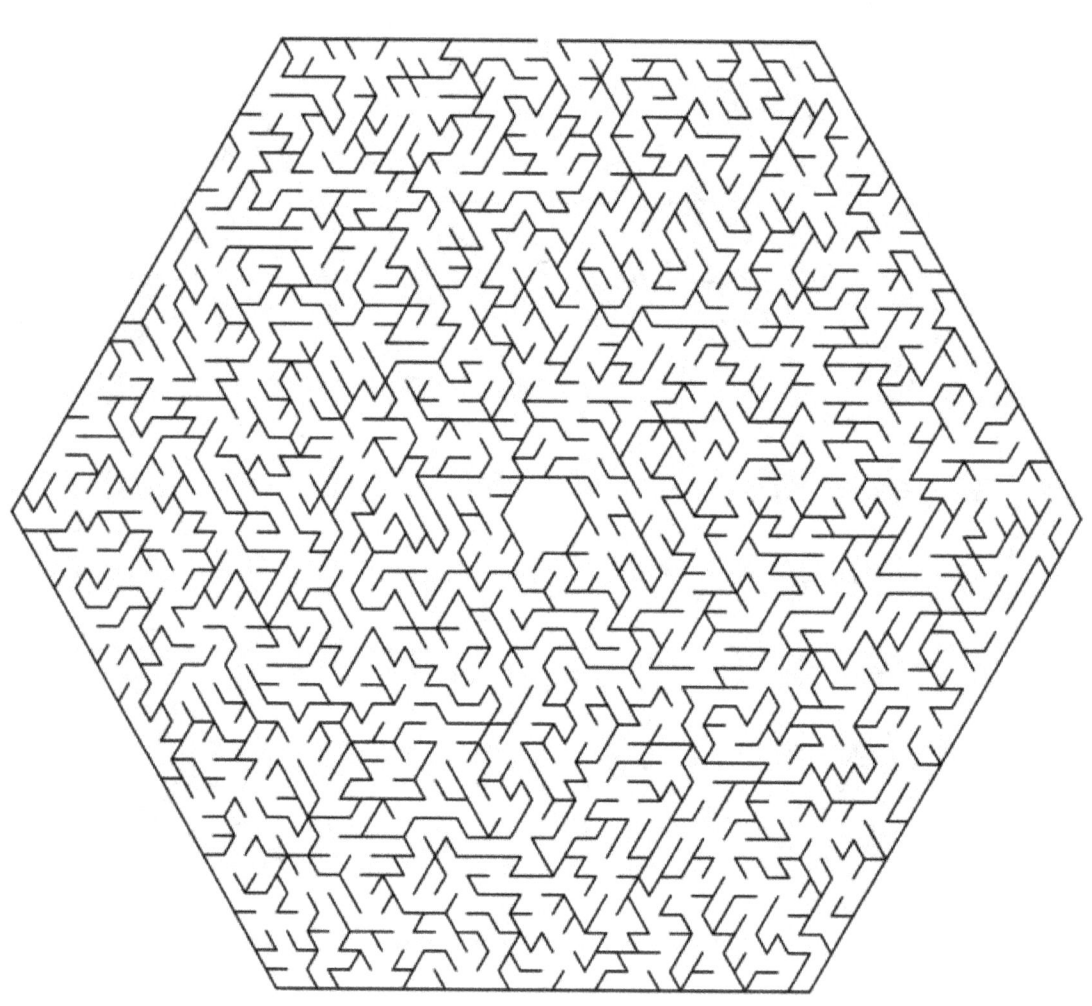

PUT A HEX ON IT #82

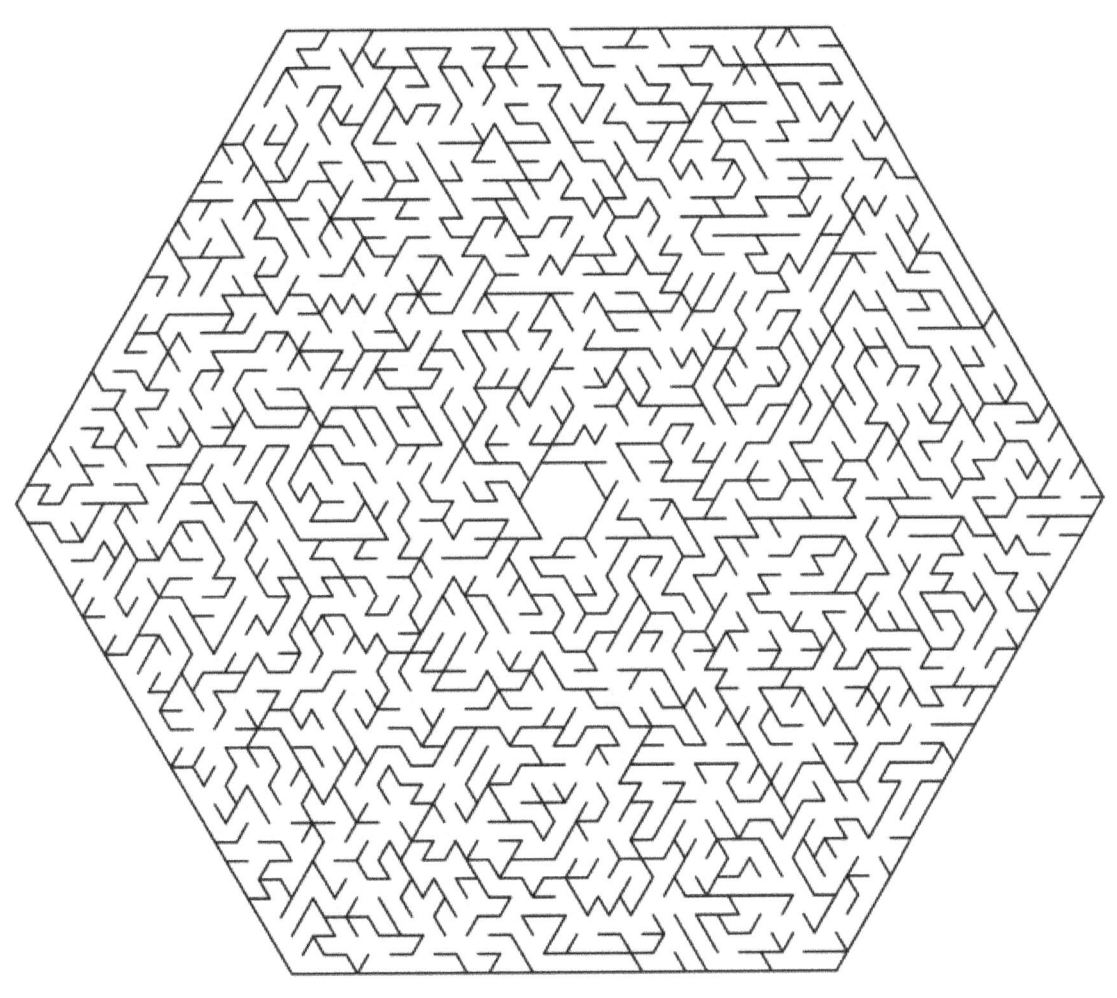

PUT A HEX ON IT #83

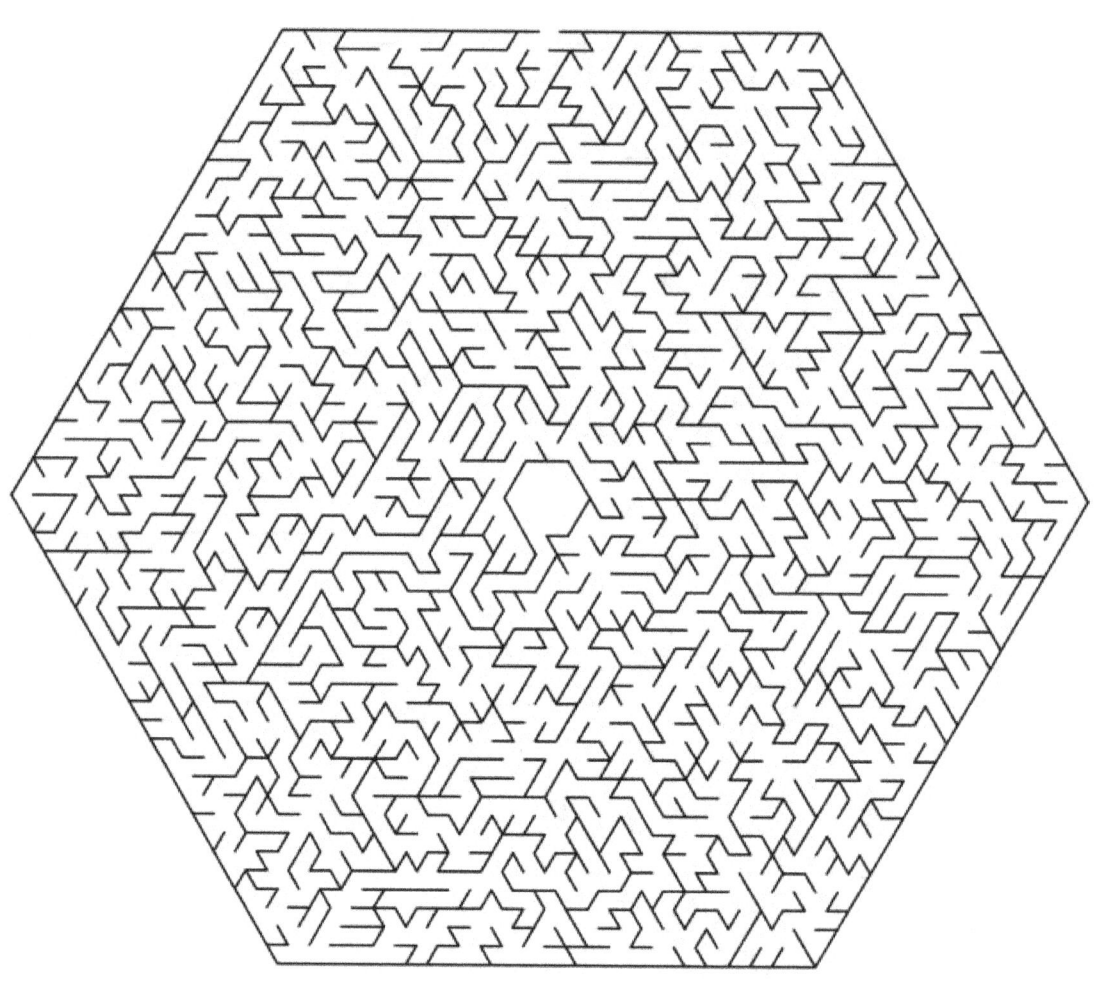

PUT A HEX ON IT #84

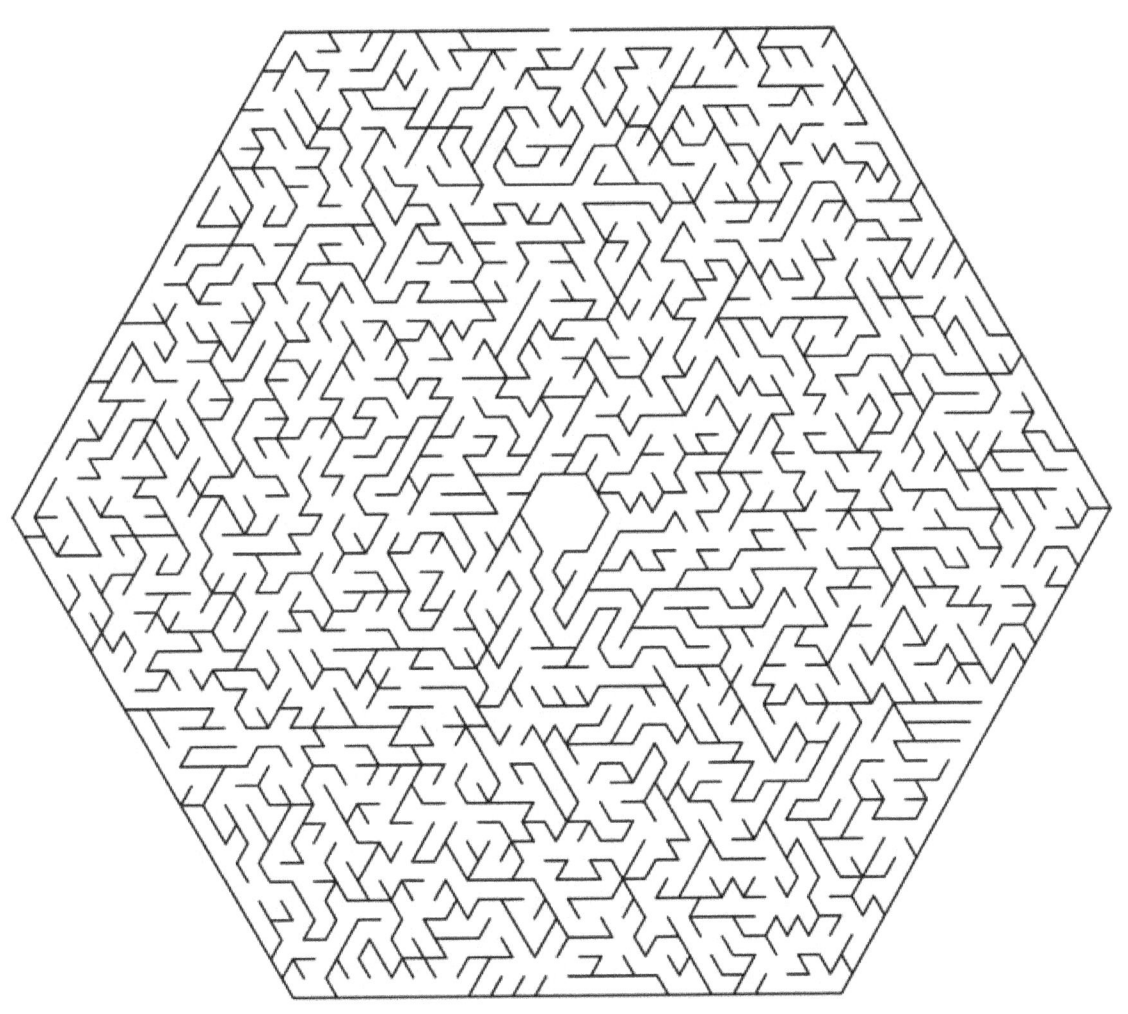

PUT A HEX ON IT #85

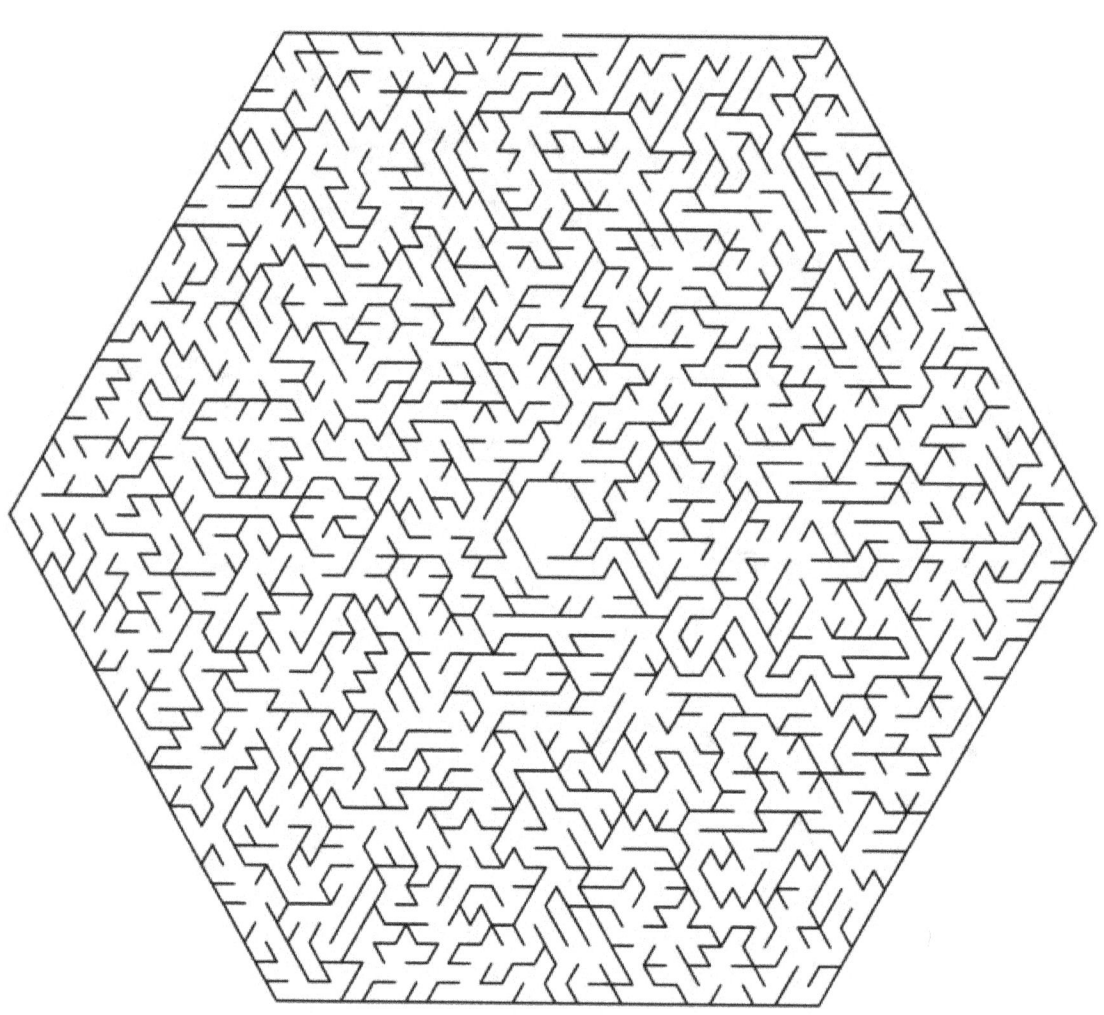

PUT A HEX ON IT #86

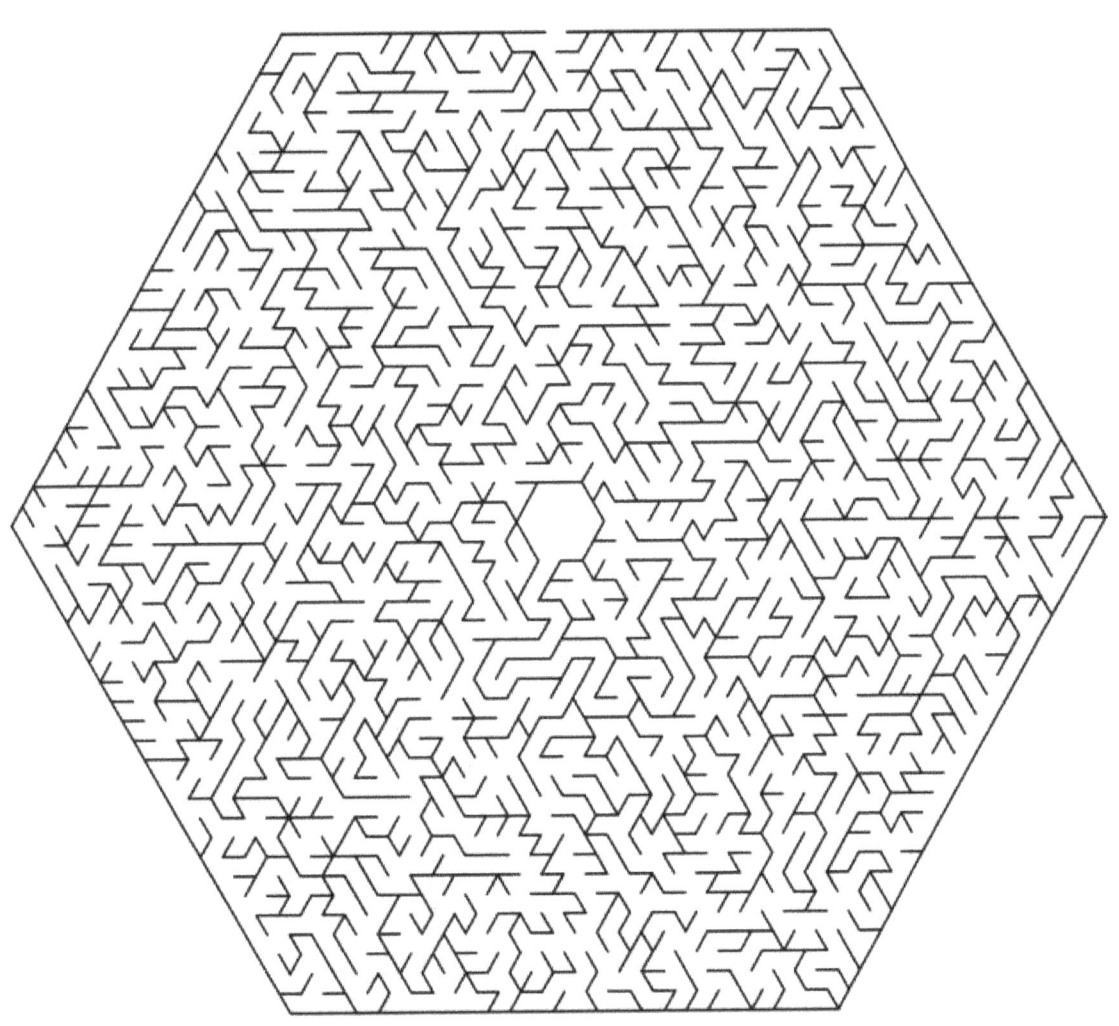

PUT A HEX ON IT #87

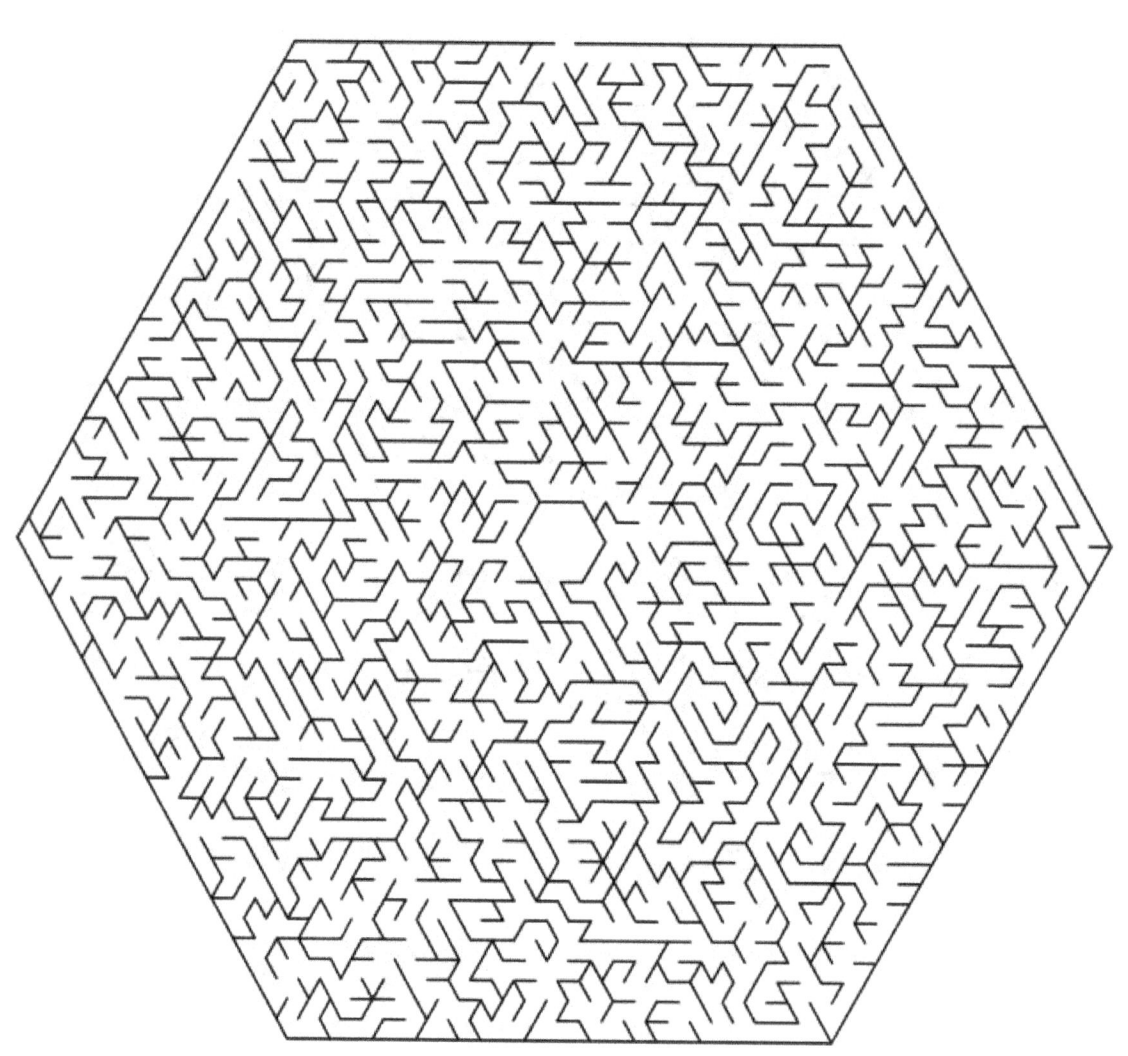

PUT A HEX ON IT #88

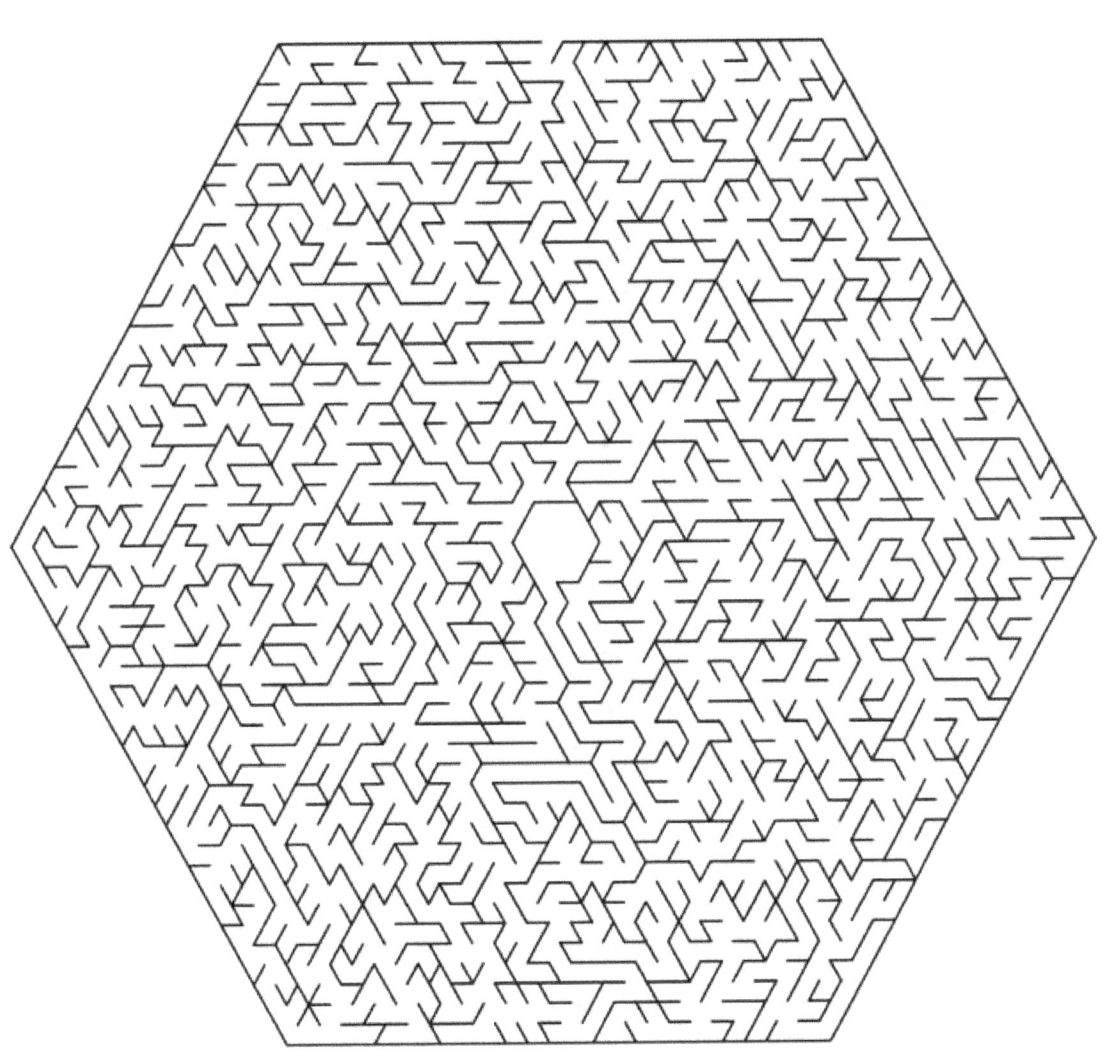

PUT A HEX ON IT #89

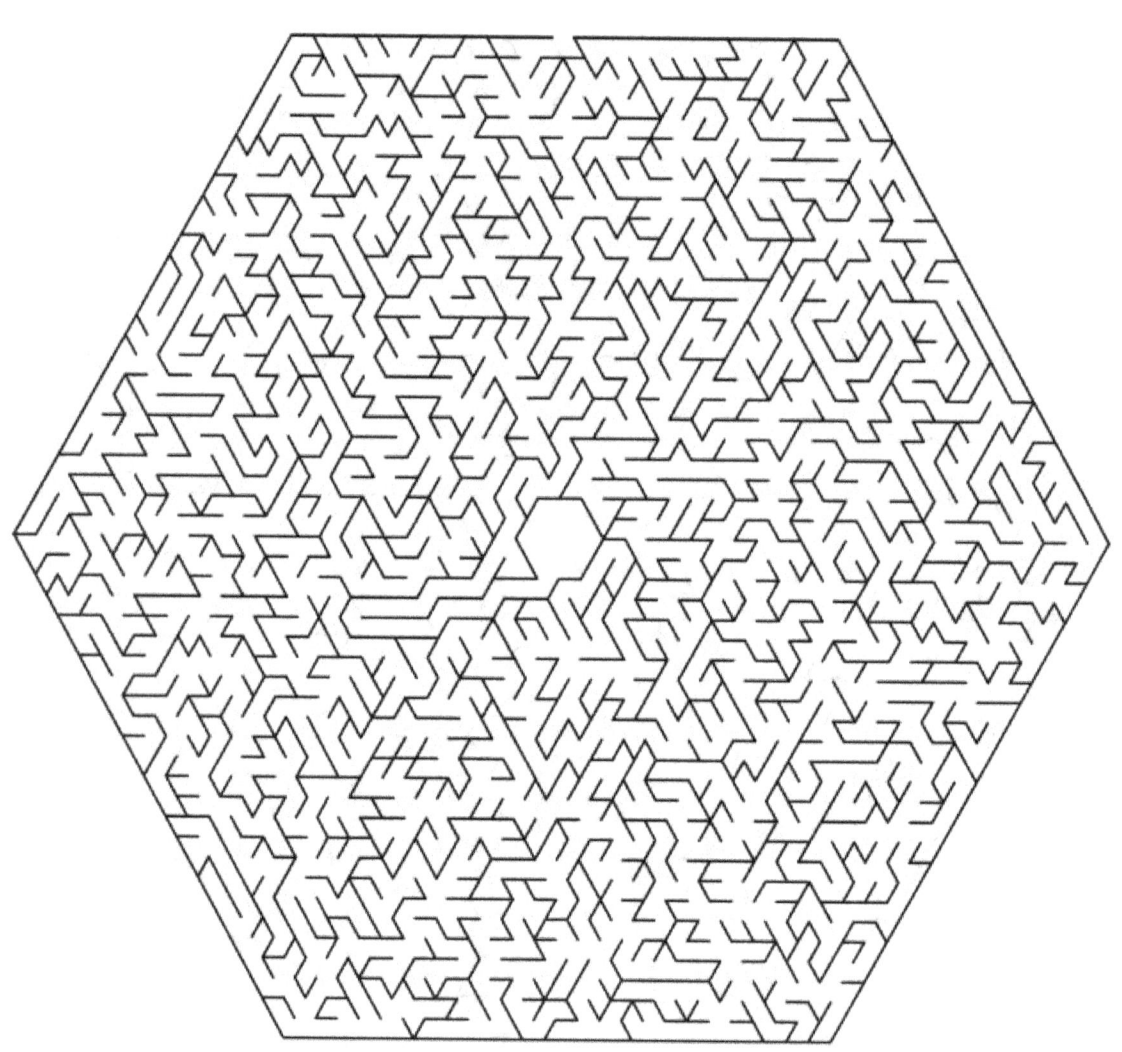

PUT A HEX ON IT #90

PUT A HEX ON IT #91

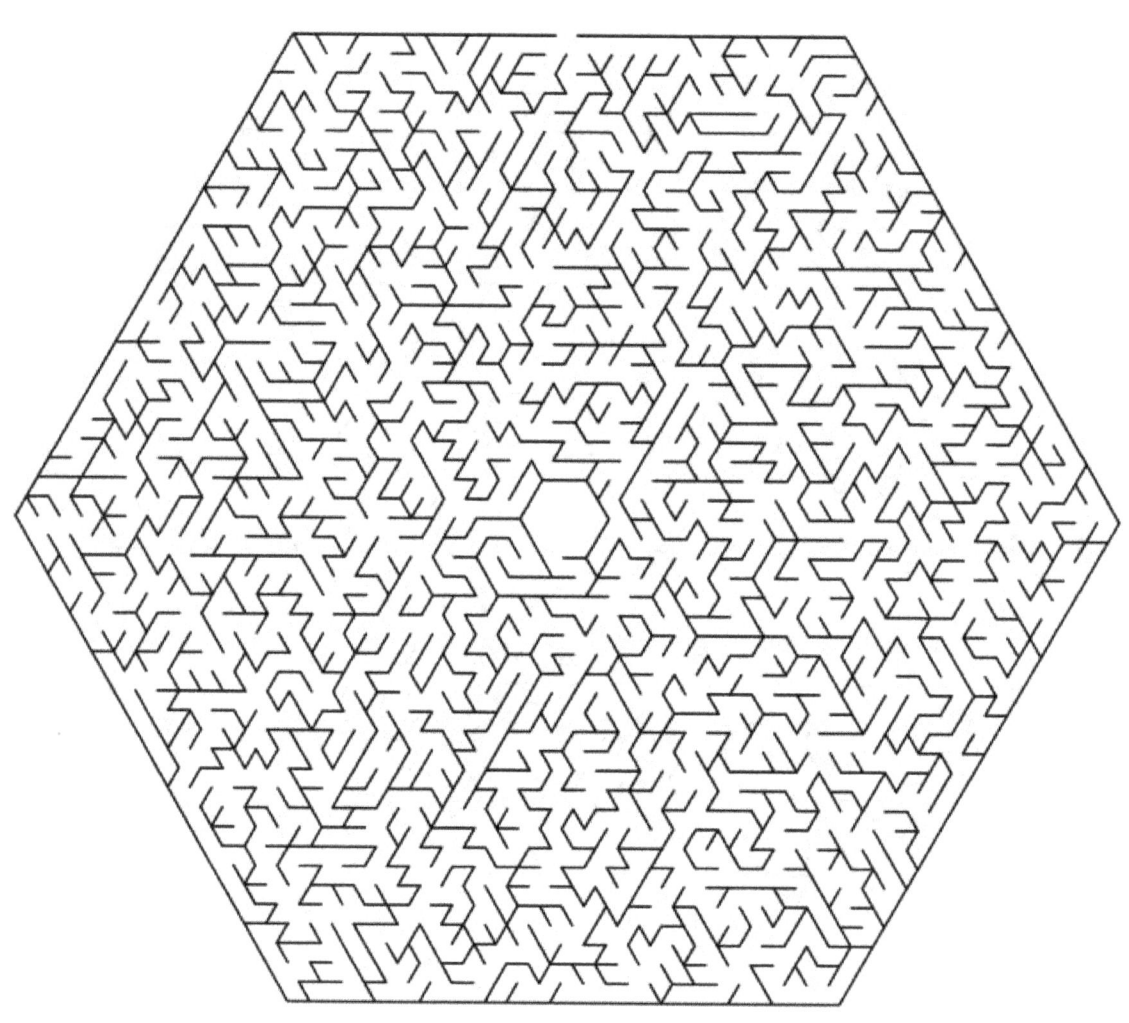

PUT A HEX ON IT #92

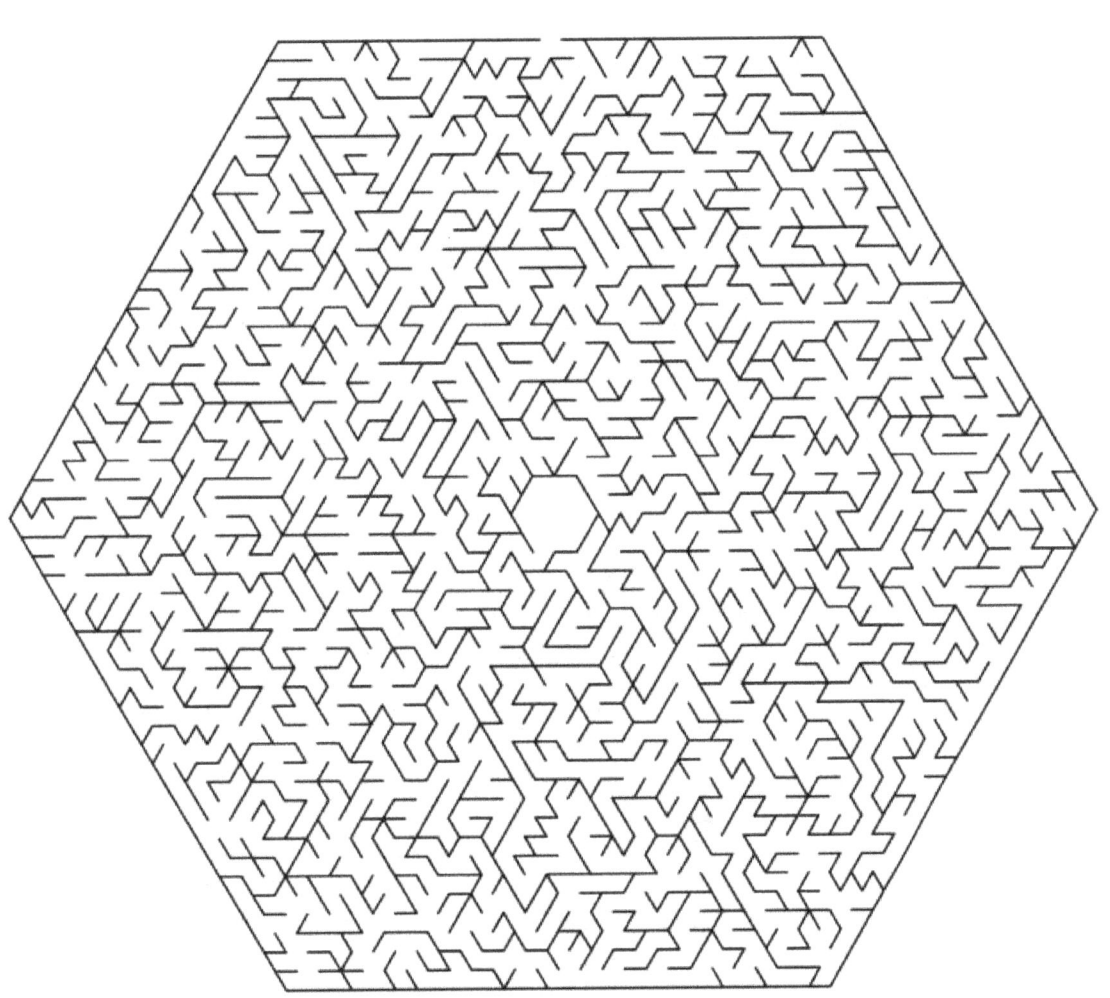

PUT A HEX ON IT #93

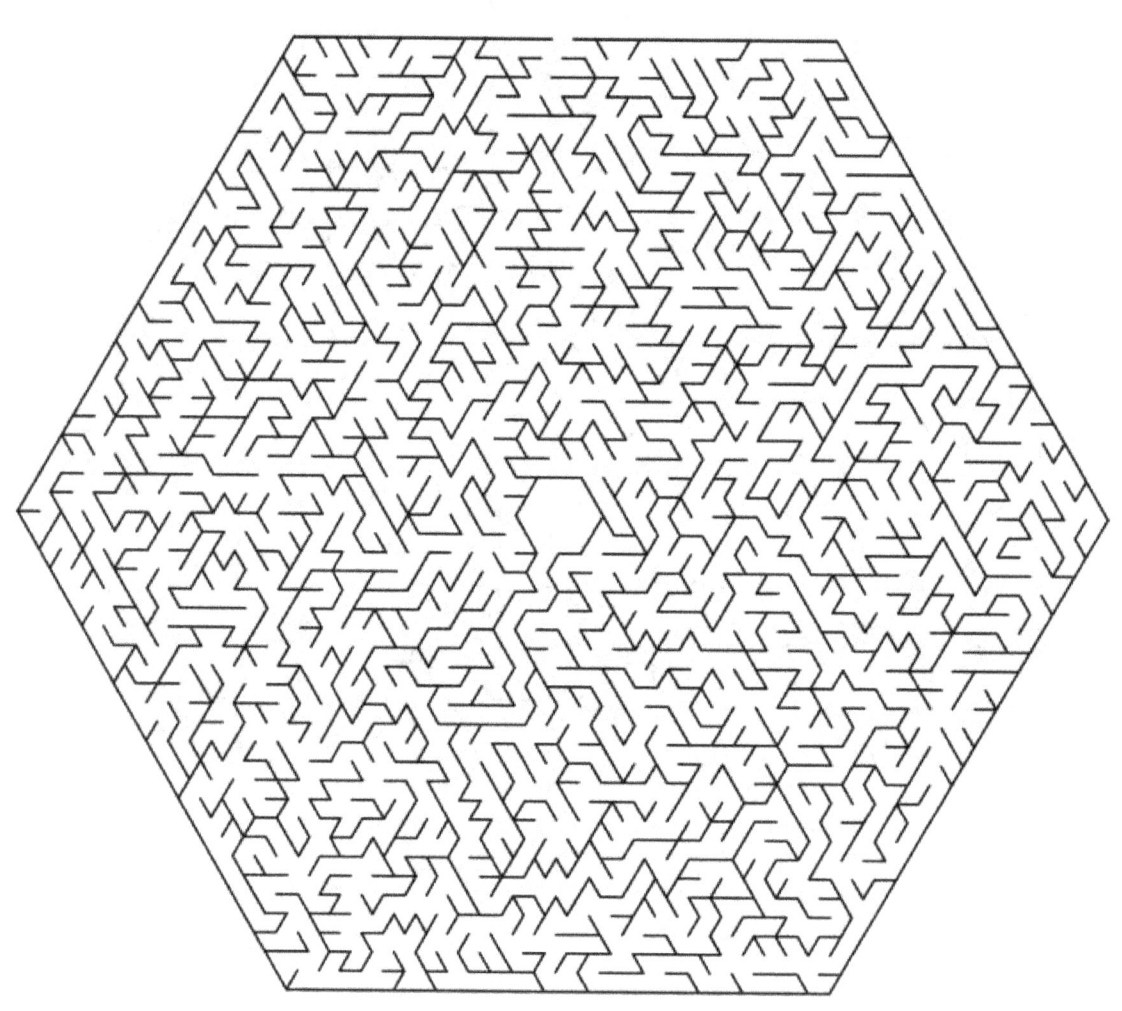

PUT A HEX ON IT #94

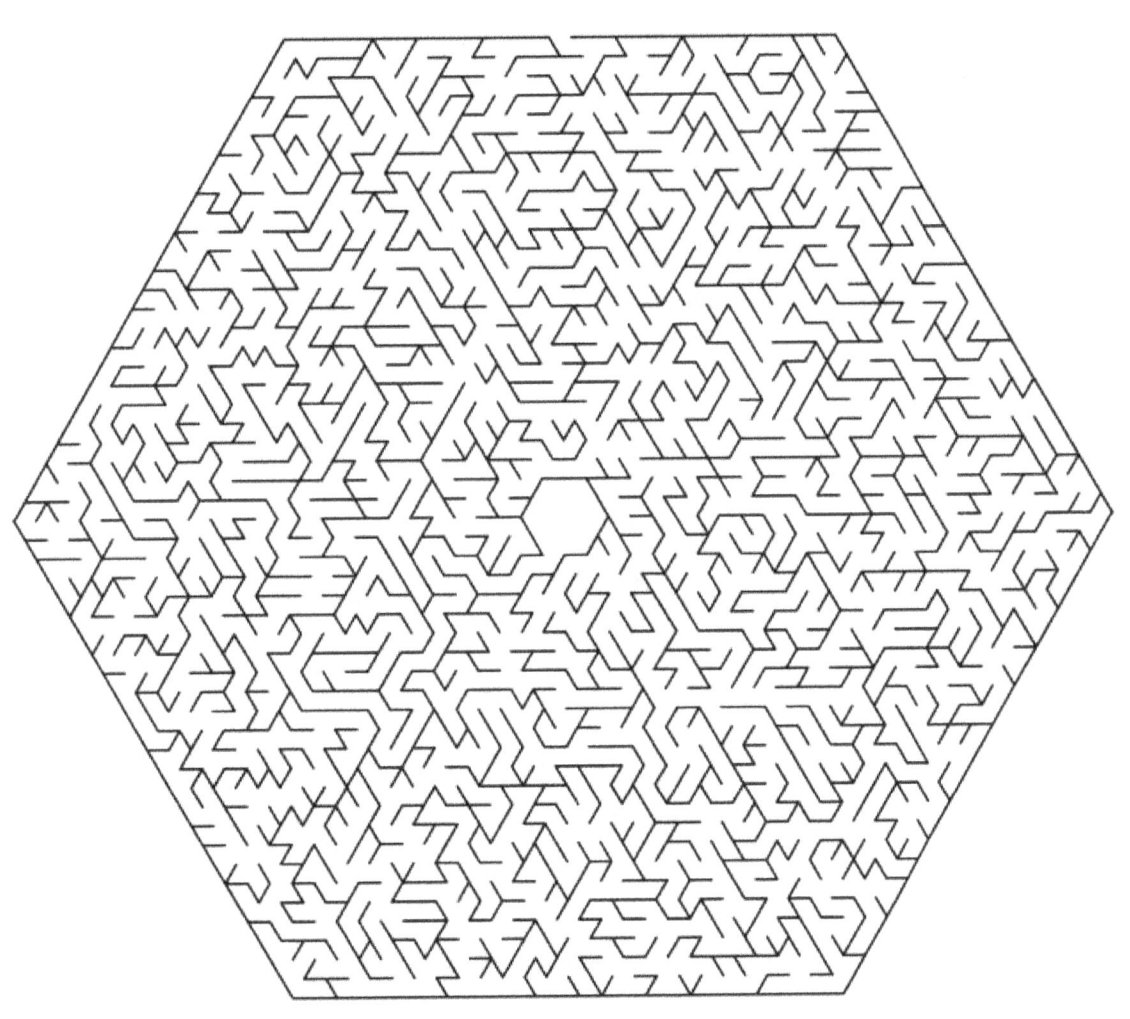

PUT A HEX ON IT #95

PUT A HEX ON IT #96

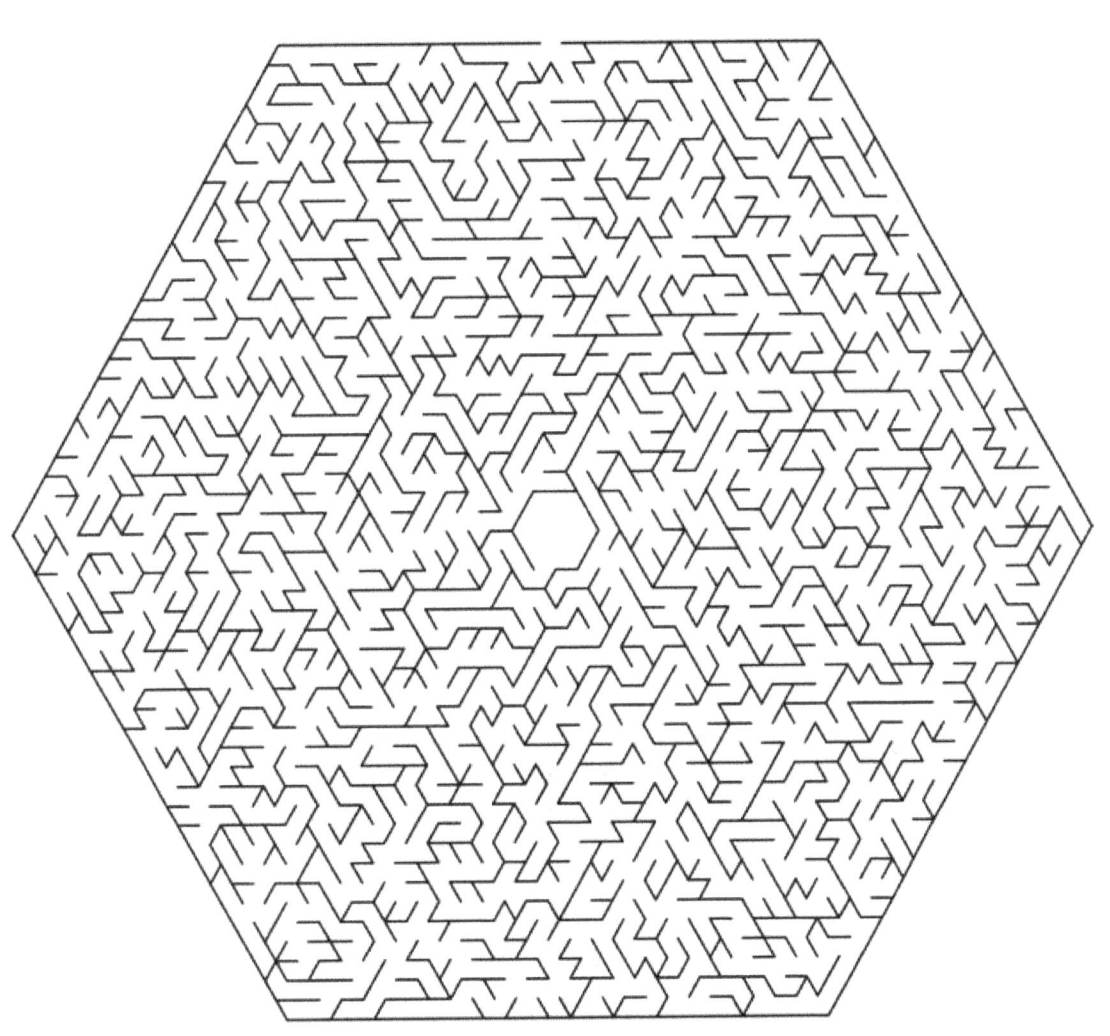

PUT A HEX ON IT #97

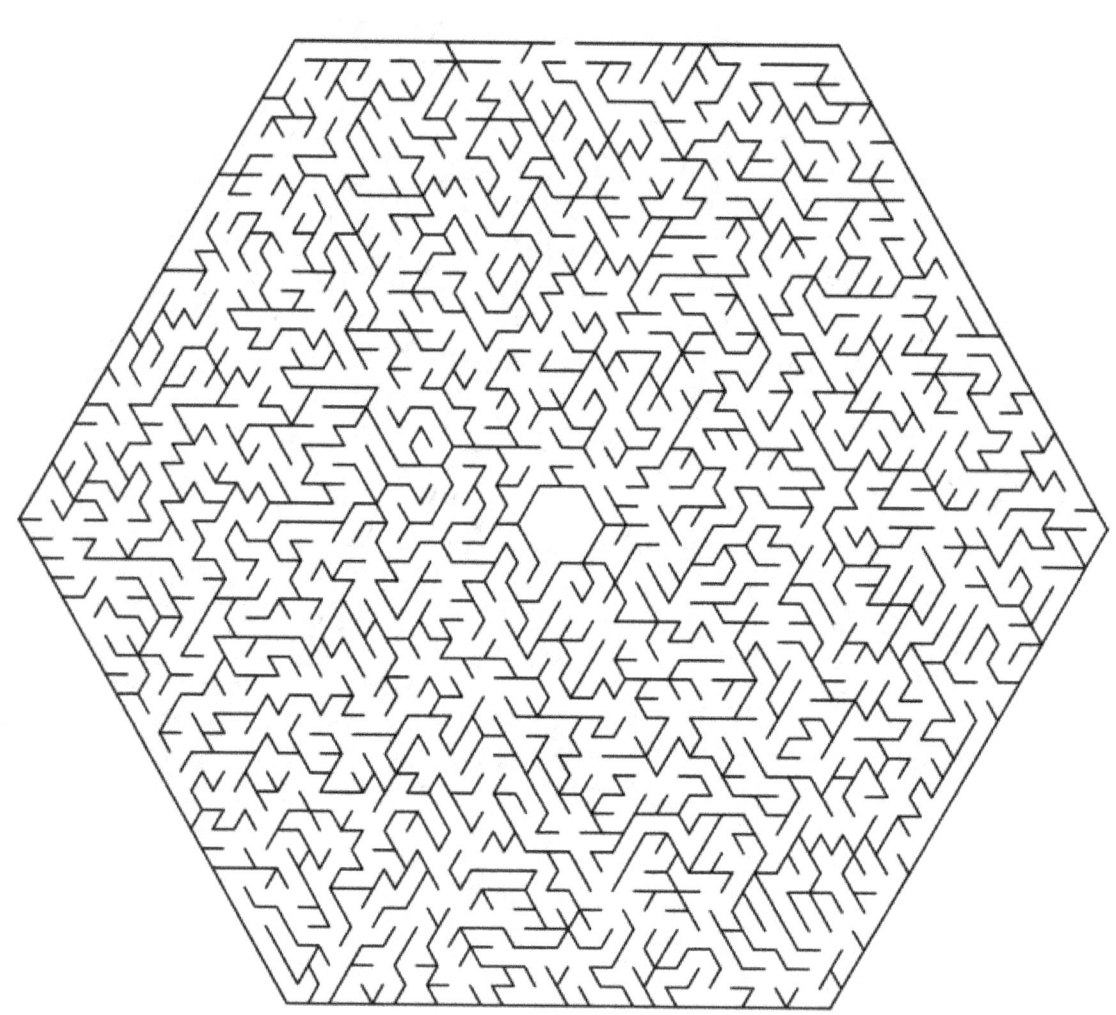

PUT A HEX ON IT #98

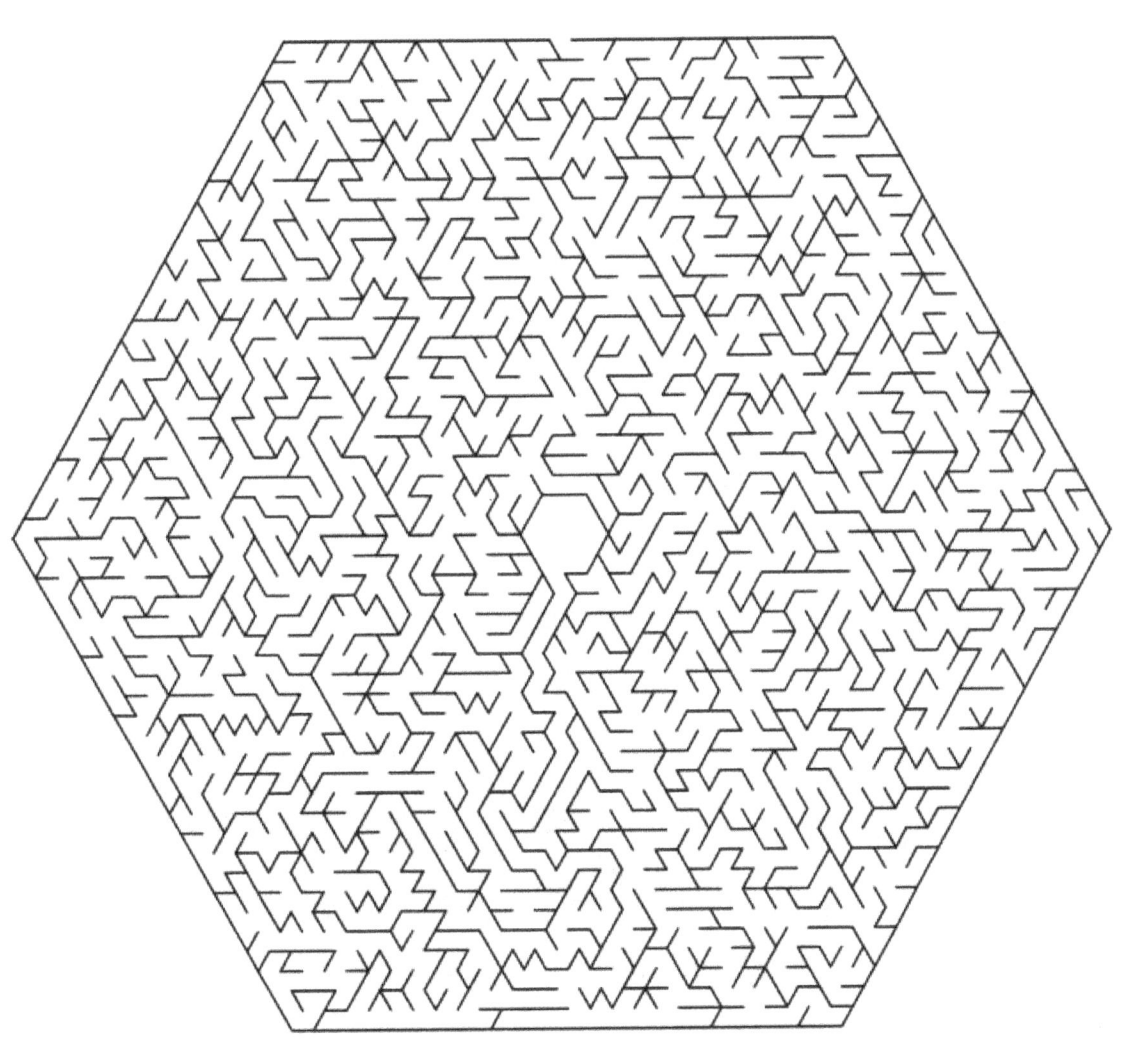

PUT A HEX ON IT #99

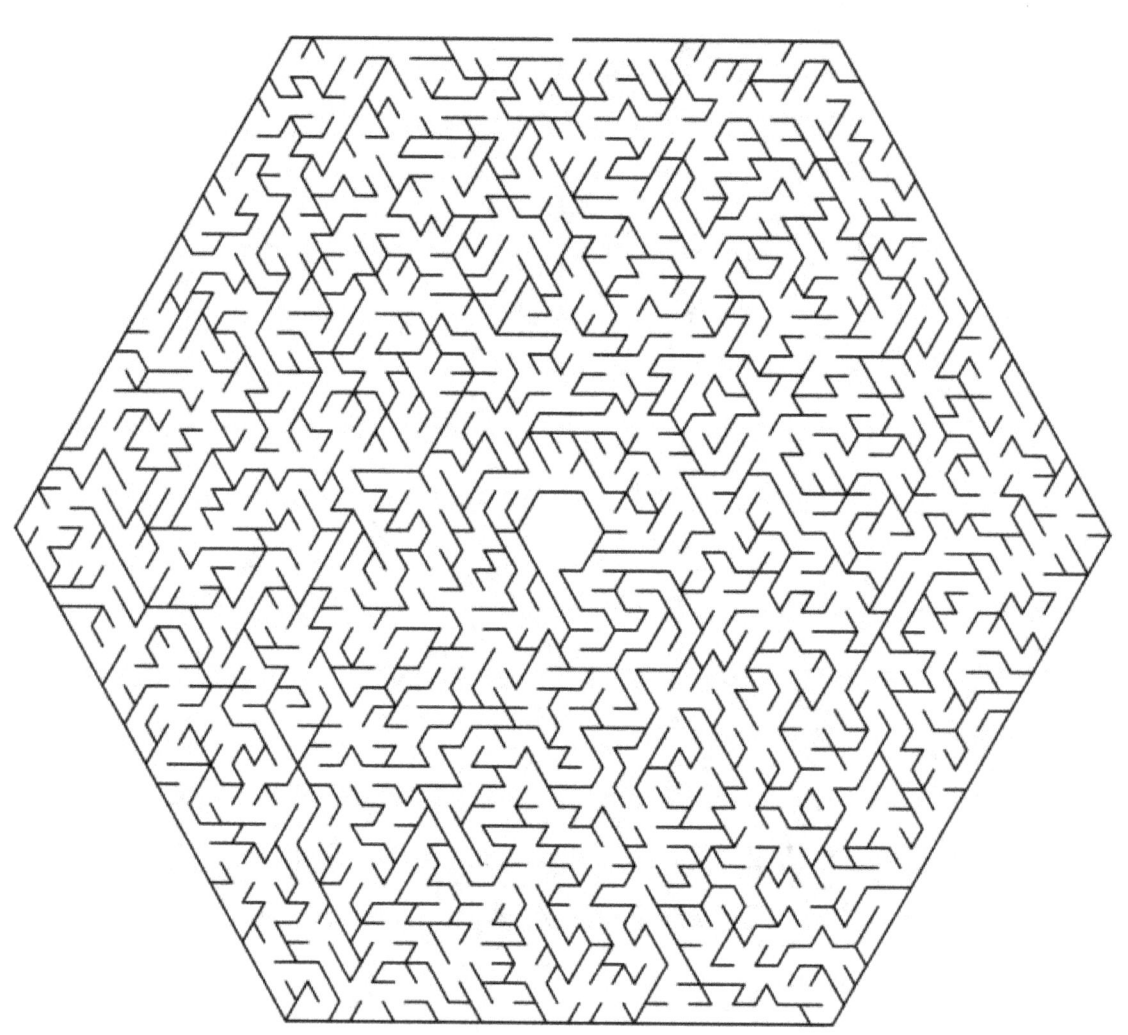

SOLUTIONS

PUT A HEX ON IT #1 - KEY

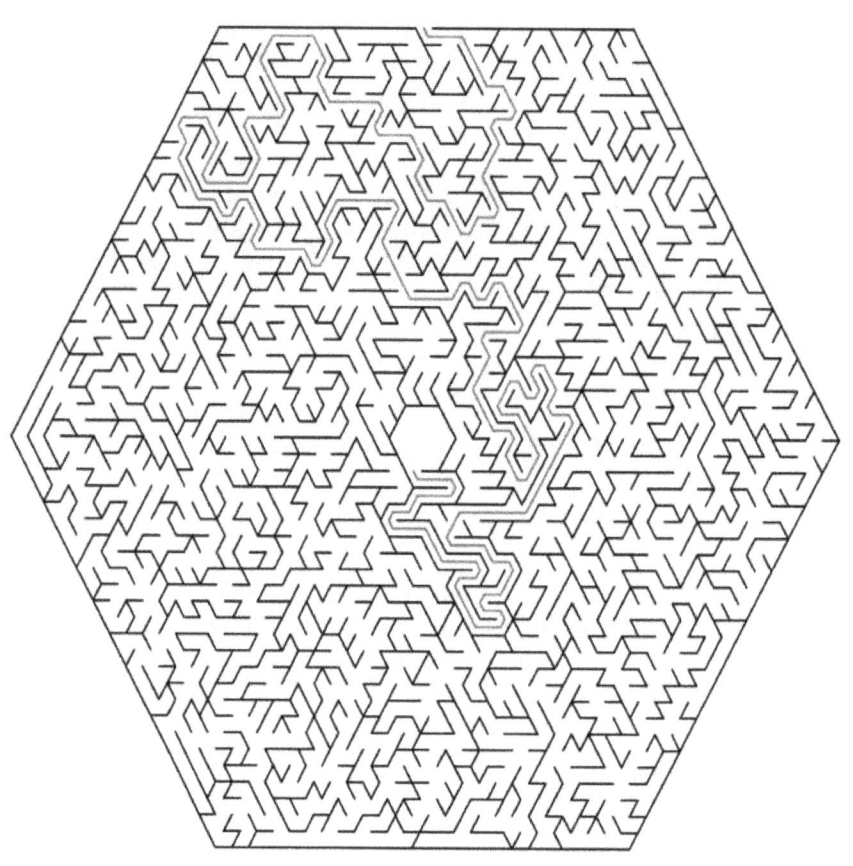

PUT A HEX ON IT #2 - KEY

PUT A HEX ON IT #3 - KEY

PUT A HEX ON IT #4 - KEY

PUT A HEX ON IT #5 - KEY

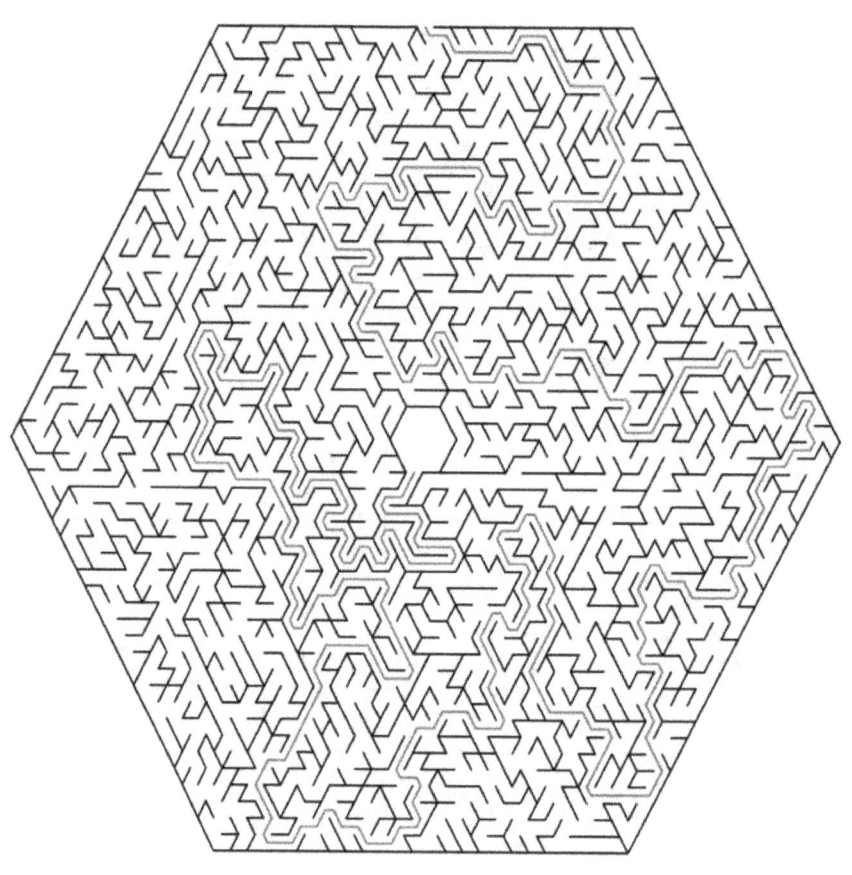

PUT A HEX ON IT #6 - KEY

PUT A HEX ON IT #7 - KEY

PUT A HEX ON IT #8 - KEY

PUT A HEX ON IT #9 - KEY

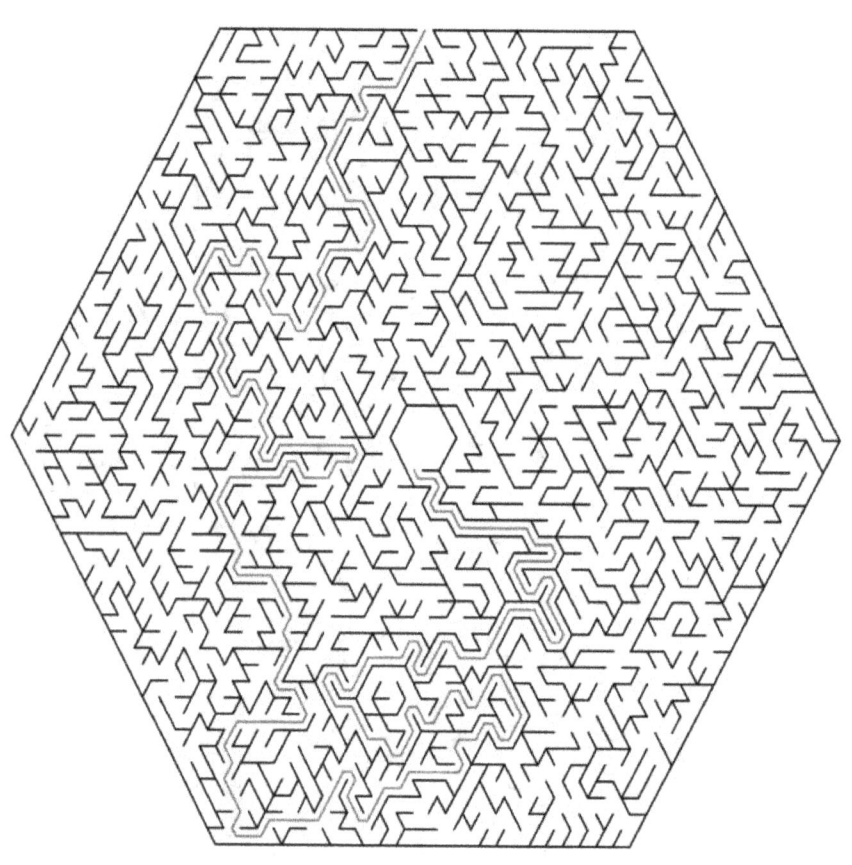

PUT A HEX ON IT #10 - KEY

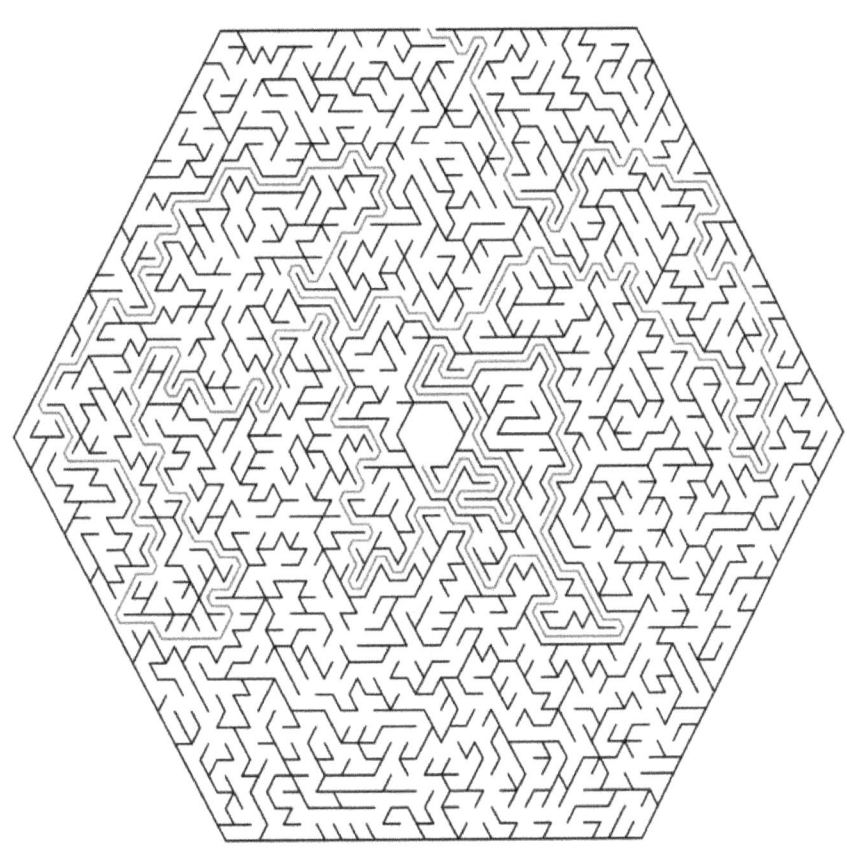

PUT A HEX ON IT #11- KEY

PUT A HEX ON IT #12 - KEY

PUT A HEX ON IT #13 - KEY

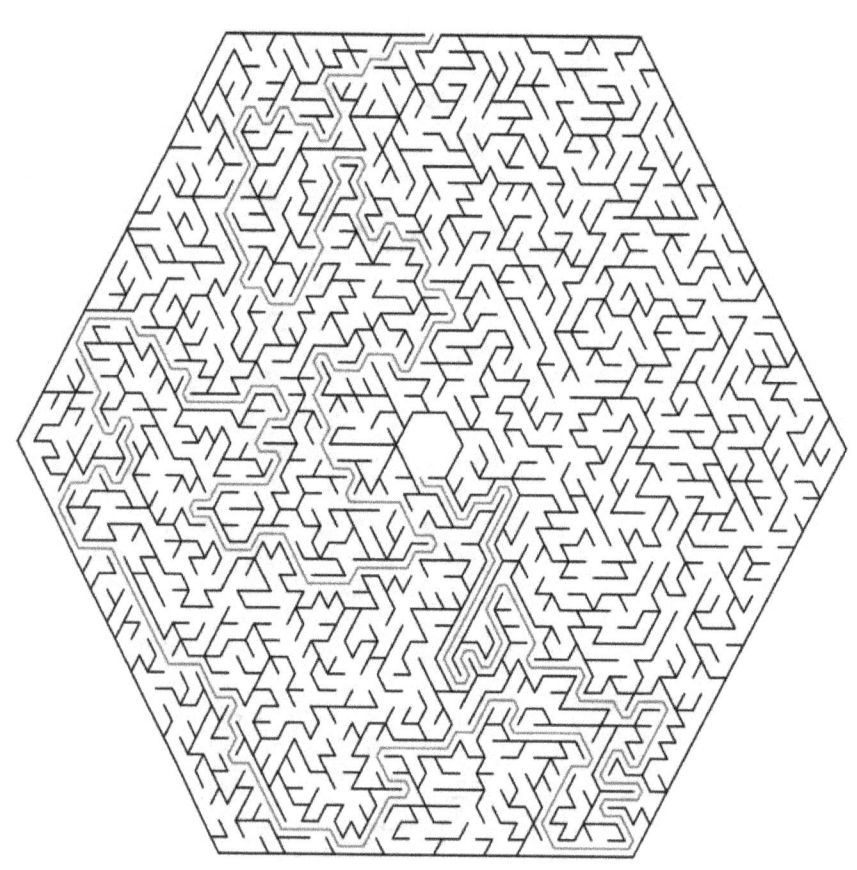

PUT A HEX ON IT #14 - KEY

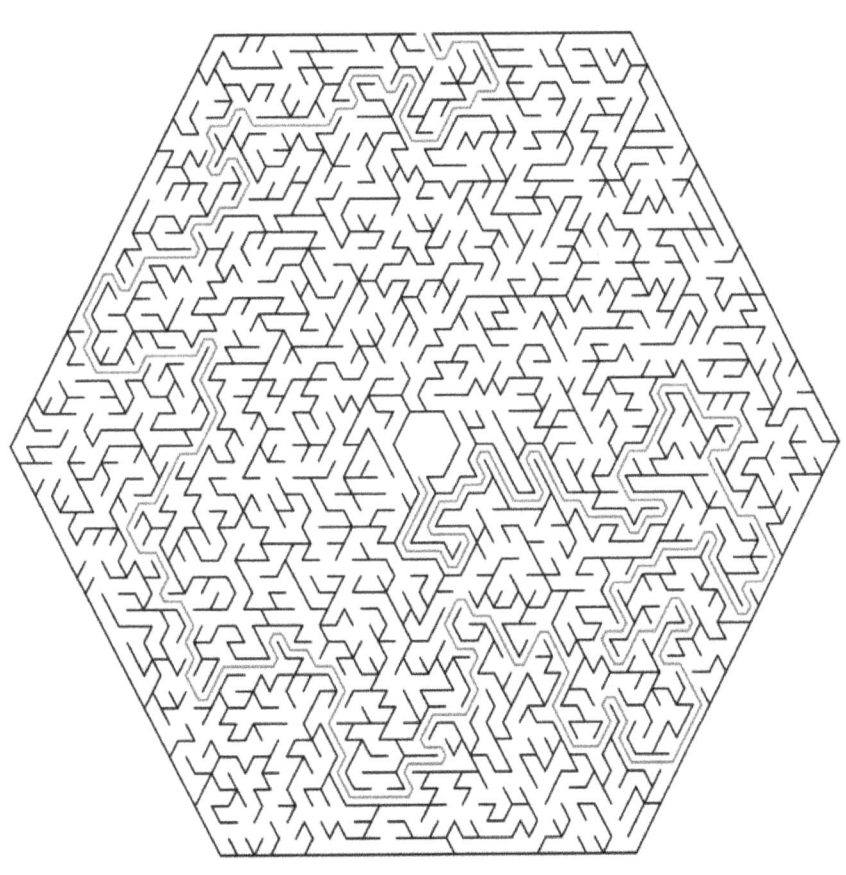

PUT A HEX ON IT #15 - KEY

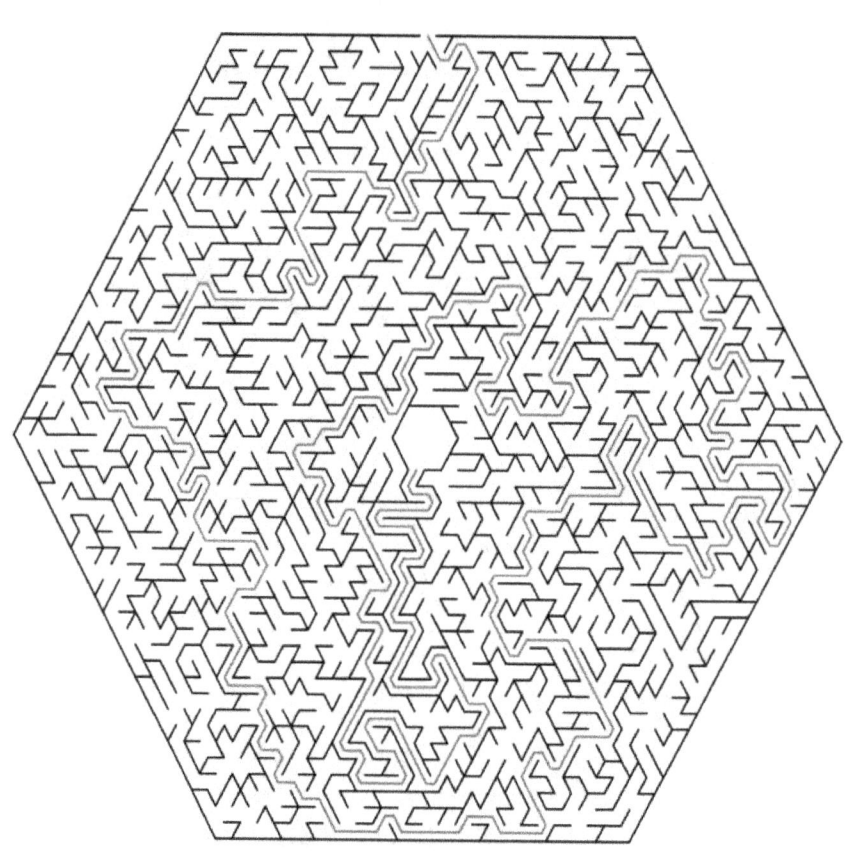

PUT A HEX ON IT #16 - KEY

PUT A HEX ON IT #17 - KEY

PUT A HEX ON IT #18 - KEY

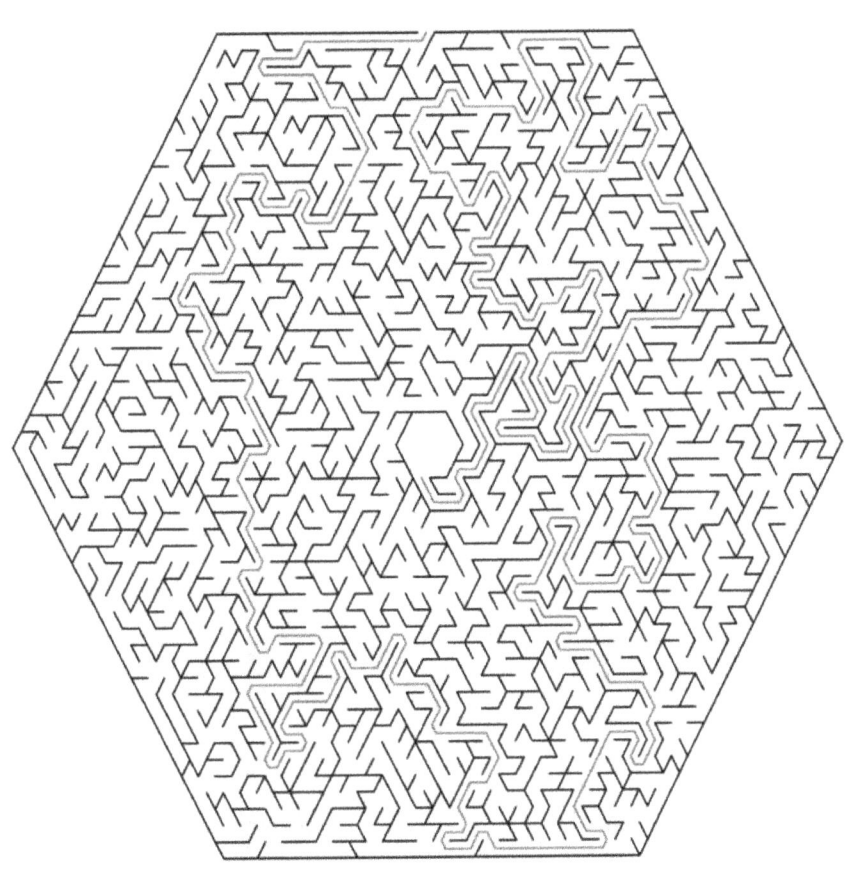

PUT A HEX ON IT #19 - KEY

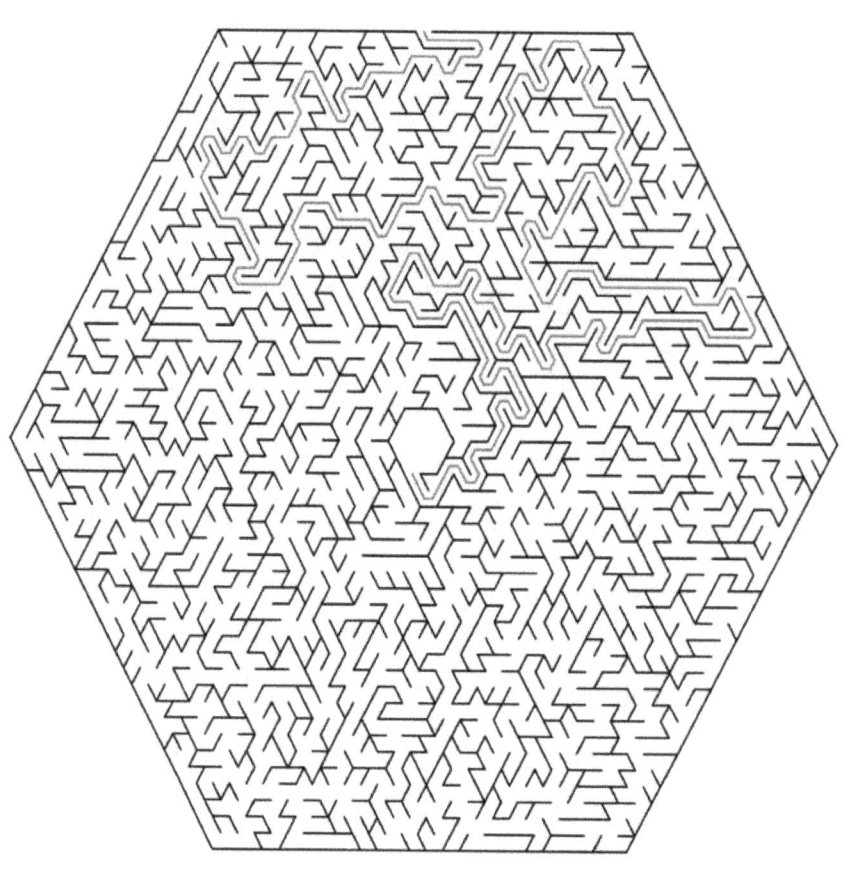

PUT A HEX ON IT #20 - KEY

PUT A HEX ON IT #21 - KEY

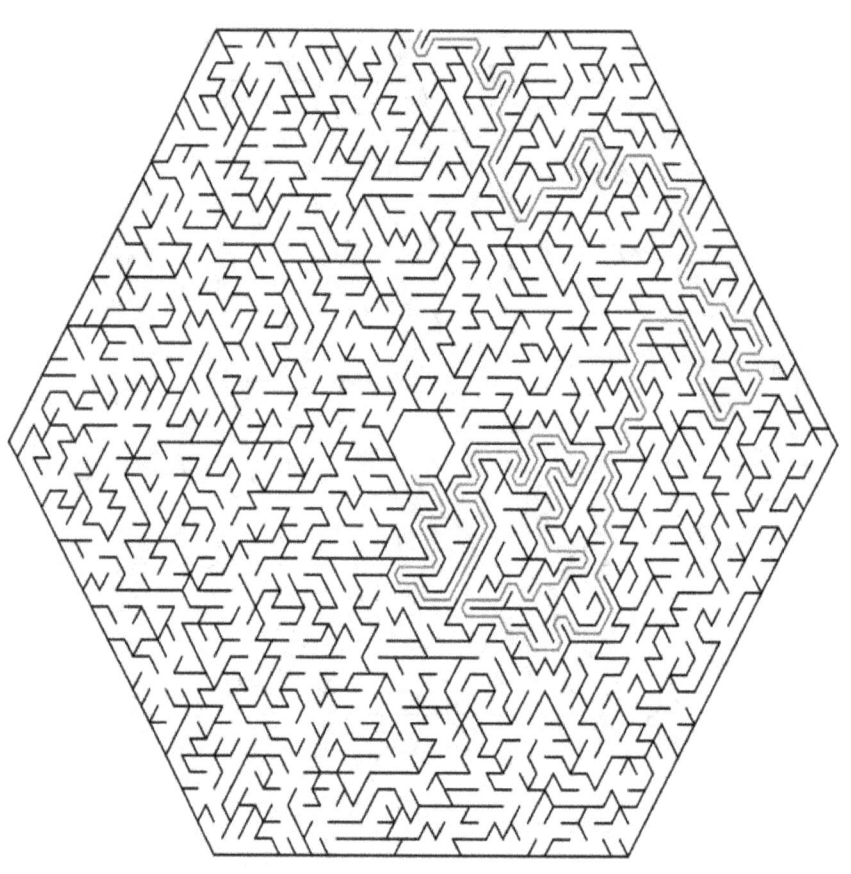

PUT A HEX ON IT #22 - KEY

PUT A HEX ON IT #23 - KEY

PUT A HEX ON IT #24 - KEY

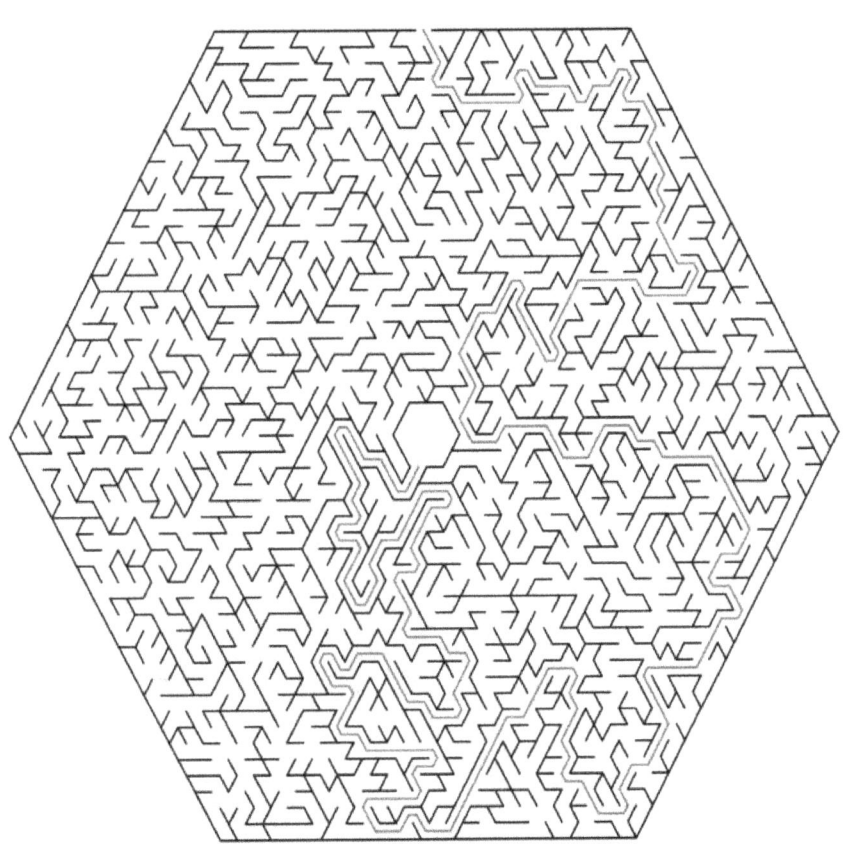

PUT A HEX ON IT #25 - KEY

PUT A HEX ON IT #26 - KEY

PUT A HEX ON IT #27 - KEY

PUT A HEX ON IT #28 - KEY

PUT A HEX ON IT #29 - KEY

PUT A HEX ON IT #30 - KEY

PUT A HEX ON IT #31 - KEY

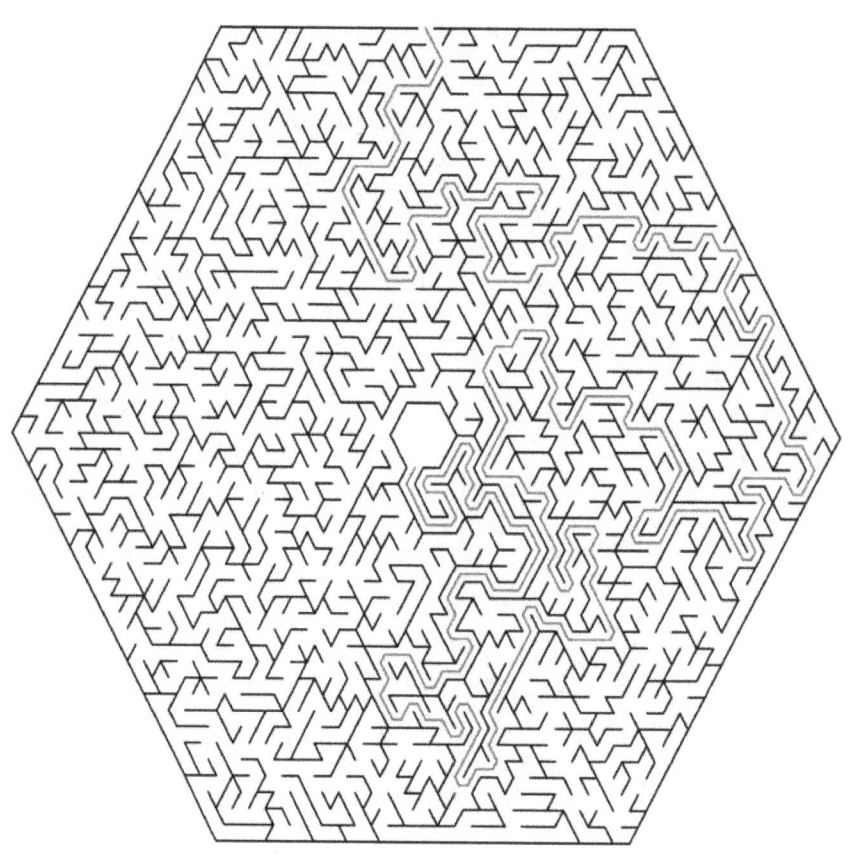

PUT A HEX ON IT #32 - KEY

PUT A HEX ON IT #33 - KEY

PUT A HEX ON IT #34 - KEY

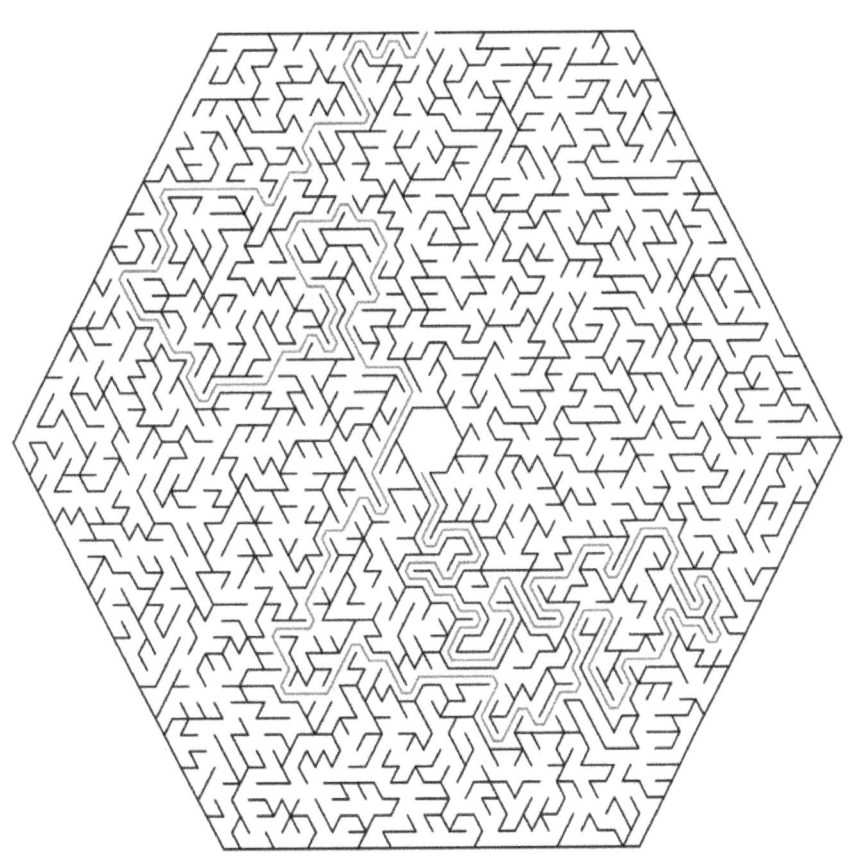

PUT A HEX ON IT #35 - KEY

PUT A HEX ON IT #36 - KEY

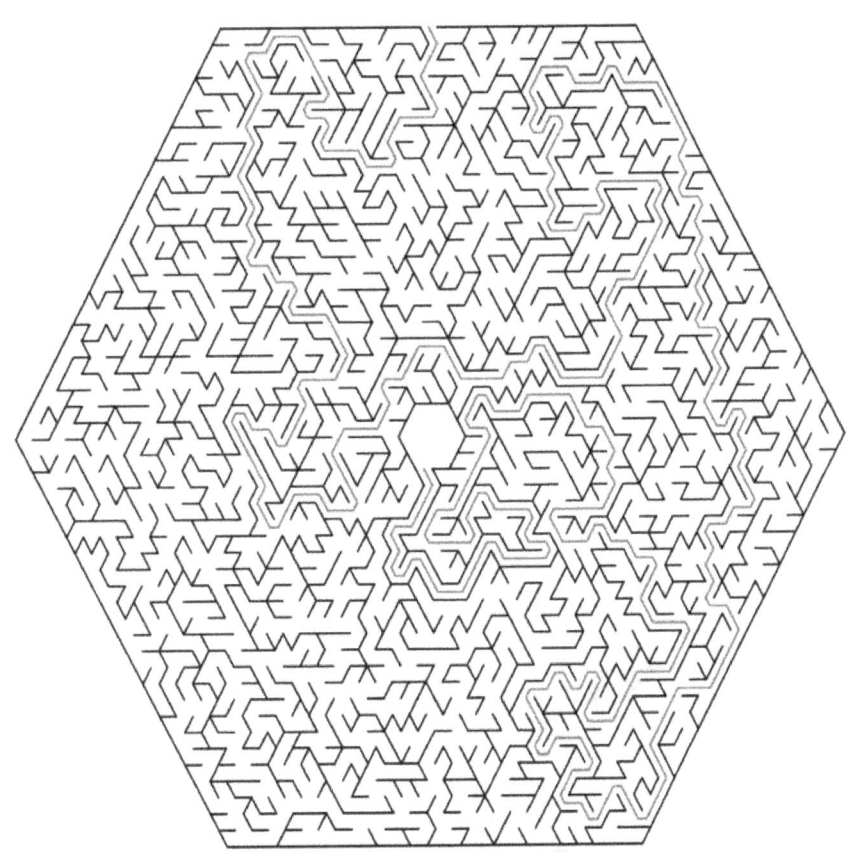

PUT A HEX ON IT #37 - KEY

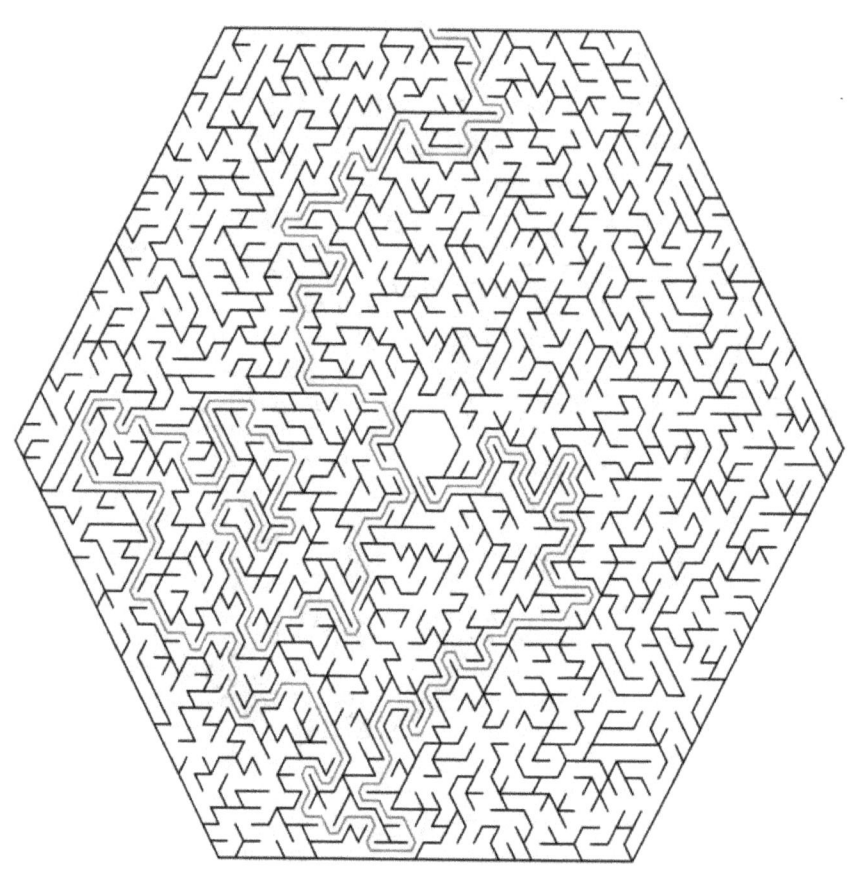

PUT A HEX ON IT #38 - KEY

PUT A HEX ON IT #39 - KEY

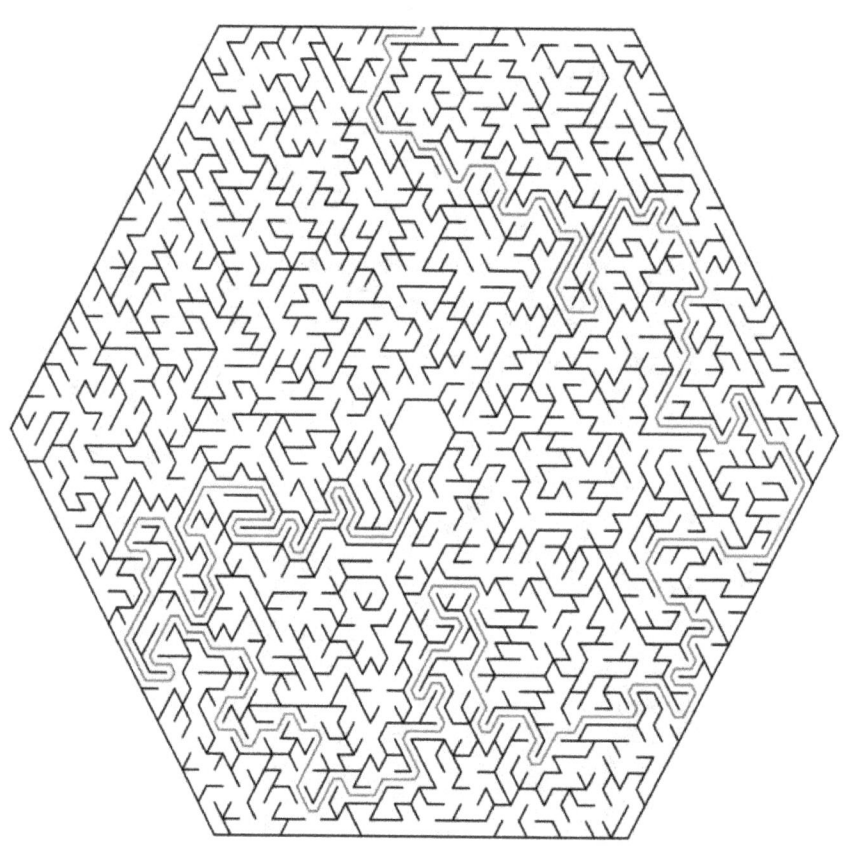

PUT A HEX ON IT #40 - KEY

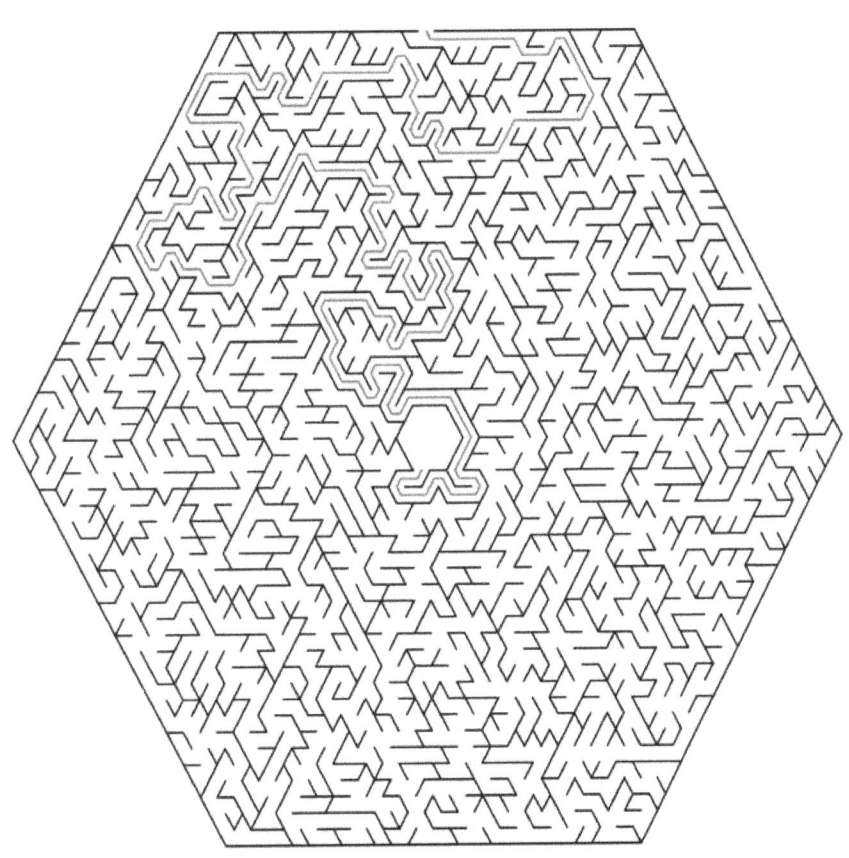

PUT A HEX ON IT #41 - KEY

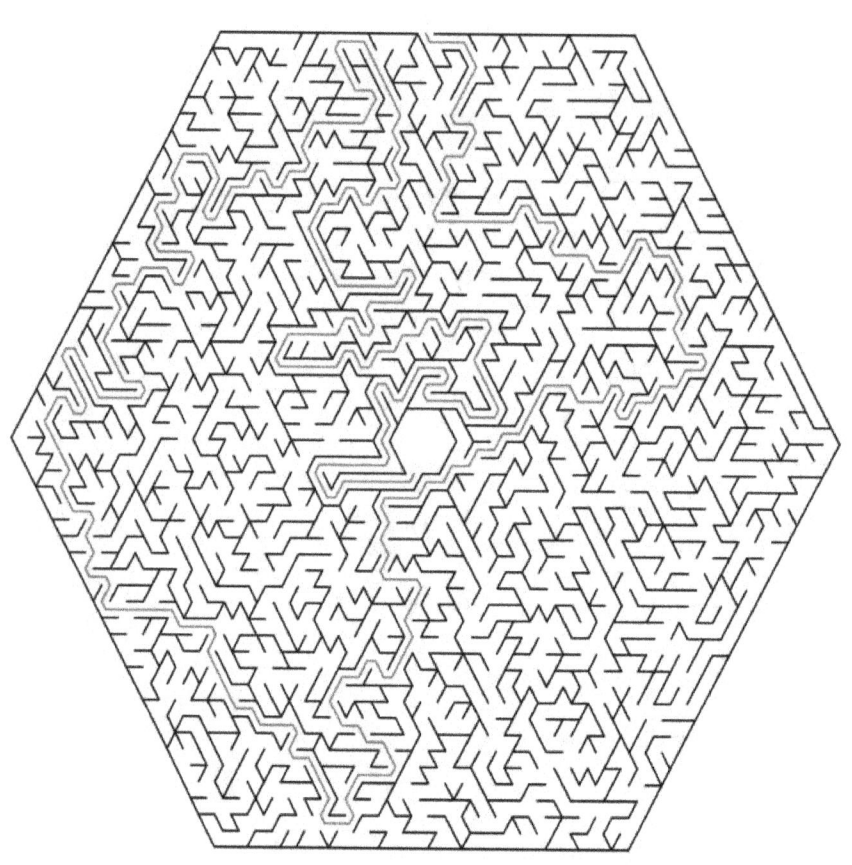

PUT A HEX ON IT #42 - KEY

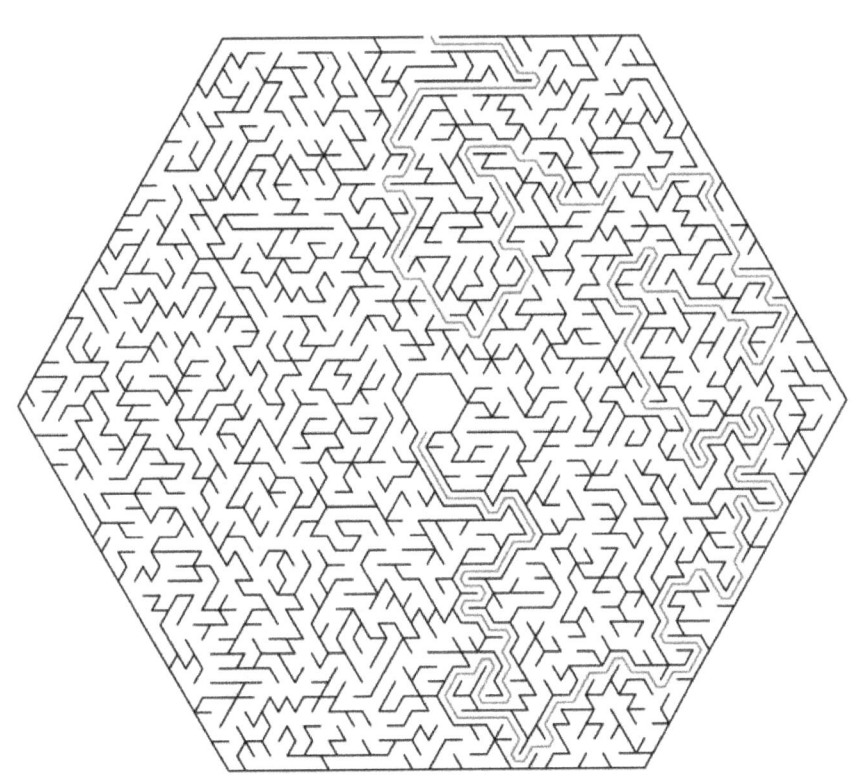

PUT A HEX ON IT #43 - KEY

PUT A HEX ON IT #44 - KEY

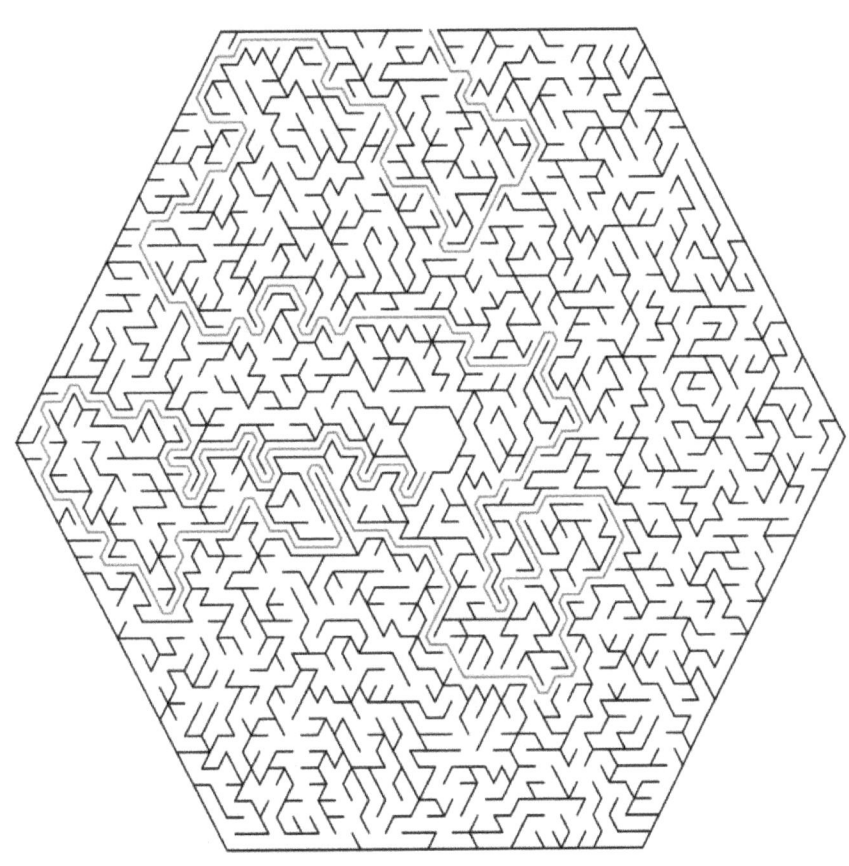

PUT A HEX ON IT #45 - KEY

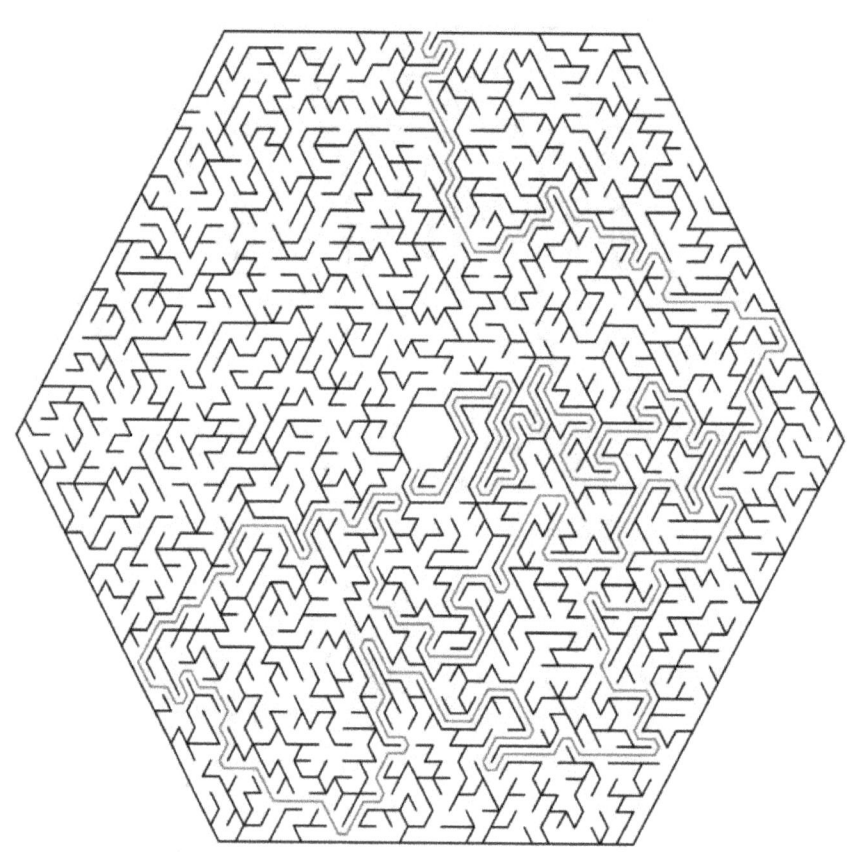

PUT A HEX ON IT #46 - KEY

PUT A HEX ON IT #47 - KEY

PUT A HEX ON IT #48 - KEY

PUT A HEX ON IT #49 - KEY

PUT A HEX ON IT #50 - KEY

PUT A HEX ON IT #51 - KEY

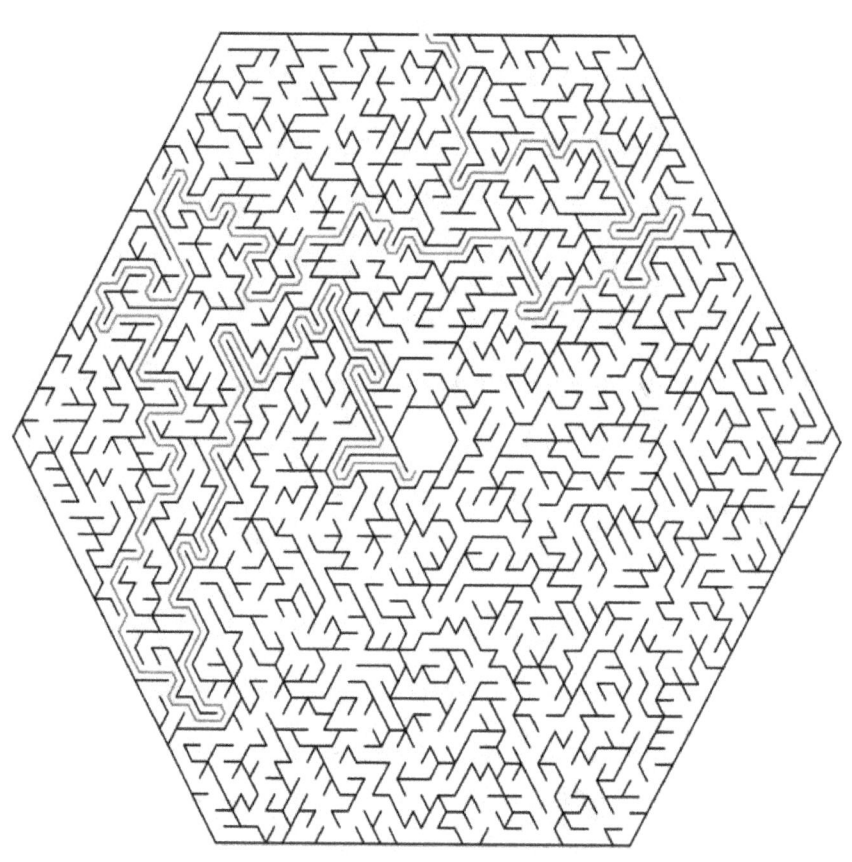

PUT A HEX ON IT #52 - KEY

PUT A HEX ON IT #53 - KEY

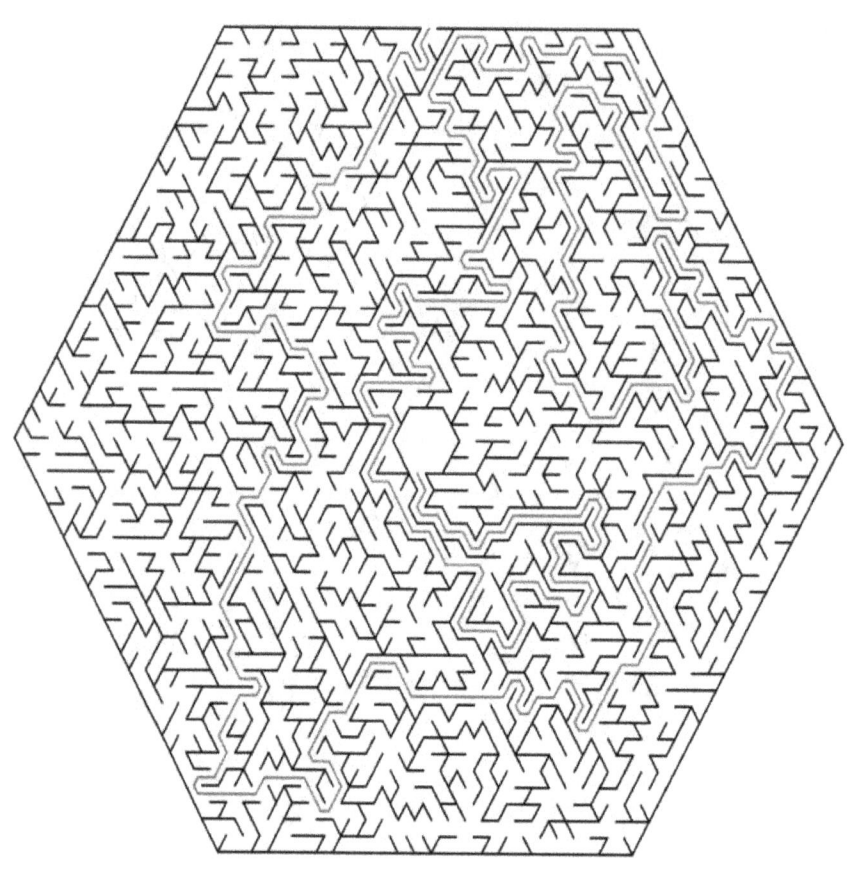

PUT A HEX ON IT #54 - KEY

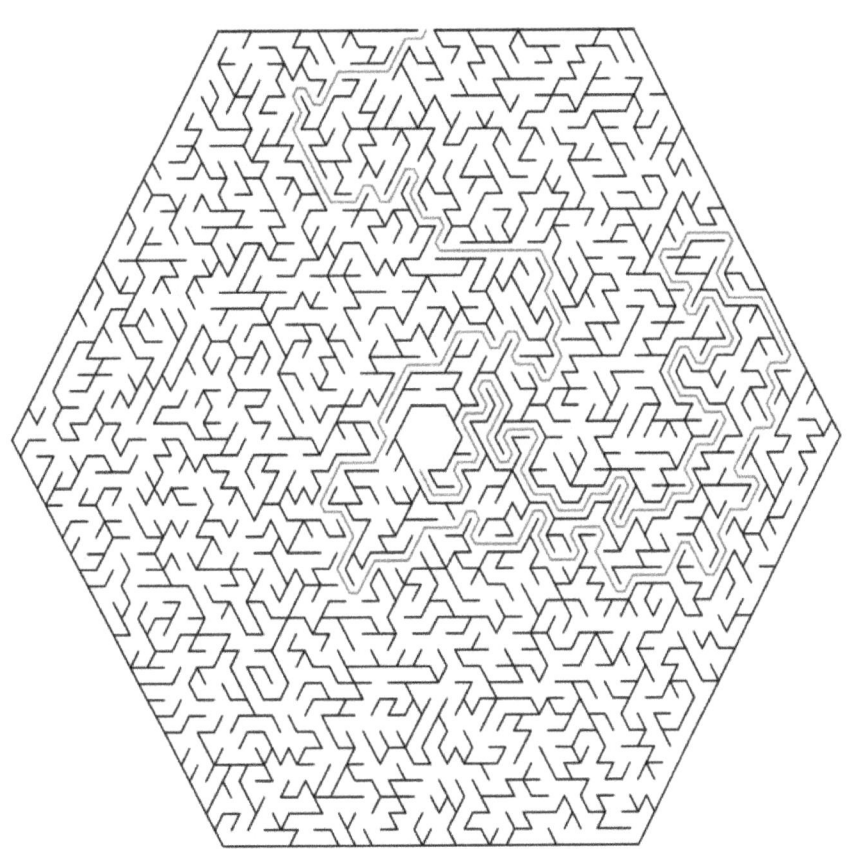

PUT A HEX ON IT #55 - KEY

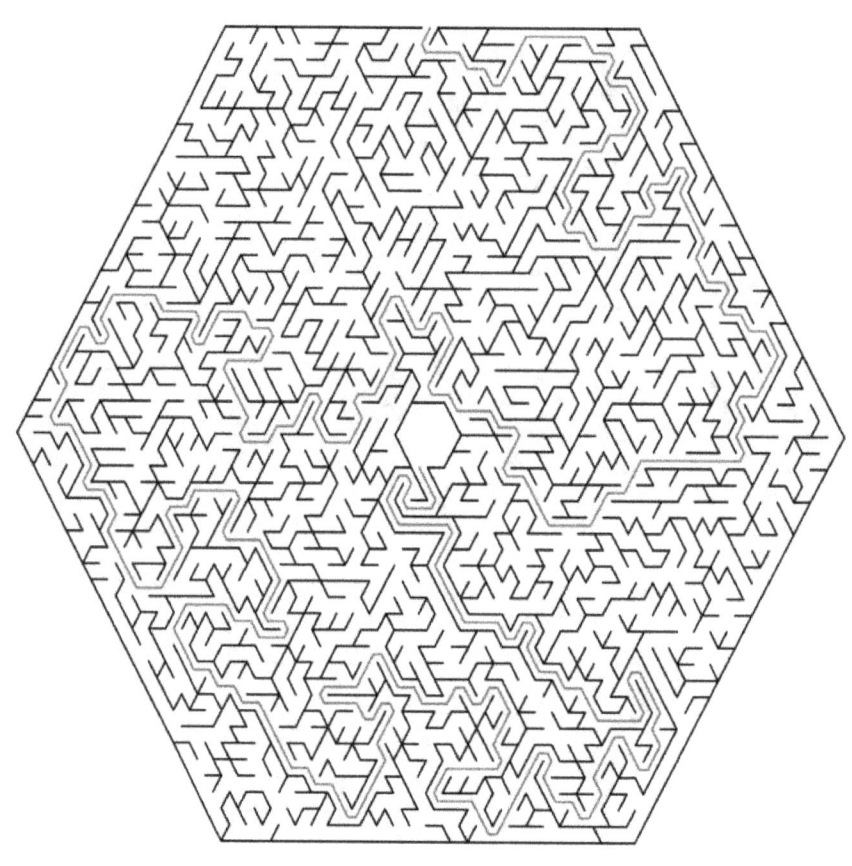

PUT A HEX ON IT #56 - KEY

PUT A HEX ON IT #57 - KEY

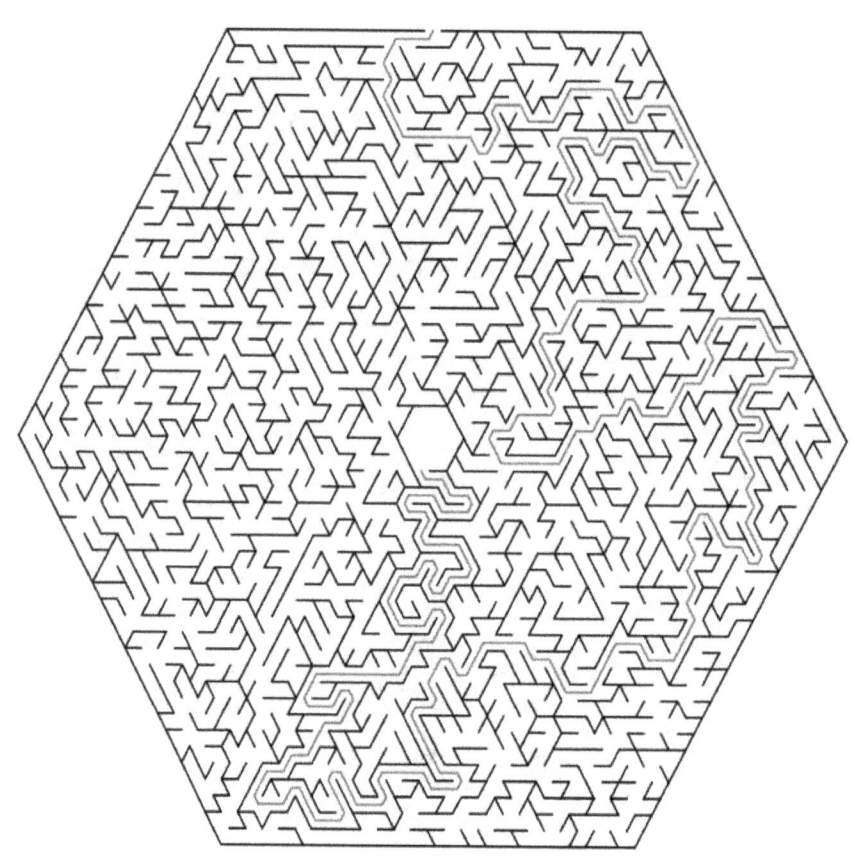

PUT A HEX ON IT #58 - KEY

PUT A HEX ON IT #59 - KEY

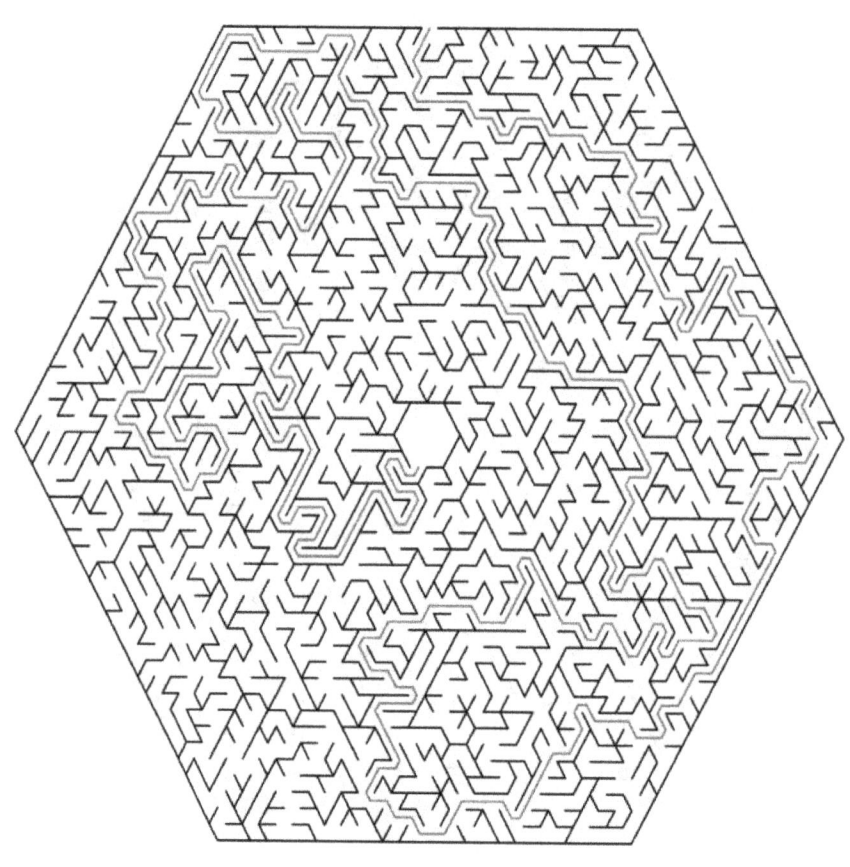

PUT A HEX ON IT #60 - KEY

PUT A HEX ON IT #61 - KEY

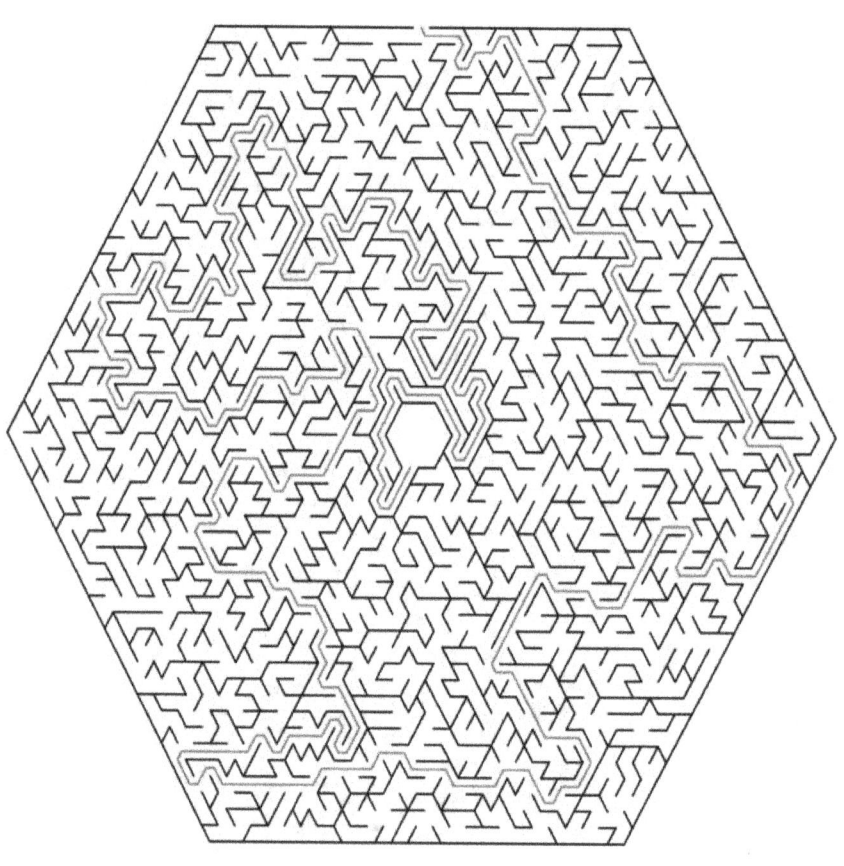

PUT A HEX ON IT #62 - KEY

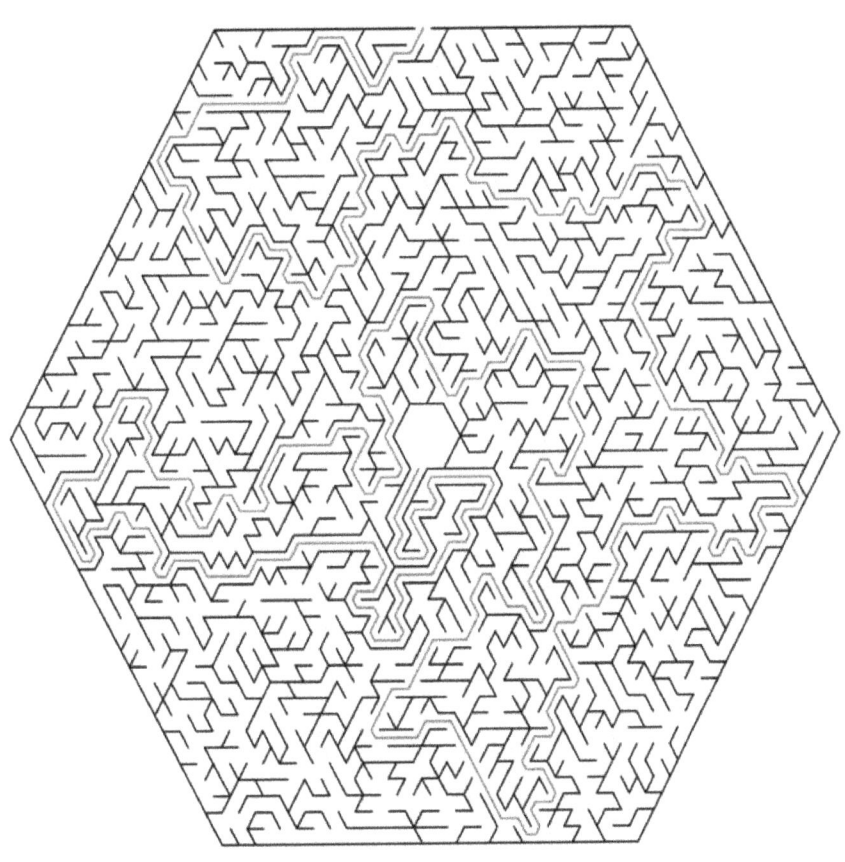

PUT A HEX ON IT #63 - KEY

PUT A HEX ON IT #64 - KEY

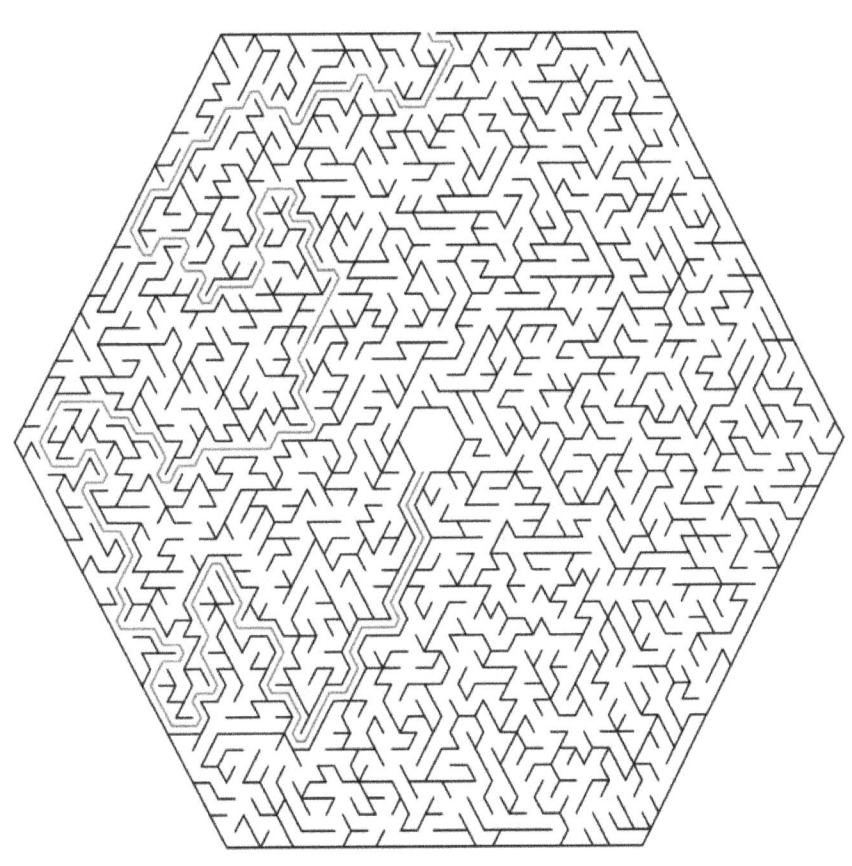

PUT A HEX ON IT #65 - KEY

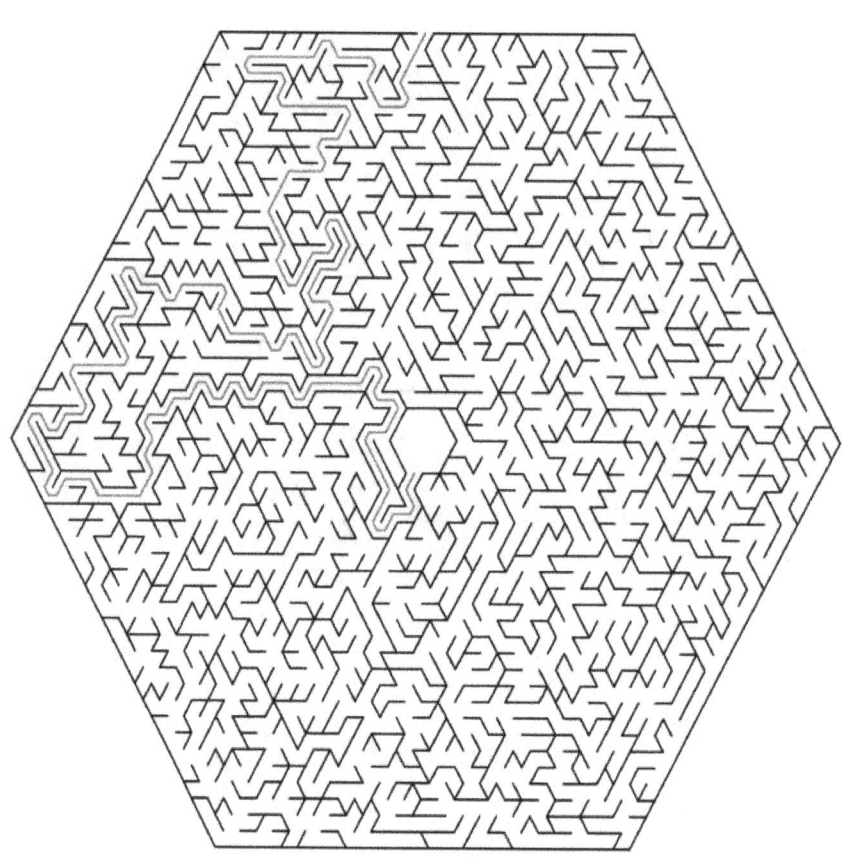

PUT A HEX ON IT #66 - KEY

PUT A HEX ON IT #67 - KEY

PUT A HEX ON IT #68 - KEY

PUT A HEX ON IT #69 - KEY

PUT A HEX ON IT #70 - KEY

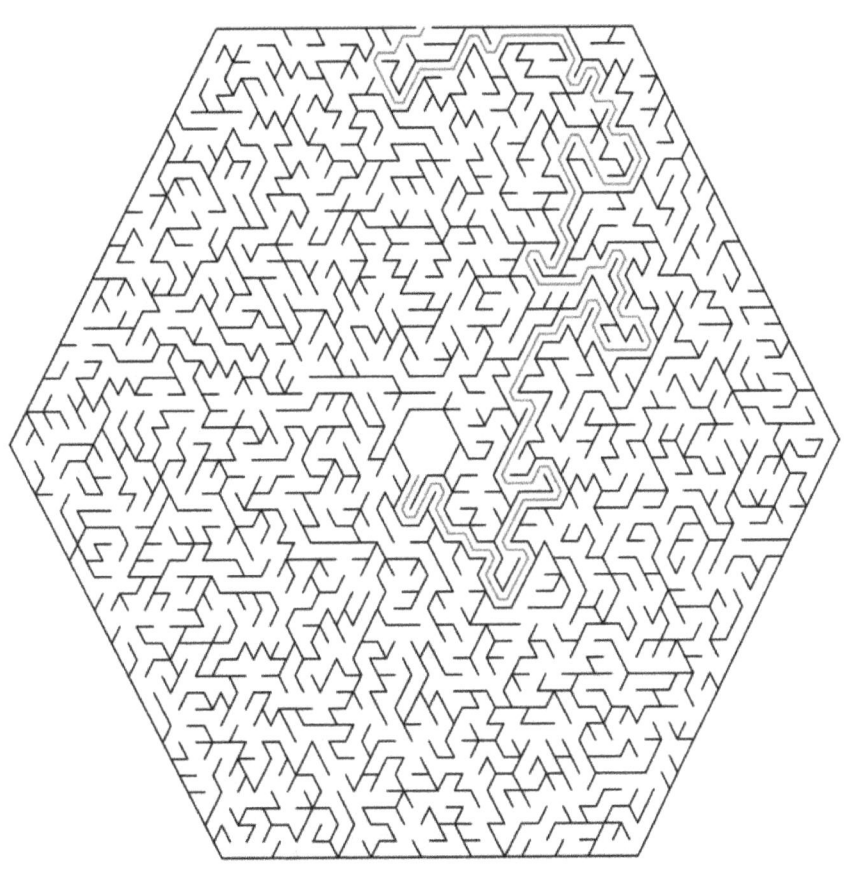

PUT A HEX ON IT #71 - KEY

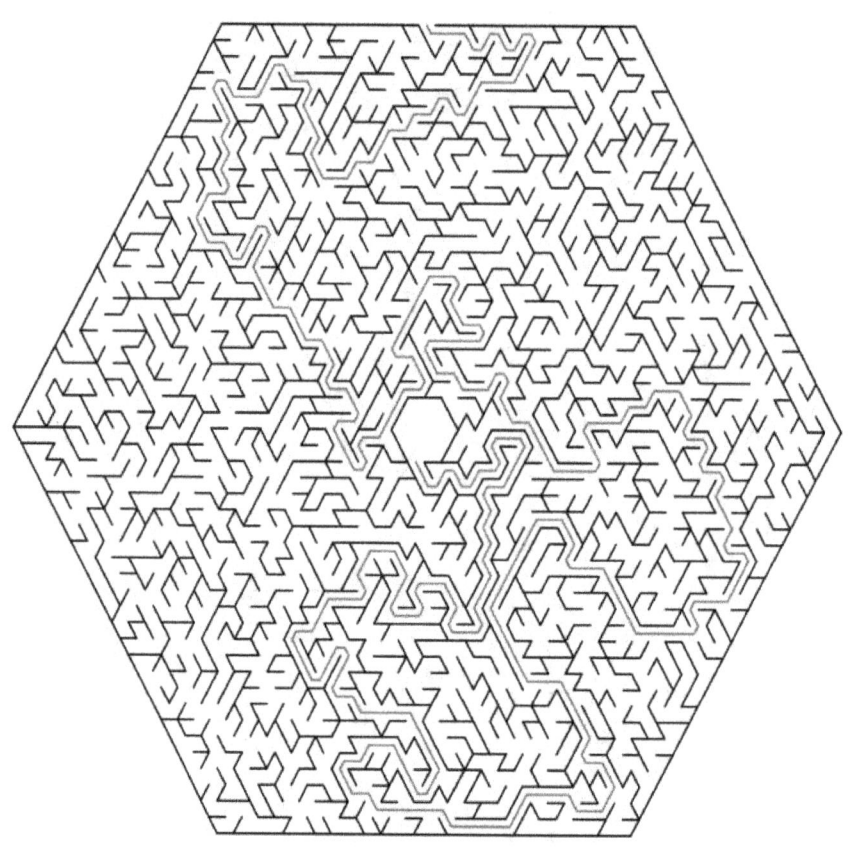

PUT A HEX ON IT #72 - KEY

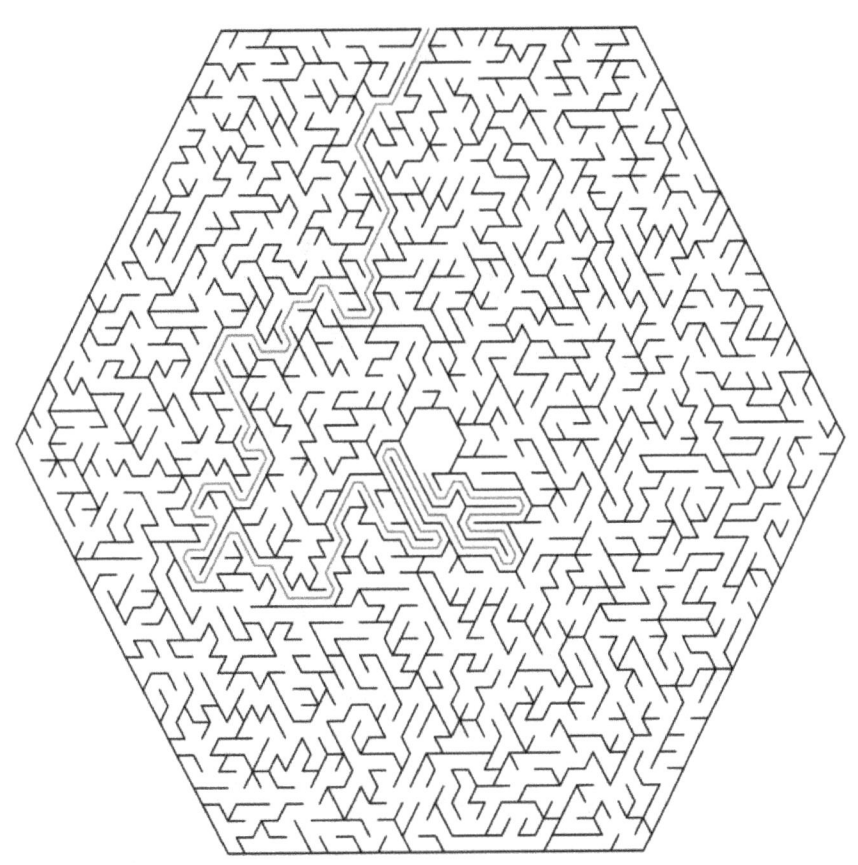

PUT A HEX ON IT #73 - KEY

PUT A HEX ON IT #74 - KEY

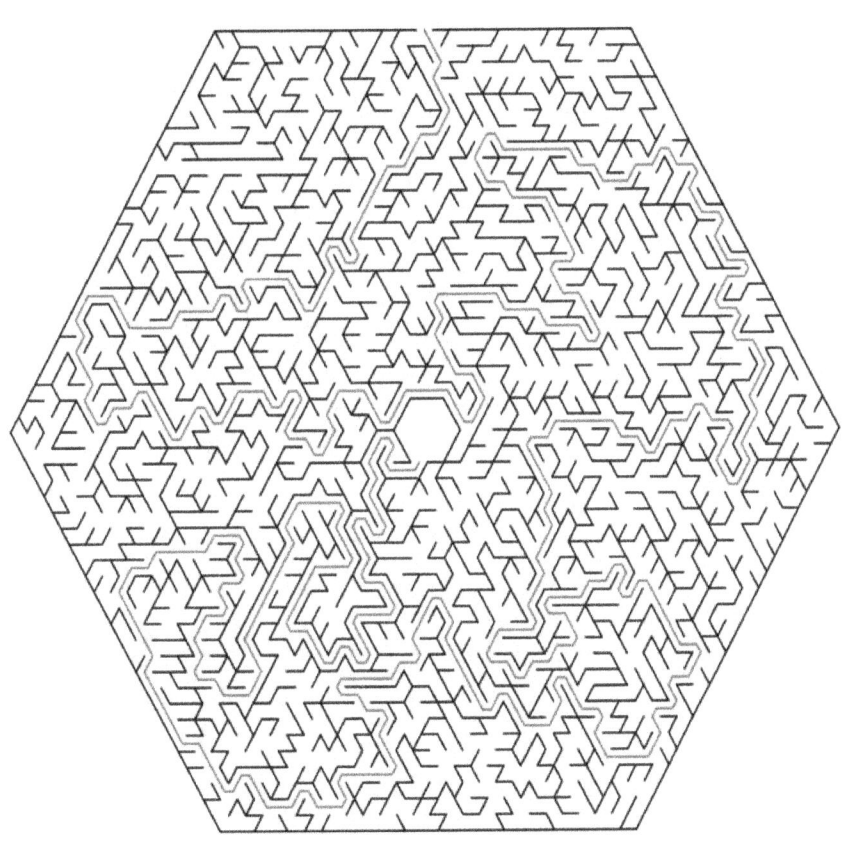

PUT A HEX ON IT #75 - KEY

PUT A HEX ON IT #76 - KEY

PUT A HEX ON IT #77 - KEY

PUT A HEX ON IT #78 - KEY

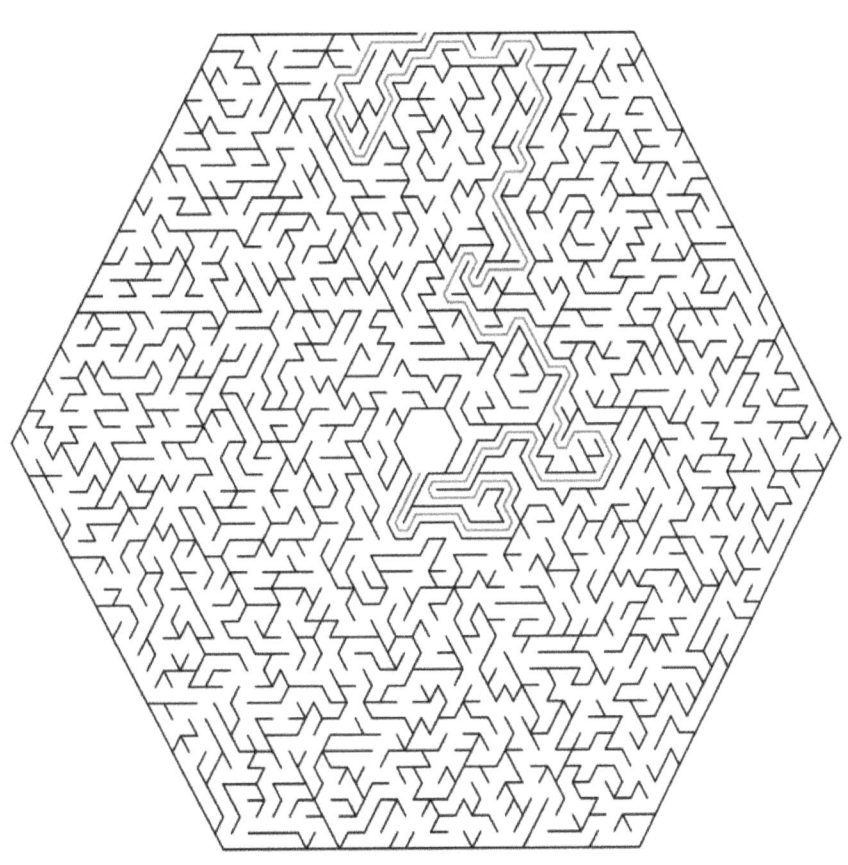

PUT A HEX ON IT #79 - KEY

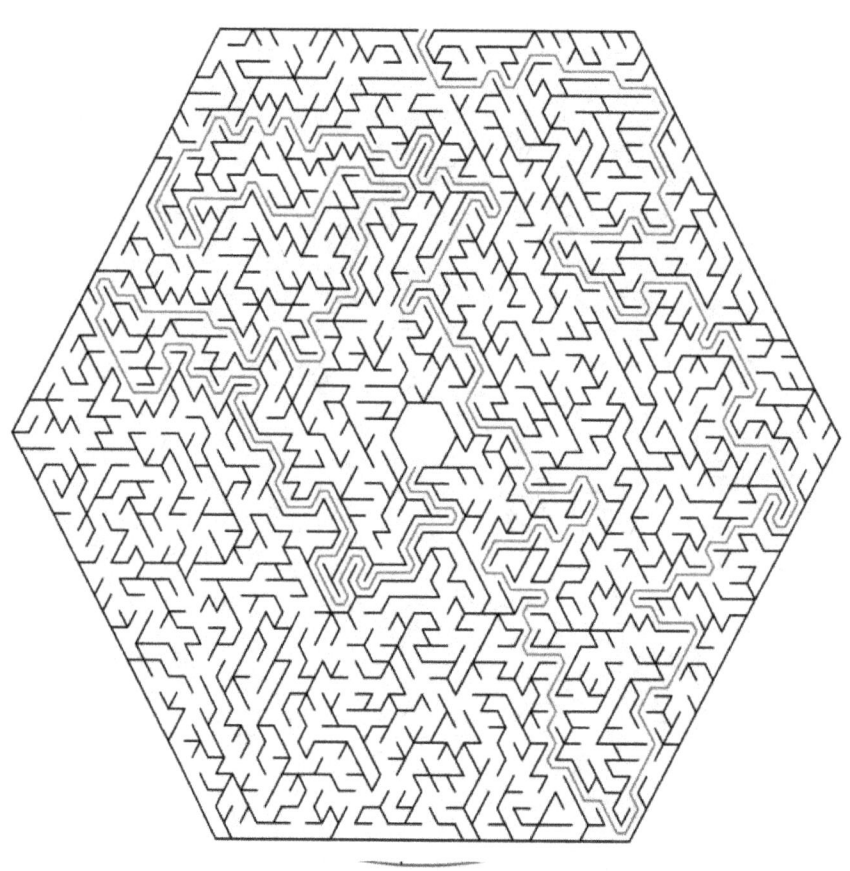

PUT A HEX ON IT #80 - KEY

PUT A HEX ON IT #81 - KEY

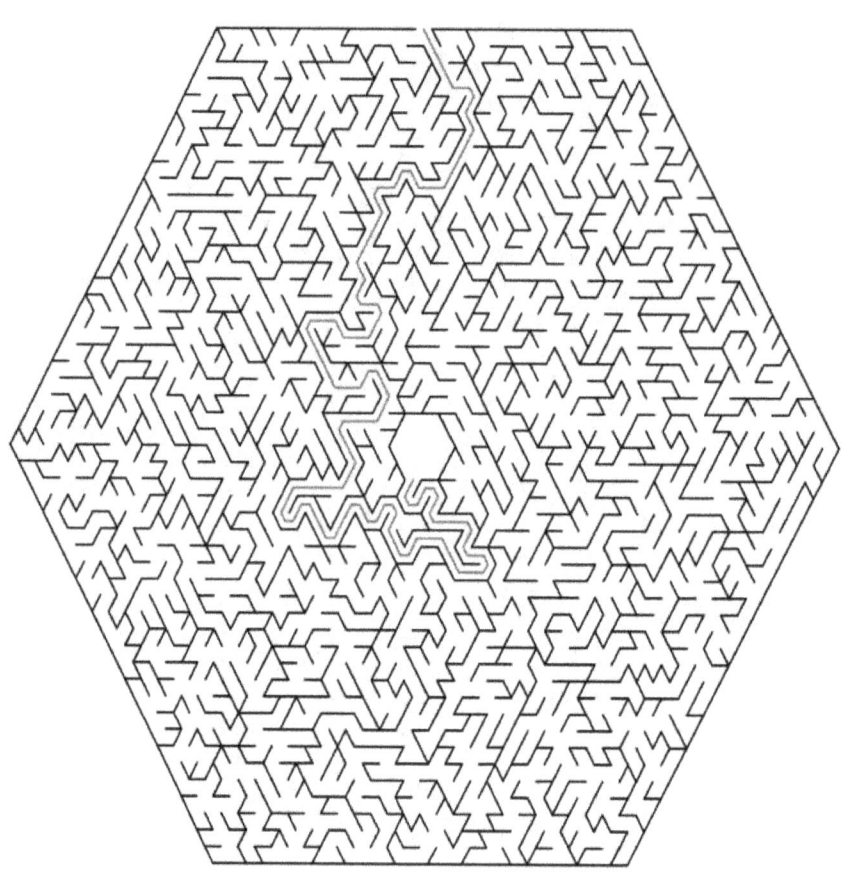

PUT A HEX ON IT #82 - KEY

PUT A HEX ON IT #83 - KEY

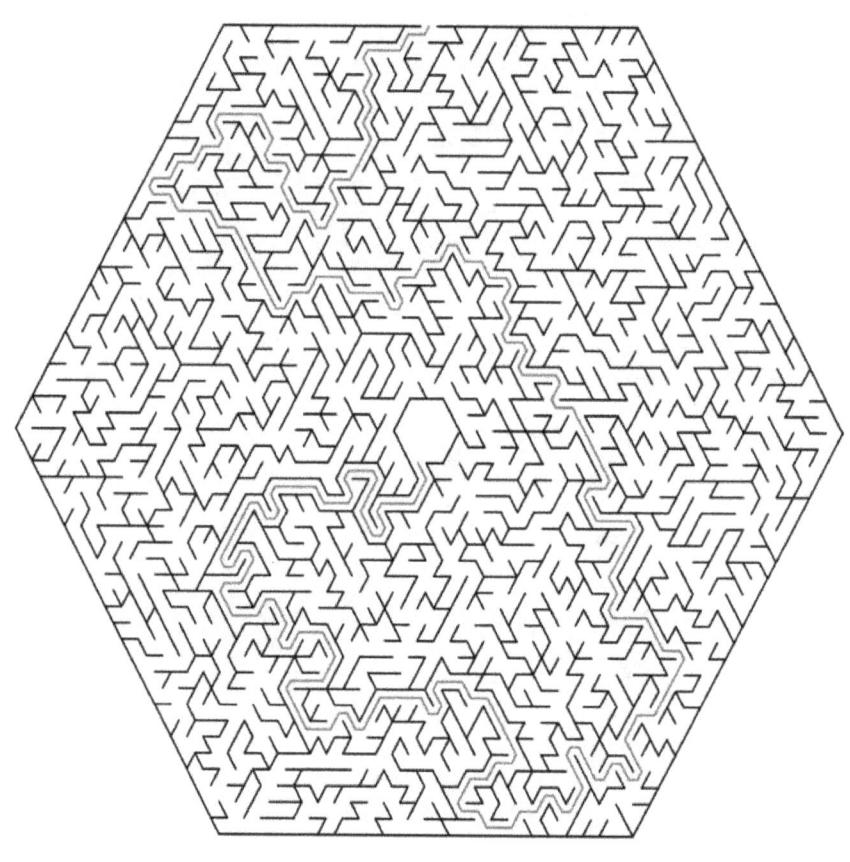

PUT A HEX ON IT #84 - KEY

PUT A HEX ON IT #85 - KEY

PUT A HEX ON IT #86 - KEY

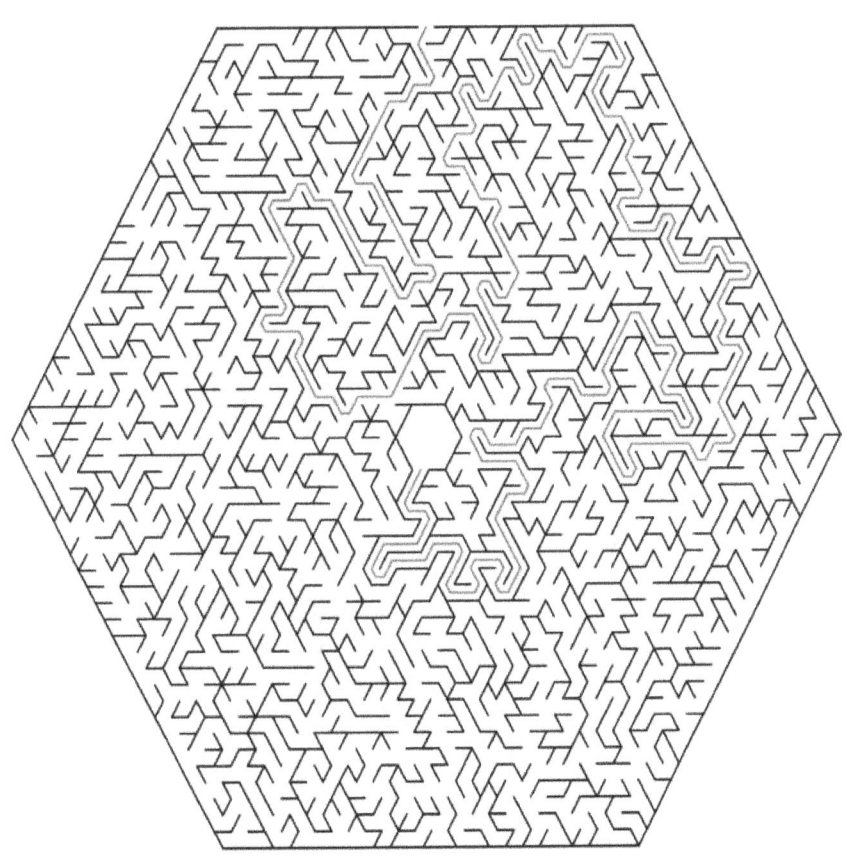

PUT A HEX ON IT #87 - KEY

PUT A HEX ON IT #88 - KEY

PUT A HEX ON IT #89 - KEY

PUT A HEX ON IT #90 - KEY

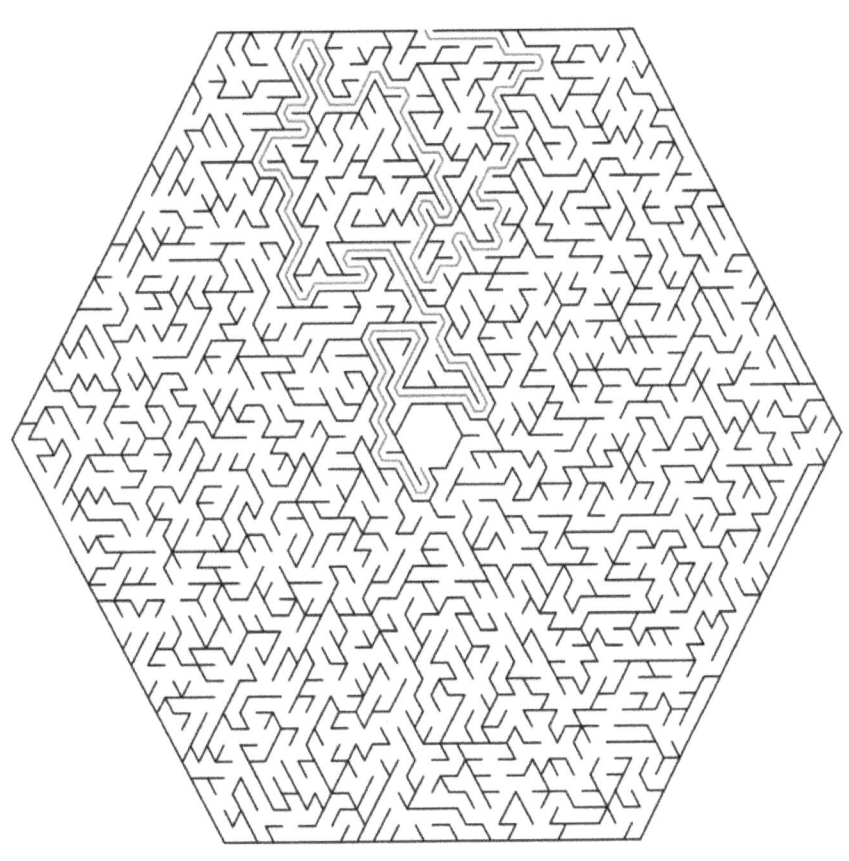

PUT A HEX ON IT #91 - KEY

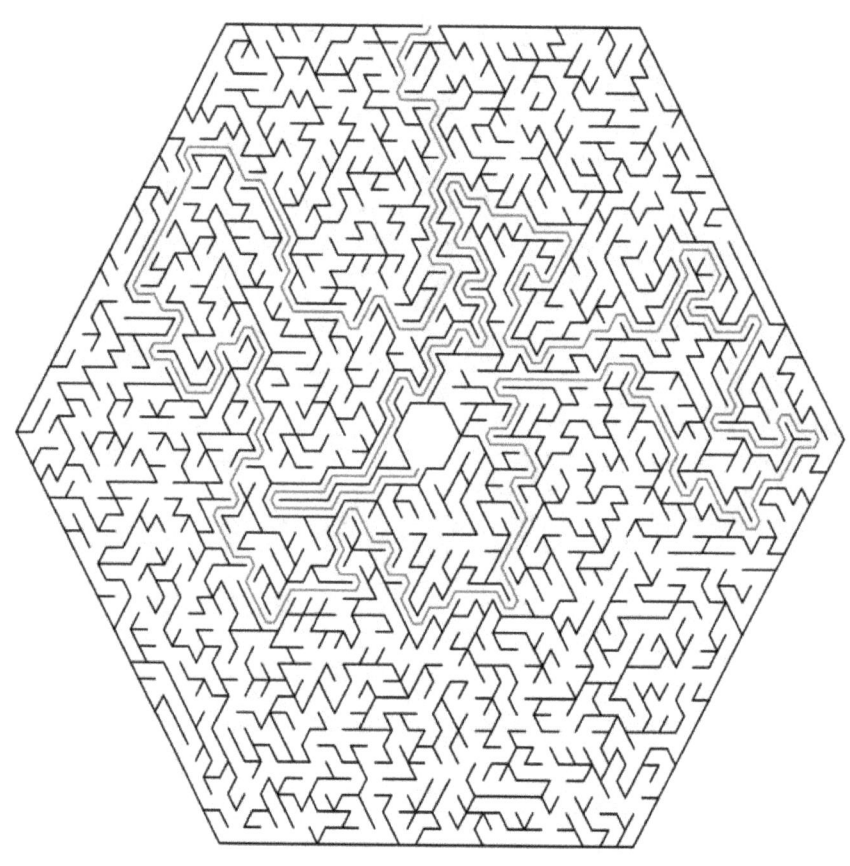

PUT A HEX ON IT #92 - KEY

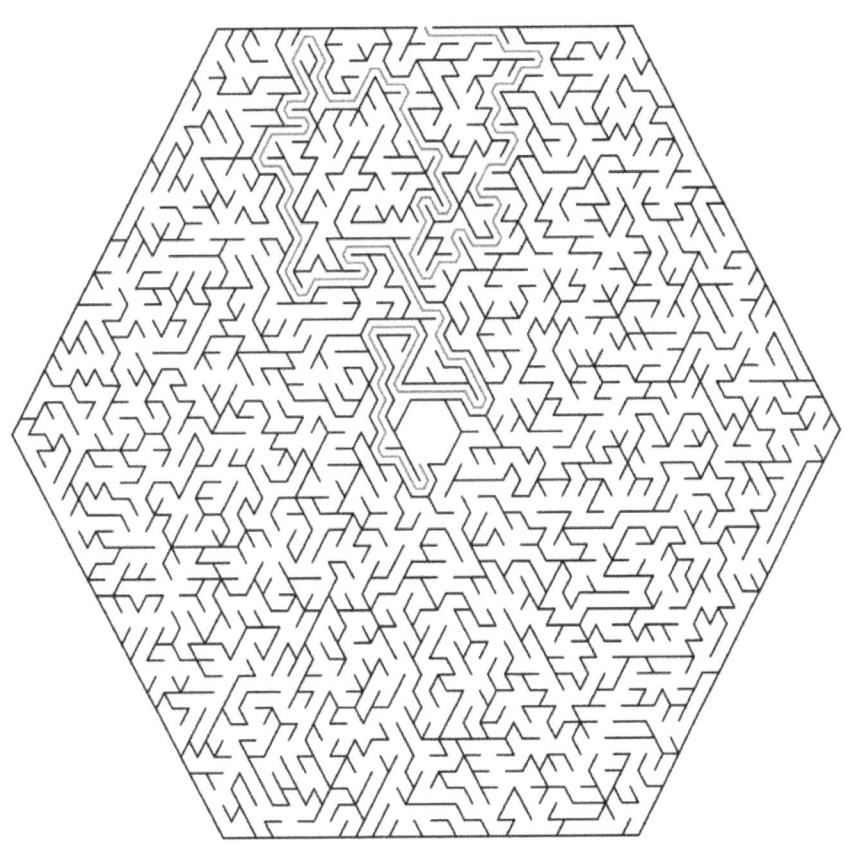

PUT A HEX ON IT #93 - KEY

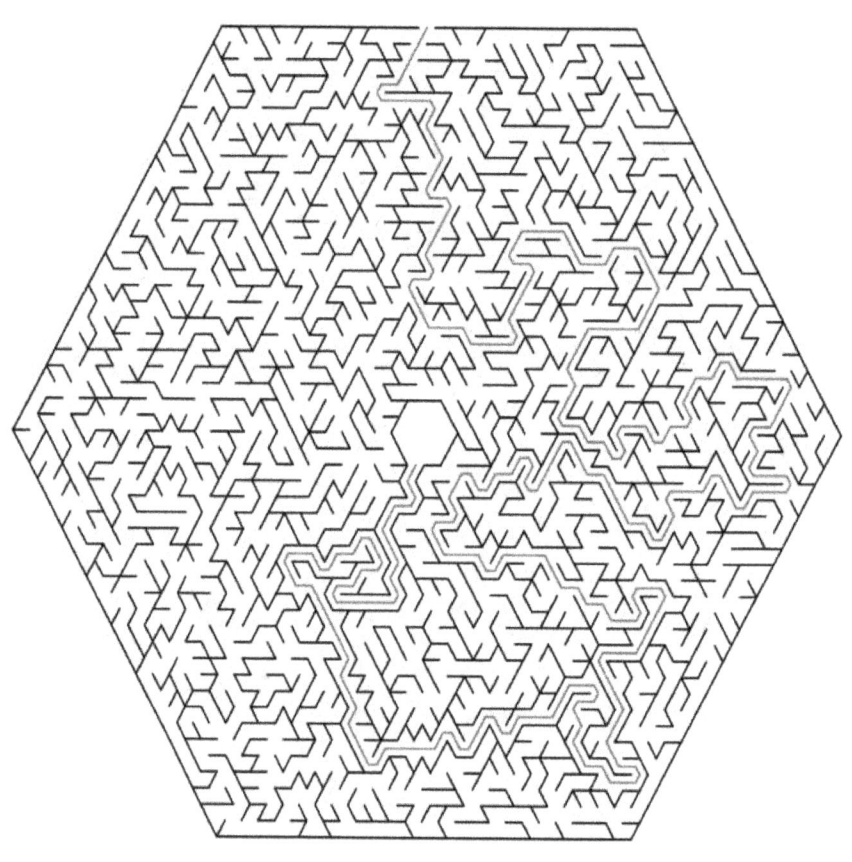

PUT A HEX ON IT #94 - KEY

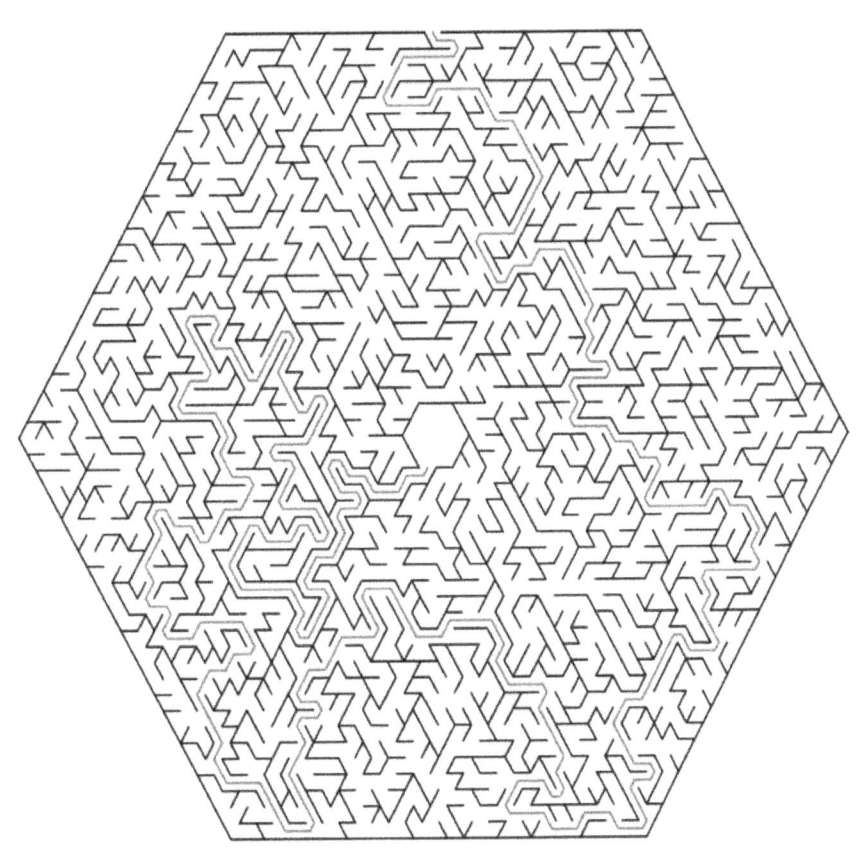

PUT A HEX ON IT #95 - KEY

PUT A HEX ON IT #96 - KEY

PUT A HEX ON IT #97 - KEY

PUT A HEX ON IT #98 - KEY

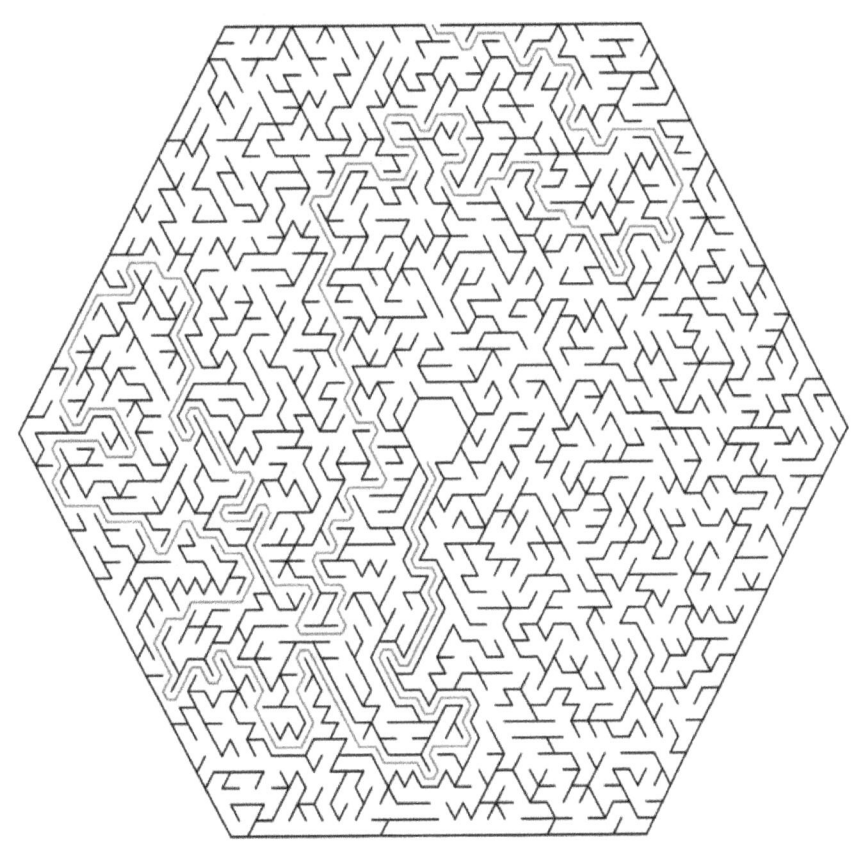

PUT A HEX ON IT #99 - KEY

More By Vibrant Puzzle Books

Puzzle Variety Easy 1
Puzzle Variety Easy 2
Puzzle Book Variety
Sudoku Easy
Maze Puzzle Book For Adults 1
Maze Puzzle Book For Adults 2

www.ingramcontent.com/pod-product-compliance
Lightning Source LLC
Chambersburg PA
CBHW081444070526
44586CB00019B/2219